Pool Care

by Kristine Blanchard

A Wiley Brand

Pool Care For Dummies®

Published by: **John Wiley & Sons, Inc.,** 111 River Street, Hoboken, NJ 07030-5774, www.wiley.com

Copyright © 2023 by John Wiley & Sons, Inc., Hoboken, New Jersey

Media and software compilation copyright © 2023 by John Wiley & Sons, Inc. All rights reserved.

Published simultaneously in Canada

For general information on our other products and services, please contact our Customer Care Department within the U.S. at 877-762-2974, outside the U.S. at 317-572-3993, or fax 317-572-4002. For technical support, please visit https://hub.wiley.com/community/support/dummies.

Wiley publishes in a variety of print and electronic formats and by print-on-demand. Some material included with standard print versions of this book may not be included in e-books or in print-on-demand. If this book refers to media such as a CD or DVD that is not included in the version you purchased, you may download this material at http://booksupport.wiley.com. For more information about Wiley products, visit www.wiley.com.

Library of Congress Control Number: 2023934944

ISBN 978-1-394-16611-4 (pbk); ISBN 978-1-394-16612-1 (ebk); ISBN 978-1-394-16613-8 (ebk)

Printed and bound by CPI Group (UK) Ltd, Croydon, CR0 4YY

C9781394166114_210423

Contents at a Glance

Table of Contents

Introduction

Swimming pools have been a staple in people's lives for hundreds of years, and just about everyone has gotten a chance to enjoy one at least once in their life. They're a place where people gather and relax, where you can melt stress away or party till you drop. But, what goes into owning a pool yourself? Just like owning any other thing in life, it's not all sunshine and butterflies, although it may seem that way from the outside. Pools can be a lot of work sometimes, and there's a lot to figure out and get used to. And if there's something I know well after my years working in the pool industry, it's that there are a lot of right and wrong ways that you can do things, and knowing as much as you can about your pool will make you a better and more confident pool owner.

What I hope to do in *Pool Care For Dummies* is provide a one-stop reference guide to answer all your questions and smoothly guide you through the many factors of owning a pool. There are so many kinds of pools that have different shapes, sizes, materials, chemicals, and climates, and all those factors play a part in how your specific pool should be taken care of. That being said, this book covers the basics of what most pools need and presents the information in a straightforward way.

If you own a pool or want to own a pool someday, this book is going to give you the answers to all of the most important and commonly asked questions. It will give you the peace of mind that this is all just a learning curve, and after you understand the why's and the how's, it's all smooth sailing from there.

About This Book

Pool Care For Dummies won't cover everything pool-related in the world, but it does cover the care that all pools should be receiving and how to do it. The different types of care and the frequency with which they need to be done can feel overwhelming to the beginner, and this book will simplify even the hardest of tasks. There are a lot of pieces and processes that keep a pool clear, clean, and safe. These are some of the aspects of pool ownership I cover in this book:

>> **The kinds of pools out there:** Not all pools are the same, that's for sure. There are inground, above ground, vinyl liner, plaster, and so on. All of these

types of pools have unique qualities that make them different from one another, and knowing those differences will help you know your pool better or help you choose the correct kind of pool for your lifestyle and needs.

>> **What makes up your swimming pool:** As a kid, a pool may have just seemed like a body of water that sustained itself with very little intervention, and sometimes that's the case. But it's because of all the pieces — from pumps to filters to skimmers — that make a pool different from a pond. By figuring out what all the parts are and how they work together, you can be a well-informed pool owner who can prevent problems and solve issues.

>> **What kind of problems you may run into:** As much as you'd probably love your pool to run flawlessly forever and ever without any extra work, it's sadly not a reality. But don't fret! You're going to learn from my experience about what to look out for, how to identify your crisis, and how to solve it.

>> **Routine maintenance:** There's nothing more important than maintaining the quality of the pool you have. When it comes to swimming pools, some avoidable mistakes can be made, and they can be expensive or time consuming to correct. I cover all the ways you can protect your investment.

>> **Opening and closing your pool:** For some people, this section won't apply to you because you are blessed with beautiful pool weather all year long. Well, for people like me who live in New England, opening your pool in the spring and closing it in the fall is a necessary act.

I've divided this book up into parts, based on these topics:

>> **Part 1: Getting to Know Your Pool:** Get all the details on what is involved with being a pool owner. I give you the lowdown on the different types of pools out there and get you acquainted with the parts that make your pool run. You also discover how to troubleshoot problems with pool parts and how to keep your guests safe when using your pool.

>> **Part 2: Hiring Yourself as a Pool Pro:** There's nothing more important than maintaining the quality of the pool you have. If you don't want to hire the pros to do it, I tell you how to do regular cleanings, open your pool at the start of the season, and close it when the season ends.

>> **Part 3: Becoming a Chemist (Well, Sort Of):** This Part goes into the nitty gritty about what chemicals are needed to maintain your pool and how to use them to keep your pool clear, clean, and safe.

>> **Part 4: The Part of Tens:** This Part offers tips on what to have on hand for your pool and how to deal with the unexpected.

My main objective in this book is to open you up to all the things you need to do and know to make a pool a relaxing and fun part of your home, rather than a nuisance. Finding that sweet spot can take time and patience at first, but after you get the hang of it, a pool is hard to live without.

Foolish Assumptions

For this book, I'm going to assume that you're buying it for one or more of these reasons:

>> You recently bought a home that has a pool or just got a pool at your existing home — and you're now stepping into uncharted territory.

>> You're considering buying a pool, and you want to see if all the hype is really worth it.

>> You want to have one trustworthy source to guide you, instead of taking all your suggestions from random blogs on the internet.

>> You've owned a pool for years and have had nothing but problems from the beginning, so you're looking for some help.

>> You're interested in the swimming pool industry as a career path, and you want to educate yourself more on things that you haven't learned yet. (If that's the case, welcome! After you're a part of the pool industry, it's a hard career to leave.)

Icons Used in This Book

There will be pictures in the margins of this book called icons, they're there to help point out specific information that you might find useful.

TIP

This icon will point out a specific trick I've figured out that can help you in the future.

REMEMBER

This is an icon that will mark important information that I want you to pay special attention to or something that you want to keep in mind if you're preforming a task recommended in the book.

WARNING

This is probably the most important icon used in this particular book, mainly because pools have the potential to be dangerous and it's so crucial that you keep your pool and your actions as safe as possible.

TECHNICAL STUFF

When you see this icon, you know I'm about to get a little techy. You can skip this information if you want, but I like to include some extra science stuff and machinery facts to help you become a well-rounded pool owner.

Beyond the Book

For a reference guide, see the online Cheat Sheet. To access it, search for "Pool Care for Dummies Cheat Sheet" at www.dummies.com. This Cheat Sheet will give you a few other fun and useful facts that you may want to know about the swimming pool you use every day.

Where to Go from Here

I've designed this book to make it so that you can easily find a subject that you want to know about and jump right to it. Swimming pools can be intimidating, so this is a way for you to get your answers quickly and with the best information.

If swimming pools are completely new to you, I suggest you start with Chapter 1, which will give you a general overview of your pool and why learning about it is so important. But if you would like to jump right in, you can skip right to Chapter 2 and begin discovering the ins and outs of pools.

You can read this book from cover to cover or you can take a look at the Table of Contents and head to any chapter that interests you. Keep this book in a convenient place so you can refer to it whenever an issue crops up (say, Chapter 12 if you're having water problems) or if you want to stock up on products in the spring (head to Chapter 14). However way you choose to use this book, I hope you find it a useful resource.

This book is meant to be fun, and to make you feel less stressed out about having a pool installed in your yard. Pools *are* fun — you just have to play your role in keeping them that way.

Have fun, and happy swimming!

1

Getting to Know Your Pool

Get introduced to the basics of owning a pool and what comes with pool care.

Discover the differences between above ground and inground pools, along with some details about saltwater pools.

Identify all the moving parts that make your pool work and how they work together.

Troubleshoot some common issues that can happen with your pool, from pump problems to filter failures.

Keep yourself and others safe in and around your pool.

Chapter **1**

Welcome! You Now Work for a Pool!

O wning a pool can be so fun — and a bit terrifying when you're first start-ing out. Either way, I have you covered! I know pools like the back of my hand, and I'm here to help you be a confident pool owner. Getting to know your pool, and its wants and needs, is a winding road. And sometimes, you'll make mistakes. My goal is to guide you and give you the tools and knowledge that you need to navigate this road. Use this first chapter as a guide for where you need to go in the book to get answers for any problems you may be dealing with and for any topics you may want to learn more about. We're in this together.

Pool 101: Basic Anatomy

When you were a kid, you probably thought that a pool was made up of two things: walls and water. That's because those are the only parts that matter for the people who aren't taking care of the pool Now, you get to see that a pool is much more than just a body of water. It's a whole network of machines and chemicals that work together to create the perfect shimmering luxury oasis that you always wanted.

The following sections cover all the parts of the pool and how they work together.

The pool itself

This is the part you're probably most familiar with, the structure of the pool.

If you have an above ground pool, here are its parts:

>> **Inside:** Made up of a vinyl liner

>> **Outside:** Made of either steel or aluminum walls

If you have an inground pool, there are several different types of construction. Some popular options include

>> Liner on a steel wall

>> Liner on a concrete wall

>> Fiberglass

>> Plaster

>> Pebble tech

Knowing what type of pool you have is important because chemical ranges and pool cleaning equipment vary depending on the surface. Turn to Chapter 2 for more details on the components that make up a pool.

REMEMBER

If you don't have a pool yet, figuring out what kind of pool is best for you really comes down to where you are and what you're looking to get out of your pool experience. You need to do some research and talk to a pool professional to discover what will work best for your budget, your location, and your lifestyle.

The plumbing

Your pool's *plumbing* consists of the pipes that connect your pool to the pump and filter equipment. Your plumbing plays a part in how many hours you need to run your pump and how big a pump you can fit. This is because your water flow can go only as fast as the pipe it's moving in. Realistically the average running time is

8 to 12 hours a day. The plumbing leads to the skimmers that catch all your surface debris, and it leads to the returns that help circulate the water and kick up anything settled on the bottom.

For inground pools, the plumbing is located underground. For above ground pools, it's located on the outside in less permanent and easily removable hoses. Unless it was plumbed with hard PVC plumbing, but that is not standardly their setup.

The pump and filter

As far as bodies of water go, one of the main things that separates a pond from a pool, besides the ecosystem, is the circulation and filtration of the water:

» **Pump:** The pump is like the heart of your pool. It's made up of the front housing with the basket, the internal parts (most importantly the impeller) and the motor. It's what brings the water from your pool into the filtration system, sends that water through all the necessary machinery, and then forces the water back to the pool. It's the part of your pool that does all the circulation, which prevents the water from becoming stagnant and, well, swampy.

   There are different pumps for above ground pools and inground pools, and they come in different strengths and sizes. They can be single speed, two speed, or variable speed, which all have their own special characteristics.

» **Filter:** Your pump wouldn't be anything without your filter. Your filter is made up of a tank that holds the actual filtering component (sand, cartridge, DE element) and, in some cases a multiport valve. It is the part that pulls out the not-clean stuff that ends up in your pool water. If you had only a pump, the water would be moving, the chemicals would be circulated, but nothing would ever clear up.

   If you have algae in your pool, all the chemicals and water circulation in the world wouldn't get your pool to clear because the algae (even if it's dead) would continue to float around in the water. The filter is there to help grab all the physical contaminants and prevent them from going back into the pool.

   There are three main kinds of pool filter: sand, diatomaceous earth (DE), and cartridge. All three have their benefits and their flaws, but all of them work to keep your pool clear.

Check out Chapters 3 and 4 for a lot of information about how these important pool parts work and how to take care of them.

The suction and pressure parts

On all pools, you will have an enter and exit port(s) for your pool's circulation. On the suction side, which is going to be where the water is being pulled in and drawn to the filter system, you have three common kinds:

>> **Skimmer:** This looks like a rectangular or square opening on the side of the pool that leads to a cylindrical housing containing a basket. The access to that basket is from the top, which may be in your surrounding pool deck, and it will be covered with a lid.

>> **Main drain:** This will be where water can be pulled into the pump from the floor of the pool. It will be covered by a circular grate(s) to prevent large items from getting sucked into the pump.

>> **Side suction:** A side suction is going to be an inch and a half-sized hole in the side of the pool covered by a grate. This can be used as a manual vacuum line or just an alternative suction for the pump.

On the pressure side, your return pipes can lead to the pool through a few different avenues. The most common way you will have the water come back into the pool is through the wall returns. They are holes in the wall that have directional eye-balls in them to guide the returning water in the right direction for proper circulation. The other options are through floor returns, which typically have pop-up heads that raise with water pressure. Those allow good circulation while also disturbing the pool floor and helping kick up and filter settled debris.

Other stuff that your pool may have

Outside of moving and filtering your water, there may be other components to your filter system that have jobs, as well:

>> **Heaters:** There are various ways to heat your pool, such as using gas-fired heaters or electric heat pumps.

>> **Sanitizers:** You can sanitize your water with a salt-to-chlorine generator or an in-line chlorinator.

Did you know that a saltwater pool is still a chlorine pool? Now you do!

All these parts will be in the same area as your pump and filter (ideally).

Going with the Flow: How It All Works

Understanding how all the parts work together as a whole will make you more comfortable with your pool. To start, you have the area where all of your plumbing begins — at your suctions. On all pools, you'll have at least a skimmer. Some other pools will have suctions at the bottom of the pool where water can be pulled in from the deepest points. These bottom suctions are excellent in improving proper circulation in your pool.

Here's the progression of water through your pool system:

1. The skimmer and suctions have the water drawn into them through the suction of the pump's motor, where it passes through the skimmer basket

    Technically *pump* and *motor* are two different terms, but commonly it is called the same thing. The pump is the entire assembly, which is the housing with the basket, the impeller, and all plastic pieces along with the pump motor. The motor is just the electrical part of the pump.

2. After the water enters the pump, it goes through one more basket that catches large debris in the front of the pump.

3. After that basket, the water is under pressure, being pushed through things instead of being sucked into things.

4. Directly after the pump, the water is forced into your filter.

    All filters work in a similar fashion in regards to water flow. The water is forced through some sort of element such as sand, fabric, or powdered diatomaceous earth (DE).

5. If you have a heater, the water is sent on to that piece of equipment.

    The water passes through and heats up at the same time so that it's nice and warm for its return to the pool.

6. If you have an additional sanitizing system, such as an inline chlorinator or salt-to-chlorine generator, the water goes through that system last before returning to the pool.

    Those two systems infuse small amounts of chlorine into the water while it passes through, and then that chlorine will get mixed into all the pool water, effectively sanitizing it.

7. The water is pushed back into the pool.

    The flow of the water coming back into the pool is strategically angled so that you get optimal circulation, no matter what kind of pool you have.

8. The cycle repeats for as long as you have your pump running.

Being a Responsible Pool Owner

If you're going to be responsible for an expensive investment into your staycation wonderland, you're going to want to know how to not only keep it clean, but to keep it safe and protected.

A pool isn't a self-sustaining environment with an ecosystem and natural water chemistry to keep it in check. It takes a bit of work to keep it nice and clean, and to make sure it's safe to swim in.

Safety first

You want your pool to be fun and safe. When it comes to pools, safety comes in two forms:

>> Using caution when dealing with chemicals

>> Providing a safe swimming environment

Practicing chemical safety

A pool and pool chemicals probably seem different to you than a science lab filled with beakers and chemicals, but they're both equally as dangerous. Chemical handling is the most overlooked part of owning a pool because it's assumed that if you can buy the chemical at your local discount supply store, it must be perfectly safe to handle. Unfortunately, that really isn't the case.

WARNING

Getting chemicals on your skin or in your eyes can cause irritation and even injury. And mixing chemicals incorrectly can result in fires, explosions, and death. These chemicals are no joke: Always handle your pool chemicals with care and never put them in the hands of a child.

Keeping your pool area safe

Keep the people and pets who will be using your pool safe. Pools have hazards that require having safety procedures in place. Here are a few points to keep in mind:

>> Create a list of safety rules for guests to follow and post them near the pool.

>> Be sure to have a secure fence either around your yard or around the pool itself.

>> Make sure safety equipment, such as a life ring, is easy to access.

>> Install equipment such as drain covers and safety covers to prevent injuries.

By taking preventative safety measures, you can guard against accidents. See Chapter 5 for details on ways to keep your pool area safe.

Proper maintenance

Pool problem prevention is always less expensive and more effective than correction. Keeping your pool well balanced and well maintained will prolong the life of every part of your pool. If you clean often, you filter will last longer. If you balance your water, literally every piece of equipment in your pool, whether rubber or metal, will last longer. If you keep up on algaecides and shocks (which I talk about in Chapter 11), you can prevent a costly algae bloom from forming. The list goes on and on — proper maintenance will save you money in the long run.

REMEMBER

Putting off weekly maintenance might mean having to spend extra time and money cleaning up a cloudy pool. When you have limited days in which to enjoy your pool, you want to be able to use the pool whenever you want. You don't want to risk using up good pool days cleaning because you let the upkeep slip. Create a good maintenance schedule and stick to it. Look to Chapter 7 and the chapters in Part 3 for information on cleaning and chemicals.

Discovering Your Inner Chemist

Pool chemistry is my favorite subject! Your pool chemistry is what will keep you and your pool safe from long-term damage. There's a little bit that goes into the balancing of all those chemicals, and figuring out how all the parts relate to each other will be the biggest hurdle. For pool chemistry to make sense, you must be familiar with the concepts related to what each chemical is supposed to do and how they react with one. Don't look at the long chemical names and become overwhelmed. Look at what that chemical does to your water to make it a safer and more comfortable environment for bathers.

Chemicals are used to sanitize and balance your pool's water. The following sections introduce you to how chemistry will work for your pool.

Keeping your pool clean and clear

Sanitation is what you do to keep your pool water clean. You add chemicals to your water to kill bacteria and other contaminants and to help keep the water nice and clear — and safe for people to swim in. When you're picking a way to keep your pool clean, you have three major types of products to choose from (which you can read about in detail in Chapter 10):

>> **Chlorine:** This is the most common and usually least expensive way to sanitize a pool. It is highly efficient because of its aggression on bacteria and other contaminates, but that also makes it known for being slightly more aggressive on surfaces of the pool and on skin and eyes. It is used as a maintenance sanitizer through tablets or powder and also can be found in a liquid form which is more for shocking (oxidizing).

REMEMBER

Saltwater pools are becoming very popular. Some people don't realize that saltwater pools still require chlorine. These pools use a salt-to-chlorine generator to create chlorine gas by splitting the sodium chloride (salt) molecules.

>> **Bromine:** Most commonly used in hot tubs, this chemical is very similar to chlorine in a lot of ways because it's also a halogen-based sanitizer (chlorine and bromine are grouped together on the Periodic Table). But it has two major flaws to it in the pool world:

- *Breaks down in sunlight:* Bromine doesn't hold up well in the sun. UV light destabilizes it and breaks it down, so the numbers drop quickly in a pool sitting in direct sunlight.

- *Costs a pretty penny:* Over the past few years, bromine has become extremely expensive, costing almost double as much as chlorine does.

If you are using bromine in your pool, it is most commonly found in a tablet form and used in a similar way to chlorine tablets as a maintenance sanitizer. It can be found in a powder form but that is most commonly seen in use for spas.

>> **Biguanide:** This bromine- and chlorine-free sanitizer was originally created to be a less aggressive hand sanitizer for scrubbing in as a surgeon. Biguanide has become a popular choice for people who want a pool that's completely halogen free. It tends to be on the more expensive side, and it certainly has a learning curve to it. But if you have money, and dedication required to use this system, you'll never want a different one because it is so soft on your skin and your pool will be looking brand new for decades.

All the products come in a liquid form with very simple dosing. You use the same amount every week of the same chemicals for maintenance. If you run into a problem, like algae or water mold, just use higher doses of the products you use weekly. See Chapters 10 and 11 for all the clean-pool requirements.

Chemicals and the importance of balancing them

Balancing your pool chemical levels is more important than almost any other thing when it comes to pool maintenance. Your pool water balance is made up of your total alkalinity, pH, calcium hardness, temperature, total dissolved solids (TDS), and cyanuric acid (CYA). All those pieces fit together like a puzzle to keep your pool from basically eating itself from the inside out.

When I say "balance your water," I'm referring to the process of getting your water to not be scale-forming or corrosive. Those two water states can quickly lead to a disaster in your system, on your surface, and on the surrounding pieces of equipment. Essentially, your goal is to make sure that the water in your pool craves no extra minerals that it doesn't have or need. Water will always try to reach some sort of equilibrium, and to get there, it requires a certain amount of minerals in its balance. If it's lacking them, it will take those minerals from anything it touches. And if it has too much, it will deposit them on all those same things.

Another important part about water balancing involves making sure the sanitizer that's killing bacteria and preventing illness remains efficient. Your pool chemistry's cause and effect will change the way the water wants to go. For example, if your acidity level is very high, the water lands on the scaling side and could create actual physical scale on the inside of things that are in your pool system. It also directly affects the speed and efficiency with which your sanitizer reacts, especially chlorine. If you have a bunch of chlorine in the pool, but it's only 8 percent efficient because of the poor balance of the other chemical components of the water, then the chlorine in the water isn't doing you much good.

Head to Chapter 9 for everything you need to know to keep your pool in perfect balance.

Practicing DIY versus Hiring a Pro

One question will always flick around in pool owners' minds, especially in the summertime: Do you hire a professional to do regular cleaning and maintenance, or do you do it yourself?

I think this is really a question based on personal preference. For instance, in my line of work, pool season is non-stop. You may be like me and have very limited time off. And when you do have it, you probably want to enjoy it. I don't currently have my own pool, but if I did, I would likely want someone to do my weekly service and even my openings and closings. It would be nice to come home and use your pool whenever you want and know it's balanced and clean without having to do anything. I would totally do that.

On the flip side, there are a lot of people who enjoy cleaning their pools. I like cleaning pools, obviously, because I do it for a living. So I understand someone wanting to do it themselves. If you have the available time to spend and you don't mind doing the work, I think everyone can do maintenance on their own pool.

TIP

Where I do recommend hiring a professional is when it comes to winterizing your pool, especially if you have a pool that has underground lines. If you're in an environment where your water is going to freeze, unless you are 100 percent confident in what you're doing, I don't recommend winterizing your pipes on your own. I've seen too many simple mistakes made because the person trying to winterize the pool was inexperienced but didn't want to pay someone (which I really do understand). But their little mistake led to a cracked pipe underneath the concrete deck. It quickly turned into a very expensive fix.

Chapter **2**

Choosing the Right Kind of Pool

When you first start the journey of picking out a pool, it's usually a battle between inground or above ground, round or oval, rectangle or free form. Although a lot of these things can come down to purely just personal preference, I've been asked my opinion on what's "better" almost every time I do a sales pitch. *Better* is a word that's left up to the buyer's interpretation. Some people may think it's better to get an oval pool because of the length, where others may think round is better for their property shape.

So, let me just break down the good, the bad, and the ugly of each style of pool in this chapter, and you can decide what's best for you.

Location, Location, Location: Inground versus Above Ground

Being a person from the Granite State (that's New Hampshire), I run into problems when it comes to choosing a good location more often than you might think. With inground pools, you obviously have to dig a massive hole. And in some areas right around where I live, the rocks in the ground make digging a hole like that nearly impossible. There are always size restrictions that you have to consider — and not just for the pool itself, but also the machinery that will be needed to build that pool. Inground pools require excavators and other construction equipment to be able to dig into the yard where the pool is going.

Of course, above ground pools also need excavation equipment and a way to bring in the stone dust or sand for the base, so both pools need ample room in their build location. The best part of an above ground pool is that, as long as it isn't over any part of a septic system, you don't have nearly as many restrictions. Above ground pool installers need to dig down only 6 feet or so — as long as they don't hit a boulder 5 feet down, you should be okay.

There's also the consideration of what kind of environment you'll be building in. For example:

>> If you're in an area that has a high water table, an inground pool may not even be a choice. Or if it is, there will always be the possibility of your pool liner floating away from the walls because water can creep in between the liner and the wall, or even the pool itself being popped out of the ground.

>> If you're in a very high wind area, like on a hill or mountain, you have to consider the effects of wind if you want to install an above ground pool. Above ground pools can handle quite a bit of turbulence, but everything has a breaking point.

>> If you're in an area near a coast, the salt in the air from the ocean is factor to consider and may limit your above ground pool options. The salts are very corrosive on most metals. The corrosion that saltwater causes will destroy a steel pool very quickly, and that damage wouldn't be covered under warranty.

No matter your location — whether it's rocky and surrounded by trees, or level with nary an obstacle in sight — it's best to meet with a professional to go over all options available to you and to find out what restrictions may be in play that you weren't even aware of.

TIP

More than a Giant Bathtub in Your Backyard: Above Ground Pools

For some reason, an above ground pool is seen as a less long-term fixture that doesn't require as much maintenance as an inground pool does. Well, my dad's pool has been up since 2004, and it's still in excellent condition because he takes excellent care of it. Above ground pools are an expensive investment and not to be taken lightly. Unless you're purchasing a $300 inflatable or easy set pool from a big box store (which I talk about in the section "Something Different: Inflatable and Easy Set Pools," later in this chapter), expect your pool to last on average around 10 years. But, with proper upkeep, you could get 15, or even 20 years of use.

All pools require maintenance and a little bit of know-how, so an above ground isn't any less work than an inground pool of equal size. (Flip to the section "More than a Big Hole in Your Yard: Inground Pools," later in this chapter, for the details on inground pools.) Above ground pools are just as susceptible to algae and chemical damage as inground pools, but they're also just as capable of providing an at-home staycation.

Looking at the benefits of an above ground pool

Above ground pools can be just as fun and relaxing as inground pools, and they can be a lot less work to get! There are a lot of perks in choosing above ground pools:

REMEMBER

>> **The less-expensive option:** The average 15-foot-by-30-foot oval above ground pool is around $15,000 to $20,000 total after being installed. That price tag includes permits, installation of electrical and filter systems, and adding water and accessories. There are some options that may be more expensive and some that may be less expensive, but standard above ground pools are always less expensive than their inground counterparts.

> If you went with a slat-wall aluminum pool (commonly referred to as an *on-ground pool*) from the manufacturers Gibraltar or Kayak, or a custom sectional wall pool from the manufacturer Radiant, then you could absolutely end up in a much higher price range. But that's where research will do you some good, figuring out what may be best for you.

>> **A temporary fixture:** Above ground pools are considered a temporary fixture by building departments, so they don't affect your property's resale value. For a long time, an inground pool was usually seen as a negative to your house's value. But with the Covid-19 pandemic, an inground pool became more of a selling feature.

> Having the ability to remove the pool with very little expense is a big plus for above ground pools. I know that, after the kids grow up and no one uses the pool anymore, homeowners often just pay to have an above ground pool torn down and use the stone dust/sand base (this is the material brought in to be the level and cushiony base underneath your liner) as a spot for a fire pit.

>> **Equal the amount of fun:** An above ground pool brings just as much fun and relaxation to you and your friends and family as an inground pool. I grew up with an above ground pool that had a simple rectangle deck, and we had a blast jumping in, swimming for hours, or just relaxing on a float. We had as much fun in our above ground pool as we did in my friend's inground pool.

TIP

Having a deck, even a small one, makes all the difference. Being able to crawl out of the pool and lay out without having to get fully out of the pool allows you to relax and hang out longer.

>> **Adaptable to most locations:** Above ground pools have a major benefit because they can work in most yards. In locations where an inground pool isn't an option — such as areas that are too rocky, or that may have a high water table or poorly placed septic system — an above ground pool may be your best option.

>> **Easy to close:** Another advantage to above ground pools is that they're a much more homeowner-friendly pool to close, when compared with inground pools. (Opening above ground pools can be just as much work as inground pools, but closing them is no comparison.) As long as you follow basic guidelines, winterizing can be quick and easy, with very little chance for winter damage. (For details on opening a pool, check out Chapter 6 and for information on winterizing, turn to Chapter 8.)

REMEMBER

Winter damage isn't always in your control, but the preventative measures to limit the risks are much simpler on an above ground pool than an inground one.

Choosing the right above ground for you

When choosing an above ground pool, there are a few factors you want to take into consideration. First is the size and shape of the pool, because you do have options! Another thing to consider are the materials that make up the frame of the pool. Then, you want to decide on how high you would like the walls to be and what type of liner will work best.

Oval versus round

An oval pool could be considered a little bit more fun than a round pool. The length is better for laps, volleyball, and splitting the pool up into a play side and a relaxing side (such as with kids and parents). Ovals also tend to be a little easier to fit in some yards. In my town, the housing lots are small, so people often opt for an oval pool because it can give you more water but take up less space. Oval pools are also easier to build a deck against, and usually allow you to get a larger deck that needs less complicated angles.

As for price, the oval is the more expensive of the two shapes for a number of reasons:

» Complex constructional requirements needed to keep the long sides of an oval pool sturdy and straight

» A special bracket system that contributes to a lengthier and more complicated install

» More expensive materials

Round versus oval

A round pool will be not only less expensive to purchase than an oval pool, but also less expensive to install. A 24-foot round pool can hold the same volume of water as a 15-foot-by-30-foot oval pool, but the oval pool can be almost double the cost to have installed.

Round pools have the effect of feeling much larger than oval pools. If you were to see a 24-foot round pool and a 15-foot-by-30-foot oval pool next to each other, the 24-foot round pool seems roomier. If you're looking to get a bigger bang for your buck, I feel that round is the way to go.

Choosing frame materials

For the frame of your pool, you have three main options:

» Steel

» Aluminum

» Resin

Steel is going to be the most common option for frame and wall choice. It is a heavy duty, durable material that is going to be the least expensive available to you. Since the pandemic, steel costs have risen quite a bit, but it is still the lowest price point option. Durability is really where this material is top tier. It can withstand a lot is wear and tear from roughhousing young swimmers! Where it lacks, is going to be the rusting factor. With proper care, such as balancing your water and being sure all leaks are addressed immediately, steel will stay rust-free and strong for years and years. What it can't handle is salt. Saltwater pools are a no-no in steel-framed above ground pools due to its seriously corrosive nature, and in most cases, it completely voids your pool's warranty.

Aluminum is a great choice because it has similar durability as steel with zero chance of rust. Now, the aluminum frame does have the possibility of corrosion from salt, so again this is not an option if you are looking to have a saltwater pool. I think aluminum is a great choice if you are going with a more traditional style of sanitizing your pool because of the fact is does not rust. Aluminum does tend to be a more expensive option from steel, since it is just a more expensive material in general, but I think the benefits are worth it.

Resin frame pools have been the way to go lately. A major reason is because it is the only acceptable frame option if you want a saltwater pool. Resin frames are not quite as durable against physical abuse such as tree limbs falling or swimmers sitting on them, but it is still a very strong material.

Does wall height matter?

Deciding on the height of your pool wall is all about preference. A 48-inch wall option has become less popular as most people want their pool as deep as possible. Most brands offer options between 52 and 54 inches. The water level in your above ground pool is going to be approximately 8 inches down from the top of the wall, so with a 48-inch pool, your water level would be around 40 inches, and so on. There is no benefit or disadvantage to getting a shorter or taller wall height outside of the water level raising a few inches with each size increase.

Liner types

When choosing your above ground pool, you will also be faced with the option of a type of liner. There are 2 main types of liners: overlap and beaded. Beaded has a choice between a regular bead and a j-hook.

An overlap liner has a wall height much taller than the wall of the pool because it gets placed up and over the wall. It is then secured with a plastic strip that sits over the liner and onto the wall. See Figure 2-1, image A, for a visual of an overlap liner.

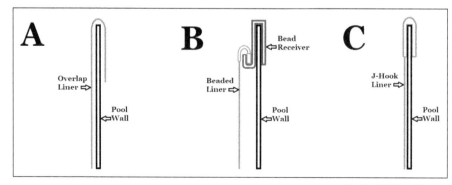

FIGURE 2-1: Types of liners: overlap (A), regular bead (B), and j-hook bead (C).

Courtesy of Kristine Blanchard

The pros of an overlap liner include:

>> They are a less expensive liner option for purchase because they have a very simple construction. They are just vinyl with no added pieces needed for install.

>> They are easy to install; they just drape (overlap) over the top edge of the wall. Because of the excess of the length on the walls, you have some wiggle room for error if the bottom of the liner is not perfectly centered.

Some cons of an overlap liner include:

>> The patterns available for overlaps are slightly limited since you can't make a straight line with the top. So, liner patterns with decorative borders along the top are not an option.

>> When the liner gets to a point from wear and tear that it needs to be replaced, the pool frame must be partially disassembled because the liner is locked in place by the top rail of the pool.

>> The extra material that folds over the wall is visible from the outside after the liner is installed.

REMEMBER

After a week of water being in the pool and once the pool has settled and the liner is in its final resting place, the excess liner on the outside of the pool can be rolled up and tucked out of sight. It is not recommended to cut the excess off, because if there is a shift in the ground underneath the pool and the liner needs to stretch a little, you want the excess liner to supply the give it will need.

If you do not want an overlap liner, you can get a beaded liner, which is when the liner itself has an extra piece of bonded material meant to snap into a track or hang on the wall. All bead styles can have a decorative straight-line border because the bead will keep the liner straight with the top of the wall. The two kinds of beads you see most are a standard bead, which is shown in Figure 2-1, image B, and a j-hook, which is image C:

>> **Standard bead:** This type has a separate track that hangs on the wall, and the bead that is on the liner will snap into that track. Installation is fairly simple. The track for the liner is accessible from the inside of the pool without having to take the pool apart. You can pull the old bead out of the track and put the new liner in the same track.

>> **J-hook bead:** The hook-like bead hangs on the wall and the railings are installed on top of the bead to hold it in place. To replace the liner, you need to disassemble the top rail of the pool to take off and put on a new one.

The kind of liner you get is determined on whether you want to see the excess from the outside, or if you want it to be easily replaceable for the possible future.

More than a Big Hole in Your Yard: Inground Pools

Here's the big question: Why inground pools? If there were no restrictions and no price tag, most people would prefer an inground pool over above ground because aesthetically inground pools are the more sought-after option. But, unfortunately, an inground pool just isn't always an option.

I go over how location can play a huge part of the decision-making process in the section "Location, Location, Location: Inground versus Above Ground," earlier in this chapter. And, of course, the environment may lean you away from an inground pool if you have only three good months to use the pool. Sometimes it's hard justifying the price of an inground pool in a seasonal environment.

But, inground pools just have a certain feel to them. They don't just become a part of your backyard. They become the focal point, and you build your yard around it. (This could be seen as a plus or a minus, depending on the person.)

WARNING

Inground pools can affect your property value, your taxes, and your home insurance. Be sure you're aware of all of those changes before committing to a $50,000 project.

Benefits of inground pools

When it comes to the benefits of an inground pool, it isn't necessarily that they'll serve a better purpose, but that they serve the purpose better. Here are a few benefits to consider:

>> **An oasis vibe:** One of the pluses is that they tend to be more aesthetically pleasing. Don't get me wrong: I know for a fact that there are some beautiful above ground pool setups. But inground pools tend to have more of a natural, oasis feeling to them because they can tie in to the surrounding environment.

>> **Much more customizable:** Of course, depending on your location and environment, not all options are available to you. But there's no doubt that an inground pool can be built to your specifications. Above ground pools do have some variety to them in this day and age, and more varieties may become

available over time. But inground pools have the ability to add water features, different shapes and depths, easier entry options, and more luxury add-ons. No matter what area of the country you live in, you have a multitude of options to choose from for your inground pool.

» **Sound structural durability:** An inground pool that's properly maintained can give you 30-plus years of memories and summer fun. There will always be wear and tear, and maintenance is absolutely more expensive with inground pools compared to above ground pools. But an inground pool is more long term and permanent than even the highest quality above ground pool.

Picking the shape of your inground pool

With inground pools coming in all shapes and sizes, it is hard to decide which is best for you. The answer really comes down to your preference. Each shape has some unique attributes to it, but just like most things, those can be a plus or a minus to different people. Here are some common shapes to consider:

» **Rectangle:** The most common pool shape, the rectangle is great for a modern and linier look. They can have 90-degree corners, or you can soften the look with rounded corners. Rectangles are a timeless shape and offer a great swimming area for laps. You customize the depths. For example, you could choose to have an extra big shallow end for more pool activities like volleyball. They are also the easiest pools to cover with both a solar and a winter cover because the shape is easy to work with. They can be long and skinny to fit a narrower yard, or they can be squarer if you're looking to just go for a dip.

» **Kidney:** A less popular shape nowadays, the kidney shape was very popular 50+ years ago. Personally, I love the look of a small kidney-shaped pool. It allows you to have a lot of swimming area without taking up as much room as a rectangular pool with the same measurements. They are still a great pool for exercise lap swimming but with more of a natural look.

» **Free form:** A free form pool is whatever you want it to be. The shape does not have to stick to any outline, and it can be as big or as small as you want. Steel wall and fiberglass pools will be limited on customizing shapes as they come in pre-built kits from the manufacturer, so this is where gunite-plaster pools really begin to come into play (see the next section). They have a natural look that gives the oasis feel people shoot for.

Types of inground pools

Here are a few very common kinds of inground pools:

>> **Liner pools:** Made with either a steel wall or concrete wall.

>> **Fiberglass pools:** One-piece shells dropped into a hole prepped for them.

>> **Gunite-plaster pools:** A rebar frame built into a dug hole, then sprayed with a gunite mixture for durability. Plaster is the most common finish layer sprayed on top of the gunite, but the finish can be pebble, aggregate, tile, glass, and many more.

All of these options really do have their reasons for being available. There isn't one kind that will work best for everyone. So, I cover some of the pros and cons to all of them in the following sections.

Liner pools

Liner pools tend to be one of the least expensive options to install. With steel-wall liner pools, you can choose from kits that have a lot of preset shape options, or you can customize the shape. (Pre-Covid, the steel-wall liner pools were less expensive than concrete-wall liner pools. But with the increase in the price of steel after the pandemic, concrete and steel may have almost the same cost.)

With liner pools, you have a lot of color and pattern options, which allow you to get the aesthetic you may be seeking. The vinyl itself comes in an array of colors, such as black, dark blue, light blue, white, and beige. Then, the manufacturer takes the vinyl and prints a pattern on top of it. Some patterns look like pebbles, sun rays on top of the water, or small tiles. You can go traditional blue; a more earth tone, stone/beige color; or full black. With proper chemical maintenance, a liner can keep its pattern for over 10 years and look just as beautiful as the day it was installed.

A big con to liners is their susceptibility to minor holes and leaks:

>> **Dog damage:** This is a common concern for people who have dogs who love to swim. Although you can train a dog to not touch the bottom or to wear booties, it's easier to just not have to worry about it!

>> **Mysterious leaks:** Finding the location of a leak in your liner can sometimes be a huge hassle. They make equipment that helps pinpoint the location of a leak, and underwater patches can be put on by homeowners. That doesn't mean it's a fun or easy task.

>> **Winter woes:** Liners also can tear from winter damage, which can lead to a devastating amount of damage that needs repair.

You'll also be forced to replace the liner at some point in the pool's life (liners generally last 10 to 15 years), which isn't an inexpensive task.

Fiberglass pools

Fiberglass pools are in the middle on the expense scale. They're usually more expensive than liner pools, but less expensive than plaster. Here are some perks to fiberglass:

>> **Durable:** You can't easily puncture it, making it an awesome choice for pets and kids.

>> **Low maintenance:** They have very little short-term or long-term maintenance, so after it's installed, you're good to go.

>> **Repairable:** In the case of an abrasion to the surface, they have repair kits (but it may never match 100 percent).

But there are a few cons to fiberglass:

>> **Not customizable:** The shells are what they are. You can't necessarily customize your pool because the shapes and sizes are preset.

>> **Size limits:** You do have options from a variety of different brands that sell different shapes and sizes, but none of them will be wider than 16 feet. The pool will need to be transported from the location it was built to the job size, and to keep transportation safe and manageable, the pool can't be bigger than 16 feet wide.

>> **The great pool escape:** Because this pool is one solid piece in the ground, if your pool isn't properly winterized in an area that has high water tables or freezing temperatures, the shell of the pool can literally pop up out of the ground. Be sure your yard is a good fit for this style pool by consulting with a pool professional.

Other than costing a bit more than a liner pool and having some size restrictions, a fiberglass pool is an excellent choice.

Gunite-plaster pools

Gunite-plaster pools are the most customizable option available because they are essentially built from scratch. They are made by digging a hole to the desired shape you want, creating a rebar frame, and then spraying a mixture of dry gunite and water onto the frame (this is done by professionals because you want the mixture to be the correct ratio of water and gunite mix). After that gunite layer is complete, you can add your surface type, which you have the choice of regular plaster (most common), colored plaster, glass beading, pebble finish, or many others. They can be built to any size, shape, and color that you can think of, which is why this style of pool is so desirable.

Gunite–plaster pools are seen all over the world, but you will notice that they are extra prevalent in warmer climates over cold ones. A few reasons for that are due to their upfront cost. It is hard to justify spending almost $100,000 on a pool you can only use a few months of the year. Also, gunite is very durable, but in freezing temperatures, it is possible to get cracks in the wall of the pool which can be pricey to repair.

All plaster pool surface types have their ups and downs, but they all share a few things in common:

>> **Cost:** This style pool is by far the most expensive option. Between the install and the upkeep, plaster is the most expensive and time-consuming type of pool.

>> **Care:** Most of the finishes on a plaster pool require some serious elbow grease during the curing process and also can take a strict chemical regiment to maintain properly.

>> **Longevity:** Plaster pools of all finishes are all also the most long-lasting inground pool option.

REMEMBER

A pool's longevity, of course, is based on very good maintenance with your chemicals, so make sure to read and read again Chapter 9. Poor chemistry could destroy an $80,000 plaster pool in just a few years.

Something Different: Inflatable and Easy Set Pools

Oh man, have these types of pools really taken off in recent years! They've been around forever but really have become a true contender in pool selection recently. Inflatable and easy set pools are many folks' introduction into the pool world. They're inexpensive, easy to set up (shocking, I know), and just as enjoyable as their sturdier and more permanent counterparts.

For these inexpensive pool options, you have:

>> **Inflatable pools:** This type will have a ring on the top that you fill with air and the rest of the pool is filled with water. Essentially, you get a vinyl bowl of water with a squishy air-filled ring on top to keep the water in.

>> **Easy set pools:** This type consists of a PVC pipe/metal pipe frame and a vinyl liner. The frame is set up into the shape and size it was designed for, and the vinyl liner hangs on the frame and is filled with water.

These pools have grown to be much more than a toy for toddlers or dogs. They're more durable and efficient than they used to be, and they're used in backyards all over the world. I honestly feel that if you're interested in trying out a pool to see whether you or your friends and family would use one enough to go for a more permanent type of pool, then it's a fantastic option.

Pros and cons of temporary pools

Entering into the pool world can be a little intimidating (especially if you read Chapter 9 of this book first, which talks all about maintaining your pool water). These types of pools offer an avenue that doesn't lock you in to a five- to ten-year commitment. Their benefits include that they

>> Are cheap and versatile

>> Come in a variety of sizes and grades

>> Are not permanent

Having the option to use it for one year and figure out whether you even want a pool long-term will save you so many headaches. But, at the same time, these pools can be adapted to run as efficiently as a standard above ground pool.

Having a lot of quality options in the temporary pool category allows you to decide whether you'll use it for one season or five. There are people who take an easy set pool and build a deck around it! You can create a landscaped masterpiece that the whole neighborhood could enjoy, using a $300 pool as your centerpiece.

Here are a few downsides to these pools:

>> **They're not incredibly durable.** They're (generally) not meant to be winter-ized or withstand any type of severe climate changes.

>> **They can't really be fixed outside of patches.** Because the pool industry sees these pools as toys, rather than legitimate pools, they don't make a lot of replacement parts for them. And if you can find replacements, they typically have to be purchased online directly from the company that manufactured the pool.

This isn't a huge deal, unless you're in a situation where the pool is nonfunctional without that part.

>> **The filters that usually come with these pools are severely undersized.** This means the filters take longer to clean up algae or cloudy water, and they don't move the water very efficiently.

REMEMBER

If you're trying to test out a pool for as little money upfront as possible, then be aware that the filters will give you more work than you would have on a regular above ground or inground pool that has a properly-sized filter. When the filter is undersized, vacuuming, filtering, and mixing chemicals is not done as efficiently and takes longer.

Tips and tricks for temporary pools

While these pools have become more popular, I've figured out how to adapt to caring for these types of pools and found a few ways to make caring for them a little easier. Consider these tips:

>> **Upgrade the filter.** I highly recommend upgrading the filter that it comes with. As I mention in the preceding section, the filters that these pools come with are really undersized and may not be able to keep up with the pool. If you have the ability to, replace the whole filter system it comes with for a new one.

TIP

You may have to use special adapters, but if you can seek out a pool store that sells these products, they can typically walk you through the setup process. I know my job here at Paquette Pools and Spas in Hooksett does it!

>> **Run your filter longer.** If you can't get a bigger filter system, run your filter for longer than the average pool owner usually does. The typical runtime for standard pools is 8 to 12 hours, with 10 hours being ideal. This amount of time will circulate the pool efficiently and turn over the water twice in most cases. The filters and pumps on easy set or inflatable pools aren't sized properly, so they won't turn over the water as quickly. I would set them to run a minimum of 12 hours a day to be sure you don't have any type of algae blooms.

>> **Practice preventative maintenance.** Treat the chemicals in this pool like you would treat a regular inground or above ground pool. Preventative maintenance on these types of pools is key because if you do end up with a severe algae bloom or cloudy water, the filters really have a hard time getting the pool back to clear and clean. If you treat the pool water regularly, circulate that water properly, and keep problems at bay, these pools will treat you very well!

Chapter **3**

The Machinery That Makes Your Pool Work

As much as I wish that chemicals and swimming alone were enough to keep your pool sparkling clear, it's not quite that simple. Your filter system is the heart of the whole pool, pumping chemicals where they need to be and keeping everything moving. Without a filter system, it wouldn't be a pool, it would be a pond! Knowing how your pool works and what everything is used for can help make you a more confident and well-informed pool owner, making your summer season as smooth as possible.

Introducing the Parts of Your Pool

When it comes to owning a pool, it can be hard to get all the terminology correct. Not knowing the names for all the parts and pieces can make it more difficult for you in the long term, especially if you ever need help from your local pool store. Most pool professionals know the lingo — and we also know the fake lingo very well! But if you learn the proper terms and names for the parts you're referring to, you can impress the pros and get the parts and assistance you need quick and easy!

The following sections cover all the common parts of your pool that keep the water pristine, and I touch base on some of the additional components that could be part of your system. I also give you insight into the many options available to you and some of the key features of each piece of equipment.

Suctions

Starting on the suction side of things, there are three main ways the water is pulled into the front of your pump: your skimmer, your side suction, and your main drain. Not all pools have all three pathways, and some actually have only one. But your pool always has at least a skimmer. Commonly, newer pools come with a skimmer and a main drain; side suctions have become less common as robotic vacuums become more popular.

Skimmer

Your *skimmer* is a square or rectangular opening on the side of the pool that contains a basket. Water flows in through the skimmer, leading to the pump, and the skimmer catches large surface debris so that leaves or other large floating litter don't end up in your pipes.

You'll have to replace some skimmer parts because of normal wear and tear. This may be something you have to do annually for things like the weir door, but in most cases the replaceable parts break down every few seasons. Common skimmer parts include:

>> Lid

>> Skimmer basket

>> Weir door

You can pretty easily identify the lid and the basket, but the weir door is a little lesser known.

TECHNICAL STUFF

The *weir* is the flap in the mouth of the skimmer that flows in towards the basket when the pool is running, helping draw water towards the skimmer basket and creating better surface suction. When the filter is off, the weir door works like a floating dam, preventing any debris collected in the basket from floating back into the pool through the mouth of the skimmer. A weir door isn't essential for proper filtration, but it sure does help! So, if your pool doesn't have a weir door, it isn't life or death — but it's worth getting a new one.

When you're looking for replacement parts for your skimmer, remember that there's no such thing as a universal basket or lid that fits all skimmers. There are, of course, some very commonly used types of skimmers (Hayward is a big one), but not all brands or even model years within brands are the same. If you need a replacement part, hold onto the old one and use it for reference. You may also find a part number on the underside of the skimmer lid. Take this part (or part number) with you when shopping (whether in-person or online) to confirm that you get the correct replacement part.

TIP

To make sure that your skimmer works properly, confirm that the water level is just over halfway up the opening of your skimmer. If you have the water level too low, the skimmer could *cavitate* (pull in air along with water). See Figure 3-1 for an example of when the water is too low. If it's too high, you may not get the best surface skimming. Right in the middle or an inch over the middle is ideal.

FIGURE 3-1:
This inground pool skimmer has a water level about an inch too low.

Kristine Blanchard (Book Author)

Side suction

Side suctions (which are holes on the side of the pool where water draws in, usually used for vacuuming) look similar to a return outlet (generally, a threaded hole in the pool; see the section "Returns," later in this chapter, for more on these pool features). Typically, a side suction is a little deeper than a return and will have a small grate over it. It works as an alternative suction port for the pump, which can be used along with your skimmer or instead of your skimmer if the water is too low, or it can be used as a vacuuming port. In Chapter 7 where I cover vacuuming, I explain how to use them in this way.

Side suctions are placed lower than the skimmer on the side of a pool, so if the water in your pool ends up lower than the mouth of the skimmer, you can simply plug or shut off the skimmer and use only the side suction. Going side-suction-only allows you to continue filtering, even if the water level drops.

WARNING

If a side suction is the only open suction on your pool, don't let anyone or anything near it — especially kids, and especially if it has no grate! The suction is incredibly powerful and could easily suck in a child's hand or hair, causing serious injury or even death.

Main drain

A *main drain*, also known as a *floor drain*, is a suction on the floor of the pool. This suction is key for good water circulation! If you don't have a main drain in a pool that has a deep end, it's very hard to properly circulate the bottom half of the pool's water. It will look like a round grated cover on the bottom of the pool; the cover creates a barrier for the actual pipe.

MAIN DRAIN SAFETY MEASURES

All pools that were built or refurbished after 2008 have two main drains in the deep end. The drains don't run to two separate pipes; they're connected underneath the pool and lead to one pipe that runs to the pump. There are two drains on all new pools to address serious safety concerns.

In 2002, a young girl named Virginia Graeme Baker was sucked into the single floor suction drain of a hot tub and lost her life. Then, in 2008, another fatal accident occurred with a 6-year-old girl, who was restrained underwater by a single floor suction drain and drowned.

In December in 2008, the U.S. federal government passed a law called the Virginia Graeme Baker Pool and Spa Safety Act. In commercial pools, the local Department for Environmental Services enforces this law, and, in residential pools, your local building department is responsible to do the final inspection. Of course, each state could have a separate governing body, but there is always someone put in place to help prevent any chance of entrapment from floor suctions ever again.

Because of this law, all new pools are required to have two main drain ports a minimum of 3 feet apart. If your pool has only one main drain on the floor, be sure it's up to date on the required type of cover. If you are not sure whether your cover is the correct kind or not, show a photo to your local pool professional.

The main drain makes a massive difference in how well the pool filters and circulates water. It's not uncommon for pool professionals (myself included) to recommend that you set up your manual vacuum at the bottom of your deep end to aid in circulation if your pool doesn't have a main drain. (See Chapter 12 for more on pool vacuums.)

If you have a main drain and a skimmer, you want to have both of those pipes open using the valve(s) in the front of your pump. Reference the upcoming section "Valves."

Returns

A *return* is exactly what it sounds like — it's where the water comes back into the pool after it goes through your whole filter system. When the water pours back into the pool, it creates the flow that guides the water to the skimmers, creating the continuous circle of filtration. Pools can come with two main types of returns: wall returns and floor returns.

Wall returns

Your *wall returns,* also known as *jets,* are the spouts that appear about 18 to 20 inches down your pool wall that shoot the water back into the pool. Most above ground pools have only one wall return, but inground pools typically have a number of them. Older inground pools may have only one wall return, but newer inground pools have at least two.

The proper way your return jets should face is at a 45-degree angle downward, away from the skimmer. This angle is especially important in above ground pools because the majority of above ground pools don't have main drains, which means that if the return is facing upward towards the surface of the pool, you don't circulate the pool fully.

WARNING

Yes, angling the return jets upward towards the surface of the water helps get the leaves and bugs off the top of the water, but it doesn't help move any water more than 18 inches down from the surface. This water movement only at the surface won't move the chemicals you add throughout the pool. And if the water doesn't circulate, it affects proper filtration.

On inground pools that have numerous wall returns, you can sometimes get away with having one return facing up towards the surface for better skimming (as long as you position all the other returns facing down). If you have only two returns, you can face one up and one down. This works best if you have one in the deep end of the pool and one in the shallow end.

Floor returns

Not all pools have a floor type of return system, but for the select pools that do, I want to make sure I cover them. *Floor jets,* or *floor cleaner jets,* are little heads that pop up on the floor of the pool. Instead of the water returning back to the pool through the returns, it flows through a mechanism that allows the water to flow through one floor jet (or a set of jets) at a time.

These systems are beneficial in some ways because they agitate any debris on the floor and kick it up towards the surface, where it can get skimmed out. Floor returns do also help with circulation if you don't have a main drain. And they're great if you have a heater! If you're actively heating the water, having it come up from the bottom heats the water much more quickly and evenly.

WARNING

The biggest downside to these floor cleaning jets is that they restrict the flow of the pump pretty significantly, especially if the pool has an oversized pump. If you imagine it sort of like a pressure washer, the water is under an immense amount of pressure and is allowed to escape through only one small port at a time. It can create quite a bit of back pressure in your filter and can sometimes cause internal damage to the pump motor from strain or the internal components of your filter.

Valves

Valve can be a broad term. There are so many kinds, such as ball valves, 3-way valves, and multiport valves. These types of valves are pretty common in the swimming pool world, so I touch base on all of them in the following sections. I cover multiport valves in the section "Filtering Through the Options," later in this chapter.

Ball valves

A *ball valve,* also called a *2-way valve,* a plastic shut-off that allows you to stop water flow with the turn of a small handle. This type of valve can be used just about anywhere you may want to shut off the water flow. Sometimes, this is on the waste line or a skimmer line; or for above ground pools or systems that are down gravity (which are filters lower than the water level in the pool like on most above ground pools) on the return lines. Ball valves have a simple mechanism and are typically inexpensive.

A benefit of ball valves is that they usually have a quick disconnect union in the center that makes it easy for you to be able to open the valve up and quickly change gaskets or washers inside the valve.

3-way (or diverter) valves

Diverter valves are another style of valve used to change flow from one pipe to another or to shut off pipes completely. There are *3-way valves,* as shown in Figure 3-2, which allow you to choose to have the flow of water go left, right, or both. These valves are also fairly common, especially in a pool that has two suctions in front of the pump. Instead of having two separate ball valves, one for each pipe, you have one and can choose which direction you want the water to flow with one single valve.

There are different kinds and different brands of 3-way valves, so if you need parts, be sure that you're getting the correct pieces!

Kristine Blanchard (Book Author)

FIGURE 3-2:
A 3-way valve that controls a skimmer (left) and a main drain (right) that goes to the pump (bottom).

Other things

When I say *other things,* I'm blanketing all non-essential equipment that may be on your filter system. The two common ones that I cover in the following sections are chlorinators and booster pumps. Both of these items are common and easy to identify.

Chlorinators

The term *chlorinator* can cover a few different things. There are tab chlorinators, both in-line and off-line; salt generators (also known as salt-to-chlorine generators); and even brominators (that last one isn't too common, but I'm sure someone out there has one).

TAB CHLORINATORS

Tab chlorinators are often canisters about 18 to 20 inches tall and 6 inches in diameter. They can be either plumbed directly into your pipes or *off-line* (which means they have small ¼-inch-thick hoses that connect to small holes drilled into the pipes). These off-line chlorinators are especially helpful if you have a small amount of space in your equipment area.

To use a tab chlorinator, fill it with trichlor-based chlorine tablets (which are made of the chemical trichloro-s-triazinetrione — trichlor for short) and set the dial on the front to your desired setting. If you're not sure what setting to choose, I usually recommend to start at halfway open. Give it two days, and then check your chlorine levels by using your kit and make adjustments as needed. You can use all different shapes of chlorine tabs in the chlorinator, whether it's 1-inch, 3-inch, or even square — it doesn't matter! If you fill your chlorinator completely, it provides most pools with five to seven days of continuous sanitation.

There are some chlorinators out there that have specific canisters that snap into them, so if you're unsure about what your chlorinator needs, check with your local pool professional.

WARNING

Don't use any other type of chlorine tab in these canisters except for trichlor. If you use ones made with calcium hypochlorite (cal hypo) or dichloro-s-triazinetrione (dichlor), they dissolve too quickly, which causes the chlorine gasses to build up inside the chlorinator and potentially explode. Also, never add any other chemicals into your skimmer that you're not specifically instructed to by the packaging of the chemical you are using. A lot of chemicals don't mix well and can cause an explosion or even a chemical fire. See Figure 3-3 for an example of what happens when the wrong type of tabs are put in a chlorinator — the chlorinator exploded!

SALT GENERATORS

The other type of chlorinators you commonly see, besides tab chlorinators (see the preceding section), are salt-to-chlorine generators. These generators are still categorized as chlorinators because they slowly release chlorine sanitation into the water. I touch base more on how salt generators work and their common misconceptions in Chapter 10.

Courtesy of Patrick McEwen

Salt generators are made up of two main components: their actual physical "cell" and the computer that operates them. Figure 3-4 shows a reference photo of a salt cell, and Figure 3-5 shows the computer for that model.

Booster pumps

In Chapter 7, I go over pressure-side pool vacuums. These types of automatic floor cleaners use the pressure of the pump to help move the unit and vacuum dirt and debris from the floor. A lot of these pressure vacuums need a certain amount of force behind them that can only be achieved through the use of a secondary pump. That's where booster pumps come in.

A booster pump doesn't have a hair and lint trap like your regular pump does, and it's plumbed separately from all other return lines. The booster pump gets its water from your regular pump, and then it pushes the return-side water into one designated pressure-side vacuum line. So if your main pump isn't running, your booster pump isn't either.

While pool robot vacuums become more and more common and energy efficient, there's been a decrease in the need for pressure-side vacuums, thus making booster pumps less needed as well.

Kristine Blanchard (Book Author)

Kristine Blanchard (Book Author)

Filtering Through the Options

Time to jump right into filters! All swimming pools have some sort of filter that helps catch contaminants and debris that's too fine to be caught by just a basket. They're plumbed in after your pump, and the water flows through them with a lot of pressure. There are three different kinds of filters: sand, cartridge, and diatomaceous earth (DE). All three of them have their pluses and minuses, but all three work perfectly fine on any kind of pool.

If you're in a position where you're going to be choosing the type of filter you'll have on your pool, it's good to be fully educated on all three options and choose one based on what you think fits your wants and needs the best. Some pool professionals have a preference, but you want to make sure it's what you want — you'll have it for years to come.

A coarse course on sand filters

Starting off strong, we have sand filters. Sand filters are known for being one of the easiest filters to maintain, but their downside is that they can filter particles only 30 microns or larger. For reference, 30 microns is about the same size as a piece of sawdust — relatively big in the particle world.

Sand filters are made up of very few parts and built to last, requiring very few annual repairs or maintenance. A lot of service companies like sand filters for that reason: They're easy to work with and winterize.

Inside the sand filter tank

You make things so much easier for yourself if you have an understanding of what's going on inside your filter and figure out what to look for if you ever run into issues. Figure 3-6 shows the inner workings and components of a sand filter. Of course, your filter might look slightly different, but the concept about how they work is the same.

If you take a look at Figure 3-6, you can see how simple these filters are:

>> **Multiport valve (#1):** This valve directs the flow of the filter through your filter.

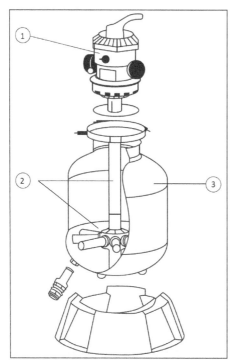

Courtesy of Kristine Blanchard

>> **Lateral assembly (#2):** On the inside of the sand filter tank. The lateral assembly is made up of the main stand pipe in the center, which leads from inside the bottom of the multiport valve to the bottom where the lateral manifold is. It also contains the actual *laterals,* meaning tubes, at the bottom. Those tubes are made of plastic and have very thin slits in them that allow water to flow through but don't let the sand pass through.

>> **Tank (#3):** The body of the sand filter.

Most pool sand filters are filled with a #20 silica sand, which is made up of finely crushed quartz stones. Quartz becomes pretty sharp when it's crushed, so you get a great filtration medium.

There are alternative media, such as glass, which is less dense than silica sand and filters down to 10 to 15 microns, versus silica sand's usual 30 microns. Glass also has a longer life in the tank before needing to be replaced. But like all things, water will wear down the sharp edges over time, and it will eventually need to be replaced.

Another alternative to silica sand is a product called ZeoSand, which is made up of *zeolites*, the minerals found in volcanic rock. The biggest benefit to this medium is that each grain has a honeycomb effect, which provides about 100 times more filtration surface area. Because of this greater surface area, ZeoSand is a great alternative to #20 silica sand and filters down to 2 to 5 microns. That's microscopic! A large downside to ZeoSand is that, in the very beginning, you have to clean the sand by backwashing. You need to clean the ZeoSand a lot when it is first added into the tank, and you lose quite a bit of water from backwashing. It's also not uncommon to get the dust from ZeoSand circulating back into your pool for weeks after it's first added, which can make your pool water very cloudy.

When you add filter media into your sand tank, make sure you follow the instructions about the proper amount to add. All filters come with a label that lists the size of the filter and the media requirements. See Table 3-1.

TABLE 3-1

Media Equivalents for a 100-lb. Sand Filter Tank

Medium	Number of Bags	Bag Size	Total Weight
#20 silica sand	2	50 lb.	100 lb.
ZeoSand	2	25 lb.	50 lb.
Glass	2	40 lb.	80 lb.

How a sand filter works

A sand filter is a pretty straightforward piece of equipment. When you set it on Filter, your water flow enters from the top of the filter and gets dispersed by a diffuser. Next, it gets forced through the sand from top to bottom. The water then travels through your laterals into the standpipe and back to the pool. While the water passes through the sand, particles in the water get caught by the grits in the sand (or whichever type of medium you use). See Figure 3-7 for a reference.

Your sand filter has two other settings that you'll use very frequently to clean the filter. One is Backwash, and the other is Rinse. You wouldn't use one without the other because when you are backwashing, the water inside the tank gets very agitated and rinsing settles the floating dirt into place and wastes out the rest. If you only put it on backwash and didn't rinse after, you would likely get a plume of dirt back into the pool.

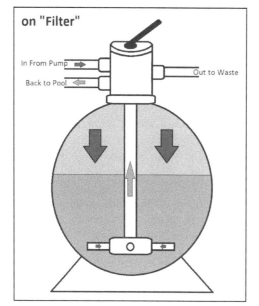

FIGURE 3-7:
The arrows
indicate water
flow; the darker
arrows show it
coming in, the
lighter arrow
is returning
to the pool.

Courtesy of Kristine Blanchard

You use these settings when the filter is so dirty that the flow coming back to the pool has weakened significantly. You can also measure how dirty your filter is by the reading on your pressure gauge, which will indicate a rise in pressure while the filter gets dirty. For sand filters, you want to wait until your pressure rises to between 7 and 10 pounds per square inch (psi) on your gauge before backwashing. So, if your pressure is at 10 psi in the very beginning of the summer, your backwash pressure would be 17 to 20 psi. Figure 3-8 shows a reference photo of backwash flow and rinse flow.

REMEMBER

While your sand gets older with each season, your starting pressure may be a little higher every spring. Mark your starting pressure in the spring by using a permanent marker or adjust the movable ring on the gauge to mark your starting pressure. Figure 3-9 shows a pressure gauge and its start and backwash points. (The filter in this figure runs at a higher pressure than most, so don't be surprised if yours never reaches 30 psi.)

TIP

A sand filter, unlike other filters, actually works a little better while the sand begins to get dirty. The large gaps in the sand grits become filled with larger particles and eventually leave only small gaps, allowing the filter to catch particles more quickly. So, if your filter pressure raises only 2 to 3 psi, don't backwash just yet, especially if the water is cloudy. This relatively small pressure increase is great for the sand and its effectiveness. This pressure tip is true for only sand filters, so don't follow it if you go with a cartridge filter (see "Pleating with cartridge filters," later in this chapter) or a DE filter (discussed in "What on earth is a DE filter?" later in this chapter).

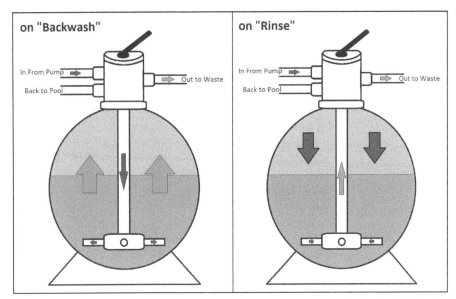

on "Backwash"

In From Pump
Out to Waste
Back to Pool

on "Rinse"

In From Pump
Out to Waste
Back to Pool

FIGURE 3-8:
The water flow
pattern of
backwash and
then rinse.

FIGURE 3-9:
A pressure gauge
with start (light)
and time-to-clean
(dark) arrows.

Perks and faults of sand filters

A great thing about sand is the ease of use. Sand filters are basically foolproof, with very few parts to maintain and steps to follow through the season. You have to backwash it when needed, which in most cases is monthly (or maybe only in the spring). And you need to change the sand out only every three to five years. Of course, that number is based on a pool that never has algae growth and is cleaned with a chemical cleaner at the end of every season or every 6 months, whichever comes first. If you have a lot of algae growth and filter it out, that heavy-duty filtering takes a large toll on the quality of your sand, and you won't get as many years out of it.

Sand filters also tend to be a relatively inexpensive option, priced around $350 for above ground pools and $550 for inground pools.

Just like anything, there's always a *but*. A sand filter is great — *but* it also has a few downsides to it. For instance, due to the fact it can only filter particles down to around 30 microns small, it has a hard time cleaning up messes that are made up of particles smaller than that. In situations where you have a large algae bloom or a lot of pollen in the springtime, the sand filter may not be able to catch the super fine particles that you see in the water.

When dealing with these situations, you can enlist a few helpers, such as clarifiers or filter aids. Basically, in some situations — not all — you may require an additional product added to the water or filter to help clean messes made up of fine particles.

Overall, a sand filter is very beneficial if you don't have a lot of time to spend disassembling and cleaning out filters, and if you want something that's very low maintenance. But with that low maintenance, you have the side effect of a medium that has a hard time with small particles in the pool and may need aids in those scenarios.

Pleating with cartridge filters

Cartridge filters are right in the middle, as far as maintenance and effectiveness go, so they're a popular option for all styles of pools. This filter has very few parts to it, making it easy to use and easy to identify an issue if you run into one.

Inside the cartridge-filter tank

On the inside of the cartridge-filter tank, you have your filtration device, a paper filter. Most above ground cartridge filters have only one cartridge in the tank, but residential inground pool filters can have as many as four. The paper cartridge is made up of a spun polyester fabric that's pleated and a plastic core in the center for durability. The cartridge is placed onto a bottom connection in the tank and usually has some sort of center insert as well, which may be attached to the tank or to a manifold. Manifolds are commonly used on multi-cartridge filters, which are meant to offer more square inches of surface area for larger pools. All the components in the filter sit tightly together in the tank, and while the water flows in, it has only one way to go back to the pool — through the fabric of the cartridge.

How a cartridge filter works

One thing you need to know about a cartridge filter is that the direction of flow in the tank can go only one way, in the direction of filtration. If the flow of the water is going in the wrong direction (which would only happen if the inlet and outlet were plumbed backwards in the system), the water would blow the fabric of the cartridge outwards, ruining the cartridge (or cartridges) immediately. The cartridge can also be ruined if the pressure inside the filter becomes high enough that the cartridge collapses. This high pressure can happen if the cartridge gets so dirty that the water can't flow through it, or if you have an above ground pool whose return shut-off valve (ball or diverter valves) didn't get opened after cleaning out the pump basket or spraying off the cartridge. Figure 3-10 gives you a visual of the way the water flows on the inside of a cartridge filter.

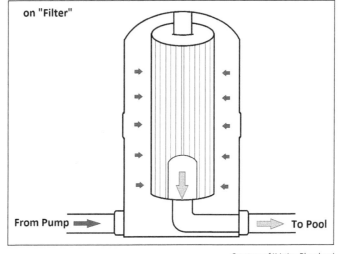

FIGURE 3-10: The darker arrows show water coming in: the lighter arrow shows water returning to the pool.

Courtesy of Kristine Blanchard

A cartridge filter is capable of filtering particles as small as 10 microns, which is pretty tiny! Considering a sand filter is 30 microns, I'd say that's a huge improvement. While the filter catches particles, the fabric on the cartridge gets dirtier and dirtier until the water can't flow through it at all. After that happens, you'll begin to see a restriction in your flow coming back to the pool and a rise in your psi on the pressure gauge. When you notice this change to your pressure, don't let it go too long before cleaning the cartridge. Because the flow on this filter can go in only one direction, unlike on a sand filter which allows a reverse in water flow for backwashing, the only way to clean it is to disassemble the filter tank, remove the cartridge, and spray it off with a garden hose.

Always allow the cartridges to dry after cleaning so that the fabric returns to full effectiveness before you reassemble the filter.

If the filter is especially dirty, it's sometimes worth using a spray-and-rinse filter cleaner. This cleaner gives the fabric a deep clean and removes oils that water can't get out on its own.

To take the filter apart, follow these steps:

1. **Ensure the tank is empty of water by removing the drain cap.**

   On an above ground pool or any filter system that's lower than the level of water, make sure you first close any valves so that you prevent the pool from draining when you open the tank.

   To drain the tank more quickly, open up the manual air relief located on the top of your filter to create a better air flow by either unthreading the small plug at the top or twisting the whole mechanism. That will vary depending on the filter brand.

2. **After the tank is empty, remove the band or ring around the center body of the tank that holds the top of your filter to the bottom of your filter.**

   There are two common ring types: One is a solid ring that threads in place and holds the two halves together and another has a nut, bolt, and spring mechanism that has to be loosened with a socket wrench to be able to remove the band. After the band/ring is removed, the top of the tank can be removed.

   There will be an O-ring in between the two halves of the tank that creates the seal and prevents leaking. Don't lose track of it and clean it if it's dirty!

3. **With the filter exposed, remove it easily by lifting it up.**

   If you're worried about how the tank goes back together, it never hurts to take photos while you take it apart.

When it comes time to put the filter back together, follow these steps:

1. **If your tank had a band/ring that held the top of the tank to the bottom of the tank, make sure that it's plenty tight.**

   With the threaded ring clamps, make sure you hear the "click" of when the ring locks in place. With a band clamp, you will have the spring, nut, and bolt mechanism that needs to be tightened back together; the easiest way is with a socket wrench.

If you don't really tighten the band clamp, the water will leak between the two halves of the tank, because you are not getting a good seal on the O-ring.

2. **Reassemble your filter by following the steps you took to disassemble it in reverse.**

   If you took photos while you took the filter apart, use those photos as a guide.

3. **After you adequately assemble the tank, open the air relief valve on the top of the tank.**

   This valve allows the air in the tank to escape while the tank fills with water after you turn on the pump in Step 4.

4. **Turn the pump on.**

   The tank fills with water quickly.

5. **As soon as you see water coming out of the air relief valve, close it by threading the plug back in place or twisting the whole mechanism down.**

   Your filter is back up and running!

WARNING

When you're putting your filter back together, everything should be tight and sealed. If you don't feel confident in the clamp in the center of the filter or the nut-and-bolt assembly on the band clamp, don't try to use the filter. It's absolutely possible that after the tank reaches its full functioning pressure, it can blow the top of the tank off and seriously injure or kill someone who may be standing nearby.

Perks and faults of cartridge filters

One major perk of cartridge filters is that the filtration on this type of filter is already three times as good as that of a sand filter. It's also less maintenance than a DE filter, which I discuss in the following section.

Its downsides are due to the same factors that make it a perk. Because of its more effective filtration, it gets dirty much faster than a sand filter, and cleaning the cartridge can be time consuming.

Another small downside is that the cartridge filter itself and the replacement cartridges can be quite pricey in comparison to a sand filter. The whole filter usually costs around $800, and each replacement cartridge costs close to $100. The cartridges last an average of three years if they don't have to filter out a lot of algae throughout the season. They do require a chemical cleaning a minimum of once a season or every six months, whichever comes first. If you get two sets of filters, you can alternate them anytime you take them out for a cleaning to get a longer life span from them.

What on earth is a DE filter?

The diatomaceous earth filter is more well-known (and more easily pronounced) as the DE filter. Some people love and swear by this filter, but others refuse to use a DE filter for as long as they live. *Diatomaceous earth* is a fine powder that you add to the filter. The powder is what actually does the filtering in this tank, not what it's attached to. On the inside of the filter are fabric covered "elements" that can be in the shape of a curved grid or a tube; both are common innards of DE filters. The issue with DE is that it has some elements to it that aren't exactly user- or yard-friendly (I get more into that in the section "Perks and faults of a DE filter," later in this chapter).

Inside the DE filter tank

The first complaint some people have about DE filters is their complex innards. There are three ways the inside of the tank can be designed, with two designs more common than the third. I go over these three designs in the following sections.

GRIDS

Grids are most commonly seen on inground filters, although certain above ground filters have grids as well.

The *grids* are a series of fabric-covered curved panels that fit into plastic manifolds. These panels are arranged most commonly in a circular fan shape and are held together with a base manifold, a top manifold, and a rod down the center to connect it all.

On inground filters, there are usually eight panels: seven standard-sized ones and one that's slightly smaller (called a *partial*). Above ground filters may only have four to six panels. Figure 3-11 shows an inground DE filter with this layout inside a filter tank with the lid removed.

A grid DE filter has a multiport valve attached to it like a sand filter (see the section "Inside the sand filter tank," earlier in this chapter). It has all the same settings and does all the same functions of this valve on a sand filter, including backwashing. Being able to clean your filter without disassembling it is a huge benefit, keeping you sane during cleanups. If there's one thing DE filters are excellent at, it's filtering!

FIGURE 3-11:
The inside of
a grid-style
DE filter.

TUBES

Besides a grid (see the preceding section), the other main DE filter tank design that you'll see uses long fingerlike tubes, rather than grids. These flex tubes are held between two plates, and the whole assembly is attached to the tank.

This style is known as a *regenerative DE filter* because you can get a little more life out of it with a bump. If the DE is dirty, you can bump the filter, which is where you push the handle on the top of the tank up and down to cause a forward and backward flow in the filter. This flow change causes the DE to fall off of the tubes and reattach, rearranged on a fresh side. If the filter is indicating a raise in pressure and that it needs to be cleaned, bumping gives you a little more time before having to do that, regenerating clean sides of the DE to prolong the time until the inevitable cleaning.

This style of DE filter has a lot of parts to it. Just in tubes alone, the filter has 72 to 120 pieces! Then you have all the screws, gaskets, and clamps that hold it all together. Having a lot of parts isn't a big deal for the first five years, but over time, while your filter's parts begin to get normal wear and tear, you realize that having all those parts can cause some headaches. You may find that wear and tear will lead to having to repair or replace small parts like O-rings or clips annually.

You can backwash a DE filter by opening up the drain cap on the bottom of the tank and bumping the filter while turning the pump on and then off a few times. It's not a perfect science and doesn't get all the DE off, but it's better than nothing.

ELEMENTS

This kind of DE filter is more common in above ground pool filters. An element looks like a cartridge filter's cartridge (but no one calls this element a cartridge to avoid confusion with cartridge filter cartridges). Although these elements look similar to cartridges, they're not interchangeable.

A DE element uses a slightly different type of material than a cartridge, doesn't have as many square feet of surface area, and is meant to have the DE powder covering it. If you use a cartridge in a DE filter and coat that cartridge in DE, it clogs immediately. If you use a DE element in a cartridge filter, your water never gets 100 percent clear, the filter gets dirty, and it doesn't clean out the pool well at all.

This style of DE filter has the water flow through it in the same way water flows through a cartridge filter — one direction! So, if it needs to be cleaned — and it will — you're taking the tank apart and spraying it down. Cleaning a DE element is less time consuming than a cartridge because an element has way fewer pleats than a cartridge — but it still takes a minute to do.

Types of media for DE filters

TIP

Diatomaceous earth is a fine powder that's made up of small fossilized shells and single-celled organisms called *diatoms.*

When you add DE to your filter, you want to make sure you're adding the proper amount. Most filters have a label that indicates the correct amount in pounds. If you're unsure, consult your local pool professionals.

To add DE to your filter, follow these steps:

1. **Set the multiport valve, if you have one, to "Filter" mode by pushing down on the valve handle and spinning it to the filter setting.**

2. **If the pump isn't running, turn it on by plugging it in or turning it on at your switch.**

3. **Measure the weight of DE that your filter label recommends.**

   Because it's measured in pounds, I recommend getting a DE scoop from your local pool store or online. One level scoop of DE in the proper DE scoop equals one pound.

4. Add the DE to your filter.

The easiest way to add the DE into your filter is to slowly pour it into your skimmer while the pump is running. You can make a "slurry" by mixing the DE in a bucket of water first before pouring it into the skimmer. That step is not necessary but, if you are pouring it in dry, don't do the full one pound all at once; add a third at a time every five seconds to avoid possibly clogging the pipes with DE.

There are two kinds of DE:

>> **Food grade DE:** Safe to inhale, biodegradable, and safe to ingest. But the shells in food grade DE are too soft to work as a filtration medium.

>> **Pool filter grade DE:** DE for a filter has to go through a heating process to harden the fossils' exoskeletons, which aid in filtration. This type of DE isn't biodegradable. Because it's not biodegradable, it won't dissolve in grass and kills the plants it lands on.

WARNING

Pool filter grade DE is incredibly dangerous to inhale. It's a finer powder than food grade DE, and it's actually sharp due to the hardening of the fossils. It's hard for the lung tissue to remove when it's inhaled, and it may actually lead to lesions, which can lead to cancer. Always handle DE like it's a dangerous pool chemical, and never allow children to handle it!

DE is an incredibly effective filter medium, able to filter down to just 2 microns. For scale, that's the same size as microscopic bacteria. A DE filter is 15 times better than a sand filter (discussed in the section "A coarse course on sand filters," earlier in this chapter) and five times better than a cartridge filter (flip to the section "Pleating with cartridge filters," earlier in this chapter).

There are alternative media options that you can use in place of diatomaceous earth:

>> **Perlite:** Another naturally occurring material, perlite is made by heating volcanic rock to incredible temperatures. It's lightweight, so you use half as many pounds of perlite as you would DE, and it's just as effective at filtration. Like DE, perlite isn't biodegradable and will kill plant life it lands on or near after you backwash the filter, but it's safe to humans.

>> **Cellulose fiber:** A plant-based product that's completely safe for pets, people, and plants — and it's biodegradable! It's biggest downside? It costs more than five times per pound what DE costs and more than double the cost of perlite.

TIP

If you like the idea of a DE filter but want to err on the side of caution for your family and plants, then consider using an alternative medium.

How a DE filter works

A DE filter works like all other filters, in the sense that the water flows into the tank, is forced through the diatomaceous earth, and then returns back to the pool. The basic concept is the same for all types of filters, but the biggest difference between DE filters and the other kinds of filters is based around the DE powder itself. The medium in this filter is so effective at filtration that it catches oils, sunscreens, pollen, algae, and even bacteria. When you have this filter system, you should never experience cloudy water. If your pool has cloudy water, you have some underlying issue, not the filter. Reference Chapter 4 for some possible causes.

Perks and faults of a DE filter

DE filters are excellent filters. They catch the smallest particles of any of the kinds of filter and keep your water absolutely sparkling clear. If you have an inground pool, your DE filter usually includes a backwashing option, which leads to a very easy-to-maintain filter.

On the other hand, due to your DE filter's excellent ability to trap all that debris, it becomes clogged very quickly if you have cloudy water from a previous algae bloom or severe pollen in the spring. And when I say quickly, I mean in a matter of hours, in severe cases.

Diatomaceous earth is also a dangerous powder to handle and can lead to health issues and the killing of plant life. But there are alternatives if you're worried about the wellbeing of people and plants. (Check out the section "Types of media for DE filters," earlier in this chapter, for the lowdown on DE risks and alternatives.)

All in all, I think DE filters have a lot of great benefits and are an excellent option for pool filtration.

What this pro prefers

If you're looking for my personal preference, I think an oversized sand filter that uses an alternative medium, such as ZeoSand or glass, is the best option. It's super easy to maintain, and you can always use clarifiers or filter aids to make it more effective at filtering.

Controlling the flow with the multiport valve

All sand filters (see the section "A coarse course on sand filters," earlier in this chapter) and all grid-style DE filters (check out the section "Grids," earlier in this chapter) include a multiport valve, which you use to control the flow of water through the filter. Because the other style filters don't have the option or capacity to handle water flowing in a direction other than the defined filtering direction, they don't need this valve.

Using your multiport valve's common settings

The multiport valve itself is very easy to use. It has a handle in the center that you push down and rotate to the desired slot.

REMEMBER

Shut off your pump any time you have to move your valve handle from one setting to another. This advice applies to all valves, but especially your multiport because the valve will leak out of all ports if your handle sits between settings.

Figure 3-12 shows a common Hayward Vari-Flo sand filter valve with almost all of the settings visible so that you can get an idea of where they all are.

FIGURE 3-12:
A Hayward Vari-Flo valve with the handle in between two settings.

FILTER

When your valve is on the Filter setting, it's indicating that the water is flowing through the tank in the normal flow pattern direction. The water flows through any media you have in the tank, that media removes particles in the water, and then the newly clean water heads back to the pool.

This setting is what your valve will be on 90 percent of the time. You use this setting anytime your pump is running it's normal 8 to 10 hours a day, and also when you are vacuuming. Reference Chapter 7 for more information about vacuuming your pool.

BACKWASH

You do backwashing when your pressure gauge indicates a 7- to 10-psi increase or if the flow coming back to the pool has slowed down significantly. When the valve is set to the Backwash position, your filter will start to clean itself, which means water runs backward through the tank. The water grabs everything out of the sand (with a sand filter) or removes the DE on the grids (for a DE filter) and throws that DE on the ground out of its waste port. (The Backwash setting is located at the bottom of the valve in Figure 3-12; the dial is covering the wording.)

TIP

To identify the waste port easily, look for the port on the valve that has a small clear plastic site glass. This clear bubble allows you to see when the water is running clear without having to stand where the water is coming out.

Multiport valves commonly have a pipe or blue vinyl hose attached to the valve, leading the water away from the equipment pad and into the woods or a remote part of your property. This attachment helps you make sure you don't flood your pool area when backwashing because you do waste quite a bit of water during the process.

When you backwash, your main goal is for the water coming out to turn clear, which signals that the majority of the debris and dirt in the filter has been flushed out. Getting your backwash water to run clear usually takes between 30 and 90 seconds, and you can judge the clarity of the water through the site glass. After the water runs clear, you want to rinse the filter (discussed in the following section).

REMEMBER

If you have a DE filter, when you backwash, you're losing a large portion of the powder that you put into the filter in the beginning. Be sure to replenish the DE you lose by adding two-thirds of the starting amount back in through the skimmer after backwashing, rinsing, and returning to the Filter setting.

RINSE

After backwashing (which you can read about the preceding section), your filter is loose, and sediment is floating freely in the water — sort of like after you shake a snow globe. So, ideally, you want to use the Rinse setting after you backwash to settle the sediment back down and flush out anything that may get past your filter media through your waste. When the multiport valve is set to Rinse, the water flows in the same direction that it does with the Filter setting (see the section "Filter," earlier in this chapter), but instead of returning to the pool, it exits through the waste line. This rinse ensures that any loose particles don't make it back to the pool in a little cloud of ick.

Getting familiar with the lesser-used settings

The following few settings are actually ones that don't involve the filter anymore.

RECIRCULATE

With the Recirculate setting, water goes into your valve through the pump port and exits straight back to the pool through the return line. This setting bypasses the filter completely; it's just moving the water, not filtering it.

You don't use this setting very often at all — in fact, you may never use it. Here are some times you might need the Recirculate setting:

» If you're trying to circulate a chemical that can't go through the filter, such as *flocculant* (which is a chemical used to help treat severely cloudy water; see Chapter 12 for more details on using this product).

» If you're working on or need to work on the inside of your filter but want to keep the water moving.

» In the spring, when you're first priming your pump up after opening (which I talk about in Chapter 6. Look for "Starting It Up.") The Recirculate setting offers zero resistance, so the pump primes more quickly.

WASTE

You'll probably rarely need to use the Waste setting. When you do, water enters into the valve through your pump line and exits directly out the waste port. You really only use this setting if you're vacuuming a pool to waste after floccing with really severe algae or sediment, or if you need to just drain the water before closing or after a lot of rain. It doesn't have any other purpose than to waste the water. For more information about vacuuming to waste, see Chapter 4.

REMEMBER

Don't confuse Waste and Backwash! If you need to drain the pool or vacuum to waste, use only the Waste setting. If you did either of these things with the multiport valve set to Backwash, you could end up ruining the inside of your filter. Even if your filter is capable of having the water flow in the opposite direction of its normal flow, they can't do it for long periods of time.

CLOSED

Use the Closed setting if you don't have a shut-off valve on the return side of a pool and the filter is below water level. The Closed setting just makes it so that no water can enter or exit the valve, stopping water flow in both directions. It's useful on some occasions, such as opening up your pump or filter on a system that is lower than the water level like with above ground pools.

WARNING

Always remember to switch the multiport valve back to Filter after you do what you need to. If you leave it on Closed and start the pump up, the water pressure coming from the pump will either blow the hose up like a balloon (and no, that's not an exaggeration) or cause the hose to pop off of wherever it's attached. Then you have a big problem, especially if you aren't home when it happens!

WINTER

Not all valves have a Winter setting marked (even Figure 3-12 doesn't). The Winter setting has the same effect as when you place the handle in between any two ports, which leaves all the ports open and allows water to drain from the inside of the valve. This prevents any water from getting trapped in the chambers and could prevent winter damage that can occur if water freezes in the valve. The reason this setting isn't marked on all valves is because all you are doing is making it so the valve is not in a notch. Sometimes it is marked for a reminder, sometimes it is not.

Picking a Perfect Pool Pump

When it comes to the pump on your pool, what pump you go with is based on the amount of suctions and returns that your pool has. It's also based on how much money you want a pump to cost you every season! In this day and age, you have so many options to choose from. Online shopping has made it easy and fast to price shop and get what you need quickly and cheaply. But shopping online also opens up the possibility of getting the wrong size or style. Knowing why you want or need one pump over another is super helpful when you're looking into a replacement.

Sizing it up

Making sure you get a pump that's not too powerful or powerful enough can be tricky. Most people might think, "I have a 20-foot-by-40-foot inground pool; I should get a 2-horsepower monster of a pump!" The problem with that logic is that if your large 20-foot-by-40-foot pool has only one skimmer and one return, a pump of that size will be too big.

A 2-horsepower (hp) pump is capable of pushing up to 160 gallons per minute (gpm) of water, but a 1.5-inch piece of PVC pipe can allow a flow of only 81 gpm. That means your pump will be attempting to force out twice as much water as the pipes can actually handle. That isn't even considering any 90-degree turns the water may have to take in the pipes, the restriction that a filter or heater causes, and if you have an eyeball in your return jet. The *eyeball* is the piece that is threaded into your return line that directs the water as it flows back into the pool. It is referred to as an eyeball because that is what the ball in the center looks like! For a reference, see Chapter 8 for a visual of the eyeball out of the pool. All of these things lead to a pump that's working too hard and a filter system that will literally crumble under that pump's power.

I've seen in many cases a 3-hp pump being put on a pool that has only one or two return outlets. You end up with a pressure in your filter of over 30 psi because the water is so backed up, it starts to push inward or outward for relief. You'll start to see leaks quickly, and things will crack that shouldn't crack. The average filter is rated for no more than 35 psi of pressure — any more than that, and it'll begin to break.

There are two variables you want to consider when determining what size pump your pool needs:

» **Minimum flow rate:** Based on how many times you want the pool to turn over completely and in how many hours.

» **Maximum flow rate:** Much more complicated to figure out than the minimum flow rate, the maximum flow rate is solely based on the plumbing underground and the layout of your inlet and outlets.

Figuring out your minimum flow rate involves just a little math (and a helpful chart). First, identify how many gallons of water your pool has. For the equations on figuring out that value, check out Chapter 9. For this example, I'm going to say we have a 20,000-gallon pool. The industry standard is to have the pool turn over two times in a day, ideally between 6 and 10 hours, and you want to find out the flow rate required for proper turnover. Use the chart in Figure 3-13 to get your answer.

Gallons In Pool	Flow Rate Required for Proper Turnover		
	6 hr. turnover (high use)	8 hr. turnover (medium use)	10 hr. turnover (low use)
10,000	27.8	20.8	16.7
15,000	41.7	31.3	25.0
20,000	55.6	41.7	33.3
25,000	69.4	52.1	41.7
30,000	83.3	62.5	50.0
40,000	111.1	83.3	66.7
50,000	138.9	104.2	83.3
10,000	277.8	208.3	166.7

FIGURE 3-13:
Figure out your minimum flow rate by using this flow rate chart.

Source: John Wiley & Sons, Inc.

REMEMBER

All of these calculations are based on getting a minimum flow rate from a pump. You could probably go a little higher in horsepower than what is recommended as the minimum, but determining your pool's maximum flow rate can be very complicated and is all based on your pool's particular plumbing. I can't help you figure out your maximum flow rate in this book because it's a unique determination for each pool individually. Always make sure that you get an opinion from your pool builder or a pool professional before you buy a large pump that might not work with your pool.

With pumps and horsepower, remember that above ground pool pumps and inground pool pumps are two very different machines. The major differentiating factor is their capability to pull the water against gravity:

>> Most above ground pool pumps are unable to draw the water up towards them, their design doesn't allow it. For that reason, you could never use an above ground pool pump on an inground pool where the filter is above water level and over 15 feet away.

>> Your inground pumps, on the other hand, are designed to draw water up to them up to 10 feet above water level. That makes them a lot more suited to handle inground pool setups.

Also, because of their differences in designs internally, such as the size of the impeller and volute, a 1-hp above ground pool pump doesn't have nearly the same power as an inground 1-hp pump. My dad once explained to me that it's like the difference between a Shetland pony and a draft horse. Sure, on paper, they're both considered a horse — but the reality is that they have substantially different levels of power.

You can certainly put an inground pump on an above ground pool if you choose to do so. Just keep in mind the difference in power and that the flow rate will be significantly higher, making the pressure higher in your filter system. But my family had a 1-hp inground pump on our little 12-foot round above ground pool, and it was great! The whirlpools were quite something.

Picking a brand

One thing I've learned in this world is that cheaper is not always better. Yes, a pump that costs you $100 less now sounds like a great idea, until you need a part. Getting parts for no-name brands of pumps is incredibly hard in the pool industry. I always feel so badly when a customer has a part I can't even find online for them, and such a simple thing means that they need to replace a larger part, or in worst cases, the whole pump!

If you're in a pinch, I do understand the need to buy a less expensive option online. But be prepared for the possibility that if something breaks, you may not be able to fix it. Even if you buy a name-brand pump online, such as Hayward, but it's not sold through one of Hayward's authorized online retailers, they won't honor the warranty. Trust me on that one — it happens way more often than you might think.

In the grand scheme of things, it's actually pretty hard to find a pump that's so off the grid that you can't get parts, but it's not impossible. I always recommend that you buy a well-known brand through a reliable source because the parts are often easily available at local pool stores or online.

Two-speed, variable-speed, and variable-flow pumps

At the time this book goes to press, the world is slowly doing what it can to become more energy efficient. Swimming pools are no different, and some U.S. states already require variable speed, Energy Star–certified pumps. In New Hampshire, where I live, as well as in many other states, it isn't a requirement yet, but single-speed pumps are becoming discontinued across the board.

So, what's the difference between two-speed, variable-speed, and variable-flow pumps? Well, it's really based on the control that you have. Pumps are rated by their gallons-per-minute (gpm) flow rate and the revolutions per minute (rpm) of the impeller and motor shaft.

Two-speed pumps

If your pool has a two-speed pump, you have the choice to either run the pump on High, which will be 3,450 rpm no matter what the pump's horsepower, or you can run it on Low, which is usually half the rpm. When you make the change from full speed to half speed, your pump will use a third of the kilowatts of electricity it does at full speed. On the Low setting, you do have to run your pump for a longer period of time, but even at twice the amount of running time, you're still looking at a savings on electricity.

Variable-speed pumps

With variable-speed pumps, you can program your pump to run at speeds anywhere from 1 rpm all the way to 3,450 rpm. You can set it to run all day on one speed, or you can have it change speeds numerous times a day. If you size the pump properly, you can run a larger pump at a lower rpm and use less electricity. It's all about savings, baby!

Variable-flow pumps

The downside to the two-speed and variable-speed pump options is that salt generators and heaters both have flow sensors in them because they require the water to flow through them at a certain speed to turn on. If you have your pump running at a low speed and your filter gets dirty, restricting the flow even further, you could possibly have the water flowing so slowly that the heater doesn't turn on or the salt system doesn't produce chlorine.

So, how did the pool world combat this problem? They created the technology of variable-flow pumps.

Variable-flow pumps have the same concept behind them as variable-speed pumps (see the preceding section), except instead of choosing your rpm, you choose your gpm. So, if the lowest gpm that your heater needs to work is 30 gpm, you can set that as your minimum, and your pump automatically adjusts its rpm to meet that gpm, even if there's something causing restriction, such as a dirty filter.

IN THIS CHAPTER

» **Diving into sand filter problems**

» **Fixing cartridge and diatomaceous earth filters**

» **Evaluating your pool pump**

» **Fixing a pool light that's not working**

» **Identifying issues with your multiport valve**

Chapter **4**

Common Problems on Pool Parts

L ike all things, your swimming pool will have some issues from time to time — whether it's cloudy water that won't correct, no matter what you do, or water leaking from somewhere it really shouldn't. It's not uncommon to need repairs on pool equipment every few years, so figuring out how to handle these things on your own can be a big money saver. Of course, these are all things that can be repaired by your local pool company — so if you're not up for the challenge, there's nothing to fret; just give them a call.

In this chapter, I cover all (or most) of the common repairs you may run into over time so that you can have some confidence to tackle them yourself.

Sandy Mishaps

Sand filters are the most common kind of filter you'll see for pools. They're inexpensive, easy to use, and easy to maintain, and they clean a pool perfectly well. They're known for common small problems like sand in the pool or a leaky backwash from time to time, and knowing what to look for can make it easy to keep this type of filter working smoothly. For a better understanding of how the innards of your sand filter work, check out Chapter 3.

Basically, the filter has four main parts:

>> The multi-port valve on top

>> The stand pipe, which runs down the center

>> The laterals, which are plastic fingers at the bottom

>> The sand inside

All of these components work together to create good water flow and keep the media (the sand) inside the filter from going back into the pool. The following sections cover three common issues that occur with sand filters, along with some tips on how to keep your sand filter running smoothly.

Finding sand in the pool

When sand escapes back into the pool or out of your backwash, more than a cup's worth at a time, consider figuring out what the problem is. Sand can be a huge pain to clean out of the pool if there's a lot of it, so don't let it get out of hand. Most of the time, when you're dealing with sand going back into the pool, check the parts inside the tank. Yes, that means the tank needs to be emptied out. In the section "Maintaining Sand Filters," later in this chapter, I explain in more detail how to do that.

To figure out how sand is escaping your filter, follow these steps:

1. **Empty the tank of sand.**

   For further instructions on how to do this, see the section "Changing the sand," later in this chapter.

2. **Give the empty tank a quick spray-down with water.**

3. **Inspect the lateral assembly for cracks.**

   As shown in Figure 4-1, this assembly includes the pipe, the laterals, and the base in which those parts all connect.

   Keep an eye out for anything that looks cracked or even broken. In severe cases, the stand pipe can have a large crack all the way up the side with actual pieces missing. You can't miss that, trust me. In less severe cases, it has a crack at the very bottom of the base of the assembly.

4. **Look for small missing pieces in the laterals themselves.**

The holes created by these missing pieces can allow a lot more sand through than you'd think, especially with water mixed in and being forced out that direction.

FIGURE 4-1:
A lateral assembly for a common kind of sand filter.

5. **Check the outside of the multiport valve for cracks.**

Your multiport valve works under a simple concept: Rotating the handle allows you to divert the water into different chambers. At the bottom of the valve, where the stand pipe attaches, you may notice cracks. That's an easy way for water and sand to go somewhere you may not want it to go. If that all looks good, something internal on the valve may be the problem.

6. **Remove the screws from the top of the multiport valve and separate the pieces of the valve.**

On the top of the valve, there are usually anywhere from six to ten screws holding the top half to the bottom half. After you remove those screws and separate the valve's halves, you see the internal chambers of the valve, as shown in Figure 4-2.

FIGURE 4-2:
Inside a multiport valve after the top half is removed.

Kristine Blanchard (Book Author)

7. **Make sure all gaskets look securely in place and that nothing appears broken inside the valve.**

   Look for cracks or distressed areas in the plastic where a piece may be broken or breaking.

8. **Reassemble and reattach the multiport valve to the filter.**

   If you take it apart and the valve looks like what you'd consider normal, there's the possibility that the valve was originally hooked up incorrectly to the pipes coming from the pool and pump. So be sure that you reattach the valve appropriately by determining that the pump line is in the pump port and the return line is in the return port. For a better idea of how to determine that, reference Chapter 3.

   If the valve is plumbed backward, meaning the pump is in the return spot, you can cause a backwards pressure that the tank isn't meant to experience, which could cause things to go where they shouldn't.

9. **Check that the sand's grit size works with your filter.**

   Filter sand is meant to be a certain grit, and anything finer may just be too small for the filter to hold back.

REMEMBER

In the process of changing sand, it's easy to break something and not realize it. If something breaks in the process of changing the sand or the sand itself is the wrong kind, the only thing you can do is start over and repeat these steps.

Fruitless sand-filter vacuuming

Vacuuming your pool is an important part of keeping it clean. However, from time to time, there may be issues with the vacuuming process when you have a sand filter. The main issue that can occur involves the debris, either small or large, coming back into the pool. I discuss why debris may creep back into your pool in the following sections.

Small debris

If you're vacuuming up small debris, such as silt, dust, or dead algae, it's very possible that the particles you're vacuuming are just too fine for your sand to filter. Silica sand can catch only down to a certain size micron, and if what you're vacuuming is finer than that, it's not going to be caught. If that's the case, vacuum your pool to waste. (See Chapter 7 for more information on how to do this kind of cleanup.)

Large debris

If you're vacuuming larger debris, such as bugs and leaves, and they're making their way back into your pool, you most likely have an issue with your filter internally. Check out the following list to figure out what the problem may be:

>> **Your sand is old.** If you're using sand that hasn't been changed or even cleaned in five years, I can pretty much guarantee that time has made your filter media non-efficient.

>> **Your multiport valve chambers aren't properly sealing.** The different chambers inside of your multiport are probably not being properly sealed off from each other, and those gaps are allowing the water that enters the valve to return to the pool unfiltered (for clarification on issues you may have with your multiport vale, see the section "My Multiport Valve Isn't Working," later in this chapter).

Make sure your setting on the valve is set to either Filter or Waste, and not Backwash or Recirculate when you vacuum your pool.

REMEMBER

>> **Your valve parts aren't working properly.** Be sure all the ports on the inside of your multiport valve are properly sealed. They're sealed by a *diverter* (the piece inside the valve that moves as you move the handle and determines what valve setting you are using) and a gasket on the inside that get pressed together by a spring to create a seal.

The spring should pop the handle of the valve into place with very little wiggle to it. If your handle is really hard to move or seems very loose once it is in place, you may need to replace parts in the valve. See the section "My Multiport Valve Isn't Working," later in this chapter, for details on disassembling your valve.

Stubborn cloudy water

Oh, cloudy water, how frustrating you can be! Cloudiness can be from so many things, most of which are chemical related (which I go into in Chapter 12). In this section, I touch base on situations where the sand filter is the source of your cloudy-water problem. With a sand filter, your issue could be simple, or it could be annoying. Figuring out the reason for the cloudiness is the first step.

If you've eliminated the possibility of a chemical cause for your pool's cloudy water, your sand filter could be the culprit for a few reasons:

» **Check the sand itself.** If your sand is old or has *channeling* (meaning the surface of the sand has hardened over time and the water has created holes through the sand) or you have the wrong kind of sand, you'll end up chasing your tail and never fixing your problem. Sand doesn't necessarily have to be old to be non-functional. If you had a pool that opened up like a green soupy mess, then the top 5 inches of sand in your filter have most likely become very inefficient, even after backwashing. In this case, clean the sand with an acid cleaner or just remove most of (or even all of) the sand and start fresh.

» **Check your multiport valve.** If the sand is in good shape and you're using filter aids to no avail, your next step is to check your multiport valve. Flip to the section "My Multiport Valve Isn't Working," later in this chapter, for the details on how to give your multiport valve the old once-over.

» **Run your filter for enough time to correct the issue.** Even with your filter running efficiently and after you add filter aids or clarifiers, severely cloudy water can take days to correct. Be sure to leave your filter running 24 hours a day until the problem corrects itself, keeping up on backwashing when your filter needs it (which I talk about in Chapter 3) and doing everything you should be doing with your chemicals (Chapter 12 can help you out with those).

Maintaining Sand Filters

As all things do, sand filters have their own set of things that you need to do regularly to keep them functioning properly. They're definitely less maintenance than other kinds of filters, and depending on the type of media you have in your *tank* (which is the body of your sand filter), you may have more or less maintenance. If you're using just traditional silica sand, then your normal jobs are due every three to six months for cleaning and every three to five years for replacing. With other kinds of media, such as glass or zeolite, your maintenance occurs less often, but it's more expensive because the media itself is pricier.

Changing the sand

Regardless of the kind of media you're using in your sand filter, they all get removed and replaced the same way. The following sections walk you through the process.

Draining the tank

Removing wet heavy water-logged sand from inside your filter is very labor intensive. Draining the water from inside the tank before removing the sand makes the process much easier because the sand is significantly lighter when dry. The draining process can take hours.

If you have a multiport valve on the top of your tank, follow these steps:

1. **Turn off your pool pump and do not turn it back on until the sand is changed.**

2. **Disconnect the filter from your hoses or pipes.**

   This step makes removing the multiport valve from the top easier.

3. **Empty the tank of water by removing the drain cap at the bottom of the tank.**

   This drain cap will resemble the one in Figure 4-3.

4. **Put your valve's handle in between any two settings so that the valve is partially open.**

   This partial opening will allow better air flow, so the water should drain faster. There should be a steady stream of water until the tank is empty.

   A trickle is okay, but just dripping isn't. If the water is only dripping, the sand or the drain is so dirty that the water can't properly empty. Unfortunately, that means you will likely need to change your sand while it is still wet.

If your multiport valve is on the side of the tank, follow these steps:

1. **Change the multiport valve to be on the setting Recirculate.**

   This will allow the pump to keep the water circulating during the sand change.

REMEMBER

   If you notice water leaking out of your backwash port on the multiport valve, you will have to turn the pump off and leave it off for the duration of the sand-changing process.

2. **Open the air relief vent on the top of your filter.**

   This will be a small threaded knob that when you unthread it, the air will be able to enter the tank.

3. **Remove the drain cap at the bottom of your filter.**

   With the air relief open on the top of the tank, the water will flow at a steady streamlike pace.

TIP

Draining the tank properly takes hours, depending on how well it's draining. I'd recommend doing sand changes in the spring, after the filter has been empty all winter, or start draining the tank the day or night before you plan to do the job. The sand becomes much lighter the drier it gets!

FIGURE 4-3:
The drain cap on a sand filter.

Opening the tank

After the tank is empty of water (you can read about draining in the preceding section), it's time to get inside the tank so that you can remove the sand (see the following section).

To get inside the tank, for filters that have the multiport valve on top, remove the valve completely by following these steps:

1. **Detach the collar of the valve.**

   Most valves will have a plastic collar holding the valve to the tank with two screws or threads. After those pieces are off, the valve is just pressure fitted to the stand pipe in the center of the filter.

2. Pull the valve off of the stand pipe.

After the collar is removed, the valve will slide off of the stand pipe. Sometimes the valve will be stuck on the pipe and may need some finesse.

WARNING

If the valve doesn't pull up easily and you're sure nothing else is holding it in place, it could be stuck to the stand pipe because it's been on there for so long. Don't shake the valve to try to release it — you'll break your stand pipe and give yourself bigger problems.

If the valve is tough to remove, twist and pull straight up on the valve with decent force. If you keep it straight but twist and pull up, it should break free without damaging anything.

TIP

If you had a hard time getting your valve off of your stand pipe, you can use petroleum jelly or O-ring lubricant to lubricate the pipe before putting the valve back on. Greasing it up will make it much easier to take off next time.

For filters that have the valve on the side of the tank, you don't need to remove the valve; instead you must remove the top "dome" piece. Some domes will thread in, some have a collar, and some have a metal clamp.

Getting the dome off can be a little tricky if it hasn't been opened in a while, and some filter companies will actually make a special wrench for their filters that gives you proper leverage for removing the top.

Removing the sand

After the multiport valve or dome is removed, it's time to remove the sand.

TIP

You can either scoop the sand out with a cup — which works but is a painstaking process — or you can use a wet-dry vacuum to suck the sand out. The sand will be heavy, so use a wheelbarrow to move it away from the filter area and dump it wherever you want. In the woods is ideal, but you can repurpose it and use it as sand on your driveway or steps in the winter, or refill holes you may have in the yard.

WARNING

When you get towards the bottom of the tank and begin to expose the laterals at the bottom, be careful not to damage them! They can be very fragile, depending on their age, and breaking them could lead you to needing a new sand filter (or at least the insides).

There will be sand under the laterals, so after they're completely exposed from the sand, you can grab the stand pipe and gently lift the whole assembly up. If you really want, you can actually completely remove the lateral assembly from the tank. Some sand filters will have laterals that fold up, and others will unthread.

Replacing the sand

After you remove all the sand that you can get from your filter tank (see the preceding section), it's time to fill it back up with fresh sand. If you're unsure how much sand your filter takes, you can find out in a few ways:

>> **Tank label:** Most tanks will have a label on the side that identifies the pounds of media requirements.

>> **Tank model number:** If the tank doesn't have a label with the media info, it should at least gives you a model number. With the model number, you can do a quick internet search to find the info you need or check with your local pool store.

>> **Estimate based on diameter:** Worst case scenario, you can use the chart in Figure 4-4 referencing the diameter of your tank to figure out how much silica sand you need.

Diameter of the Tank	Pounds of Sand to Add
16 inches	100 lbs
18 inches	150 lbs
19 inches	175 lbs
20 inches	200 lbs
22 inches	250 lbs
24 inches	300 lbs
27 inches	350 lbs
30 inches	500 lbs
36 inches	700 lbs

FIGURE 4-4: The silica sand amount for different tank sizes.

Source: John Wiley & Sons, Inc.

REMEMBER

If you're really not sure how much sand to get, just keep in mind that you want the tank no more than two-thirds full but no less than half full. You want the sand to have the optimal amount of surface area, so on spherical tanks, you'd go halfway. On cylindrical tanks, you can go halfway to two-thirds of the way full.

Putting the sand back in is trickier than it sounds, especially with filters that are filled from the top. To fill the tank back up with sand, follow these steps:

1. **Make sure the stand pipe is in the center of the tank.**

   They make a guide tool for this process if you need it.

2. **Cover the hole in the stand pipe while you add sand to the filter.**

   If you don't cover the hole, sand can get down it and will shoot back into the pool when you turn the pump back on.

   To cover the hole, you have some options:

   - Plastic wrap or aluminum foil secured with a rubber band

   - The guide tool

   - A rubber expansion plug, such as the type you'd use for winterizing a pool

3. **Pour sand into the tank carefully to cover the laterals.**

   Pour the sand in gently when you're covering the laterals back up. You can even fill the tank halfway with water if you want because the water will soften the force from the sand as it falls. If you dump the sand in too quickly, the weight of the falling sand could break one of the laterals, and you wouldn't know until you turned the filter on and sand blew back into the pool.

4. **After the laterals are covered, pour the sand in more quickly.**

   Level out the sand with your hand while you go.

Putting your sand filter in its place

After the tank contains the proper amount of sand (see the preceding section), it's time to put everything back together.

Make sure your valve is facing the correct way before you fully secure it down, and check and lubricate any O-rings that you see in this process.

After you get your tank back together and your hoses back on, start up your filter on Backwash — not Filter! The sand, or any media that you use, will have dust in it that needs to be cleaned out. If you immediately turn the valve back to Filter, you'll have a beautiful dust cloud shooting into your pool. No one wants that! When you backwash, I recommend running it for longer than you normally would (backwash until the water comes out clear; see Chapter 3 for more details on how to backwash and rinse properly). You can switch from Backwash to Rinse a few times until you're positive that you got all the dust out.

After the sand has been backwashed and rinsed, you can switch your valve back to Filter, and you should be up and running until your pressure gauge indicates it's time to backwash again! You can learn all about that in Chapter 3.

Cleaning the sand

Sometimes, changing the sand isn't completely necessary. You're able to clean your sand by using an acidic cleaner, just like you would clean a DE or cartridge filter. I recommend cleaning the filter sand every six months (or at the end of your season, if you're in a seasonal climate). An acid wash will break down grime and oils that make your sand channel or become inefficient.

After you have your sand cleaner, follow these steps:

1. **If your skimmer has any chlorine tablets in it, take the basket out of the skimmer and run the filter on the Filter setting for 30 minutes.**

   This step cleans out any residual chlorine.

2. **Set your multiport valve to Backwash.**

3. **Pour the sand cleaner into the skimmer on your pool.**

4. **Turn your pump on.**

   Let the chemical get into your sand filter while the filter's set on Backwash.

5. **As soon as you see the cleaner color coming out through the backwash sight glass, shut your pump off.**

   I talk about the backwash sight glass in Chapter 3.

REMEMBER

   All brands of cleaner will have a different amount of time to let the chemical soak in the sand, so refer to your specific cleaner's instructions. But as a general rule, the minimum I would wait is 2 hours and the max I would wait is 12 hours.

6. **After the cleaner has been sitting in your sand for the correct amount of time, turn on your pump, with it set to Backwash.**

   Keep running the pump until the color of the chemical is completely gone from the sight glass.

7. **Run your pump with the multiport set to Rinse to be sure there's no residual chemical cleaner left in your filter.**

8. **Turn your pump on with your multiport setting on Filter, like normal.**

Cartridge Calamities

Cartridge filters are a type of filtration system that uses a pleated piece of fabric wrapped around a plastic core. The water flows through the fabric into the core where it is guided back to the pool; the fabric does the filtering.

One of the pluses of a cartridge filter is that they're pretty simple in the inside, so when it comes to having issues with them, it's very easy to identify the culprit.

Vacuuming to no avail with a cartridge filter

It's a common mishap with all filtration systems: You vacuum your pool all nice and clean, but either while you're vacuuming or the next day, you notice the debris settles right back on the pool floor.

Well, if you have this problem with a pool that has a cartridge filter, that can really be because one of two things needs attention:

» Your cartridges

» The manifold that your cartridges fit into

It's not often the cartridges themselves are the issue, but you want to check everything.

To properly inspect your cartridges and manifold, follow these steps:

1. **Drain your tank.**

    For most pools, you drain your tank by unscrewing your drain plug at the bottom of the tank and letting the water drain.

WARNING

    If you have an above ground pool, be sure the hoses coming from your skimmer and return are off or plugged; otherwise, your pool will drain too!

2. **Remove the top of the tank.**

    After the tank is empty of water, remove the ring or clamp that's holding the bottom and top of the tank together, and then take off the top.

    The top should come off pretty easily in most cases, but I've definitely come into contact with filters that gave me a really hard time. If the tank top is really hard to remove, you can use a thin flathead screwdriver to wedge and twist between the two pieces to break the seal. Be careful with this procedure, though. If you damage the top or bottom part of the tank badly enough, it may not seal back up properly, and you could end up with a leak.

WARNING

Don't use the manual air relief on the top of the tank for leverage — it will break off.

3. **Remove the cartridges.**

After the tank is open, you'll be greeted by your cartridge(s). In some filters, you'll have just one; others may have two or even four.

On the tanks that have more than one cartridge, you're going to have a plastic manifold that holds all the cartridges together in one spot. Make sure that you take the manifold out and remove the cartridges, then begin inspecting.

4. **Spray the cartridges with water to remove large debris and dirt.**

Because they're already out of the filter, spray the cartridges clean so that you can get a clear look at them.

5. **Inspect the top and bottom of the cartridges.**

The top and bottom of each cartridge is a hard plastic, which is easy enough to inspect — just make sure there are no cracks.

TIP

If you do find a hairline crack, sometimes you can seal it with a clear RTV silicone and it will hold up. Beyond that, replacing the cartridge is the best course of action.

6. **Look for tears in the cartridges' pleated fabric.**

The hard part is looking for these tears. A tear can be as small as a dime and still cause you problems, so be sure to inspect them thoroughly.

If you find a small tear, smaller than a quarter, you can sometimes use high quality duct tape to patch it. Unfortunately, this is a bandage fix and the cartridge really should be replaced.

7. **Look for cracks on the manifold.**

Those cracks — even hairline ones — under pressure will open up, and the water, along with any debris in the water, will flow through the path of the least resistance.

8. **If you do find a crack, replace the broken manifold.**

Although the ideal solution is to replace the whole piece, a temporary fix can sometimes be done by using silicone or patch putty. It's a bandage on the problem, but it'll usually hold things together until you can get a replacement.

9. **Check for any tears on the internal emergency air relief screen.**

The screen will be on the top of the manifold and will look like a tube covered in a sock, or a metal screen like the ones in your window. Tears in that can lead debris back to the pool, so if there are tears you will want to replace the air relief. Patching it or plugging the hole is not ideal, because the purpose of this part is to prevent built-up pressure in the tank. It is a safety feature, and it should always been in good working order.

TIP

If after inspecting the cartridges and manifold, you can't find an obvious culprit, I recommend securing everything back together — and make sure it's nice and snug. Sometimes, the cartridges just simply moved from their designated spot in the filter, allowing water to flow in places it wasn't supposed to. If that's the case, put it all back together, start it up, and the problem should be solved.

Cloudiness in a cartridge-filter pool

If your pool is properly sanitized and balanced, then blaming your filter at that point is acceptable. With a cartridge filter, there can be a few causes for cloudy water. Check out the following reasons for unclear water, along with some possible fixes:

>> **Your filter is just old or dirty (or both).** Start by taking your cartridge out (see the preceding section) and hosing it down really well. Maybe even use a spray-and-rinse filter cleaner, which you can find at your local pool store. Thoroughly cleaning your filter will ensure that you're working with the best condition of your filter you can get.

TIP

If your cartridge is over 12 months old and has never been chemically cleaned, it's possible that your filter may have such a buildup of dirt and oils that it can't be saved. Having a new replacement filter handy will ensure you're not setting yourself up for failure.

>> **Your filter isn't running long enough.** Check your filtration times. If you're running your filter for only five hours a day in the middle of summer, that's not enough time.

After your pool has become cloudy, you should run your filter 24 hours a day until it's clear — but definitely run it a minimum of 12 hours a day.

>> **Your pool has particles in it that are too fine for your filter to catch.** If you're running your clean filter for 24 hours a day and see no changes to the water clarity, it may mean that the particles are too fine. A cartridge filter can filter out very fine contaminates, but that doesn't cover everything. In this case, move onto using clarifiers to aid in clearing your problem up. For tips on choosing and using clarifiers, see Chapter 12.

If your pool is still cloudy after addressing the issues in the preceding list, it's possible something internally in the filter is causing the water to bypass the filter. I go over popping open and inspecting your cartridge filter in the preceding section. Problems in the filter itself can be the cause of many ailments.

Common cartridge-filter upkeep

There isn't a whole lot that goes into maintaining these filters during the summer. In general, you can follow the schedules in the following sections.

Once a month

Spray out your cartridge once a month. Even if the pressure doesn't raise on the pressure gauge (see Chapter 3 for info on checking your pressure and knowing when your filter is dirty), that doesn't mean your cartridge is clean and working well.

REMEMBER

This is especially important after pollen season, small or large algae blooms, or pool parties. All these things will cause dirt or oils to build up on the fabric of the cartridge and ruin its efficiency. I can't tell you how often I go to clean out a filter at the end of the season and find that it's just caked with grime. A dirty filter will not only affect your pool's clarity, but it will also ruin your filter prematurely.

Every three months

Chemically soak your cartridges every three months. The oils that build up on the fabric won't come out with just a quick rinse. They need to be washed with an acidic cleanser. I recommend using a filter cleaner that's designed for cartridge or DE filters because those cleaners tend to be the most efficient and safe way to complete this process. Soak the filter cartridges over a few hours, or even overnight.

TIP

Keep two sets of cartridges for your filter so that you can easily swap a clean set and continue running the pool while you clean the others.

Fixing DE Filter Problems

A diatomaceous earth (DE) filter is a type of filter that has a fabric covered element on the inside, and that element gets coated in a fine powder called diatomaceous earth (DE). The DE itself filters the water as it passes through, and the element simply gives the DE a place to stick to. I feel like if you own a DE filter, you either love it or can't stand it. I, for one, think they're an amazing filter if you don't mind a little extra work sometimes. When a DE filter works correctly, it kicks the butt of any other filtration option out there. It's so effective that it's capable of filtering out microscopic bacteria. But, with the design of these filters, they're not always the easiest to take care of. They can have a lot of parts, and that can mean a lot of chances for problems.

Getting dirt all over your pool floor

Here's the number one complaint about DE filters: They can easily develop issues that lead to either debris that you vacuum out appearing back on the pool floor or diatomaceous earth itself showing up in the pool. Both of these things can happen for the same reasons.

There are three types of DE filters out there:

>> Almost like a cartridge filter element, but with slightly different fabric and pleats

>> Grids that are mostly found in a circular fan formation

>> Long fabric-covered tubes which are affectionately known as *fingers* or *tentacles*

REMEMBER

DE is a very fine powder and can make its way through even the smallest of holes. So what may seem like a minor tear or crack to you is likely to still be the culprit behind any DE leaks.

In the following sections, I cover common problems that each type of DE filter may have.

Issues with a cartridge-like filter

With the type of DE filter that comes in a cartridge-like element, the reasons for DE or debris escaping back to the pool is the same as for a cartridge filter (see the section "Cartridge Calamities," earlier in this chapter). If you have this type of filter, look for the following:

>> Check whether there's a crack in the top or bottom plastic of the cartridge itself, or a small tear in the fabric of the filter.

>> See whether you have a missing or torn internal air relief screen, which is where air from inside the tank can escape back into the pool, so it doesn't build up.

WARNING

A missing or torn screen would be a big cause for filter failure. Because this air relief is a safety feature in the tank to prevent too much air pressure from building inside the tank, it's best to replace it rather than try to patch it.

Issues with filters that have grids

For filters that have *grids* — which can either be curved or flat panels — there's even more room for small errors. The common kinds of grid filter will have eight individual panels that all attach into a top plastic manifold and are held together with a bottom retainer and long rods. The assembly, when put together properly, will slide down onto the stand pipe in the tank, and everything will be sealed tightly. If you're getting dirt or debris back into the pool, it could be for a number of reasons:

TIP

>> **A tear in a grid:** These can be tricky to find, and honestly, it's kind of a pain. To get a proper look at all the grids, you have to empty the tank, take the whole grid assembly apart so that it's all separated, thoroughly spray it all down so that it's nice and clean, and only then you can inspect for tears.

Tears in grids aren't always super obvious, so be sure to check under any folds, along the bottom where the spine of the grid is, and along all edges. A tear can be as small as a pinky nail — keep your eyes peeled.

>> **A crack in the manifold:** Inspect the plastic manifold that all the grids fit into. Small cracks can be repaired with silicone or putty, but those are temporary fixes until you can get a replacement part.

>> **A tear in the air escape:** If the air escape has a tear in it, your best plan of action is to just replace it. Temporary fixes don't really work and can affect the function of that part.

>> **A problem with the stand pipe in your tank:** Look for the O-ring at the top; you want to make sure it is in place, tight against the pipe and not cracked or broken. You also want to inspect the pipe itself for cracks, and to make sure it is not too loose inside the tank.

>> **Not properly rinsing the filter after backwashing:** The filter gets very rustled up, and so does the debris and DE, during backwash. And if you don't follow a backwash with a rinse to settle all the loose stuff, it's not uncommon for it to find its way back into the pool.

A GOOD TIME TO CHECK THE FABRIC INTEGRITY

While you're looking for tears in either your cartridge or DE filters, you can check the integrity of the fabric to see whether they're due for replacements anyway. The best way I've found to check a filter fabric's integrity is to run a hard object, such as the tip of a pen with the cap still on, in a straight line across the fabric, using a small amount of pressure. If the grid fabric is still in good shape, you won't get any tearing. If it's due to be replaced, the fabric will tear easily because of dry rot.

Issues with filters that have long tubes

In the case where you're dealing with a DE filter that has long tubes inside of it, rather than the grids (as discussed in the preceding section), the places you check are different but just as simple.

To start, you want to drain your tank, remove the insides, and spray them off nice and clean.

After you rinse all of the filter elements thoroughly, inspect the assembly for tears or holes in the tubes, or for cracks in the large plates. You need to place the assembly tubes on the ground and spread them apart to inspect the plates properly. Hairline cracks in these plates can cause a lot of mess in your pool, especially when you first start up the pump or after bumping/backwashing.

With the tubes, the most common thing that happens is the glued ends of the tubes begin to fail and open up. That's definitely a big problem because an opened tube can cause a huge amount of water, dirt, and DE to escape into the pool.

Dealing with a DE filter giving you cloudy water

A DE filter is capable of filtering out microscopic bacteria — things so small you can't see them with your naked eye. If your pool has enough contaminates in it that you're able to see that it's dirty, that's quite a lot of the DE filter is letting through.

So, if you have a DE filter and your pool water is cloudy, follow these steps to try to correct the problem:

1. **Test your pool water.**

    Make sure your pH, alkalinity, cyanuric acid, and calcium hardness are in their proper ranges. See Chapter 9 for more information on all that testing.

2. **Shock your pool.**

    Shock your pool (See Chapter 11 for more information on shocking your pool), using the proper amount of pool shock. Read the instructions that come with the chemical you are adding and add it correctly.

    TIP

    If the cloudiness is bad enough that you can't see the bottom of the pool, my recommendation is to double the dose of shock you are adding.

3. **Check the pressure on your filter and Backwash, if needed (for steps on how to backwash, see Chapter 3).**

   The pressure can be checked two ways, one is by the flow coming back into the pool. If it feels weak, that is an indication that the filter is dirty and restricting the flow from the pump coming back to the pool. The more accurate way to check is to look at your pressure gauge. This is a gauge on the top of your filter with a needle indicating what your current pressure is reading (psi). If your filter is dirty, it will be 7 to 10 psi higher than when the filter is nice and clean. If you are not sure if your pressure gauge works, don't have a pressure gauge, or don't remember what your starting pressure was, you can set your multiport valve to Recirculate (if you have a multiport valve) and see if the flow coming back to the pool increases. If it does, that indicates that the filter was causing a restriction in flow and needs to be cleaned.

4. **Run your pump for 24 hours with your DE filter set to Filter.**

   If you don't see a significant enough difference after 24 hours of the filter running continuously, be sure that your circulation is going in the right direction. Chapter 3 goes into all the circulation details.

If it appears that your pool is increasing in clarity after you follow the preceding steps, run your filter on the Filter setting for another 24 hours. If you don't see any change after 48 hours of running the filter, and there's no spike in your filter's pressure, there's a very good chance something is wrong with your filter.

Routine DE filter maintenance

All filters have maintenance tasks that should be done on a routine basis. For DE filters, you have to clean it not only during the season, but at the end of the season, too. Because these filters can catch every little thing, they catch oils, pollen, and dead algae that can clog them very quickly. Follow the schedule in the next sections to keep you DE filter running smoothly.

Once a week

The most important thing to do with your DE filter is to check the pressure as regularly as possible, a minimum of once a week. If you're amidst a cleanup from an algae bloom or pool party, check it every day until is the pool is clear. These filters will get very dirty very quickly, and if you don't see it happening, the pressure can build so high in the tank that it can crush the pieces inside. The pump may also still be trying to pump the water full speed, but the resistance in the filter will cause the motor to burn up. I've seen both of these things happen firsthand, and there were a lot of parts that broke and needed replacing. To learn more about what your pressure should be at, see Chapter 3.

REMEMBER

If the filter pressure becomes too high, be sure to backwash the filter the proper amount of time and add the correct amount of DE back in. If you're unsure on how to backwash and add in DE to your filter, check Chapter 3. If the filter is really dirty — say the water coming out the backwash is green from algae — I recommend taking the filter apart and spraying down the insides thoroughly.

Every three to six months

Chemically clean the fabric parts on the inside of your filter about every three to six months, depending on the quality of the water in that time. Chemically cleaning your DE element will keep the fabric of the grids or tubes from becoming clogged with oils that you can't just spray out. The oils can come from all sorts of things. You'll notice a difference caused by oil buildup mostly if you clean out the filter, put new DE in the tank, and your starting pressure is higher than it used to be at the start of the season with a clean filter.

To clean your filter element(s), remove the internal parts of the filter and spray them with water to clean off dirt and old DE.

After the internal parts of the filter are cleaned off, use an acidic filter cleaning wash on them. You can either put the wash and filter into a bucket of water to soak or spray the wash directly onto the fabric of your filter. This cleaning process may take a few hours, so do it when you know your pool could survive without proper circulation.

Pump It Up!

A pump is used to circulate the water in your pool. Without a pump, your pool would never filter or mix up chemicals; it would be a swamp! The reality is that yes, this is a slightly more complicated pool component to work with than your filter because it is more mechanical and harder to disassemble. But it's not impossible, and it's something that you as a pool owner can handle (if you want to). I want to touch base on a few of the common things that can happen to your pool pump and what usually causes them. The following sections give you a brief overview, but I think they should really be able to help you self-diagnose and even repair your pump.

Air in the lid

When your pump is running and it's perfectly sealed, the spot on your pump where you have the lid will be so crystal clear that you can't even tell there's water in it. Your pump should run with no bubbles or foam in the water at all. There are two main causes for air in the housing where the lid is, which I go into in the following sections:

>> You're pulling in air from somewhere in the pump or in your suction pipes.

>> The water level in the pool is too low, causing *cavitation,* which is when the pump is pulling in air along with water because the water can't keep up with the flow the pump is causing.

Pulling in air

If you're sucking in air, it can only be from the skimmers or suctions in the pool, going to the front half of the pump. It's like drinking through a straw that has a crack in it. It's much easier to pull air than it is to pull water, and it's a consistent amount of air any time the pump is running. If your pump is pulling water, but there is a crack and it can pull air, it will always pull air from that spot any time it's running. The reason the air is entering only the front half of the pump is because all the other parts of the pool — such as the filter, your returns, and your heater — are having the water pushed into them, not drawing the water towards them. So if you're going to be drawing in air, it will only be on the suction side of the pump. See Figure 4-5 for reference.

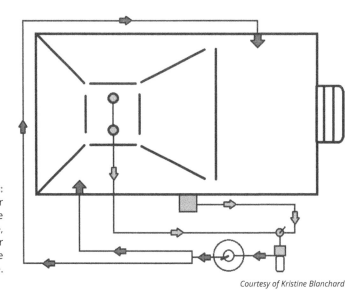

FIGURE 4-5: The lighter arrows show the suction side, and the darker arrows show the pressure side.

Courtesy of Kristine Blanchard

If your pump is pulling in air, the spot on your pump you'll see it is in the lid. The air bubbles can range from a few small scattered ones to a sloshy washing machine-looking mess. A few scattered air bubbles is typically not something to go too crazy about; most of the time, that will work itself out — and if it doesn't, you can try just tightening the lid down a little more on your pump.

If you have water that's sloshing around, that's a sign of a lot of air being pulled into the pump, that is enough air for the pump to almost lose its prime (meaning it runs completely dry and can't pull enough water to keep the flow going). Follow these steps to find the reason for the air being pulled into your pump:

1. **Check all O-rings and plugs on the pump.**

   The first thing that you want to check, especially if this is the initial spring startup, is that all O-rings and plugs are in good condition and properly sealing. There's an O-ring or gasket in the lid of the pump, one in unions (which are quick disconnecting nuts for easy removal of pool equipment; not all pools use unions) if you have one in the front of your pump, and the drain plugs on the pump (there will be two) that I go over in Chapter 6.

   O-rings and gaskets should have no cracking and should fit snuggly in their spots. If you see any cracking or damage, replace the O-ring to get a better seal.

TIP

2. **Turn off all but one of your suctions.**

   If you have a pool similarly set up to the one in Figure 4-5, where you have two or more suctions (such as a main drain and skimmer; or skimmer, main drain, and side suction), start by turning all but one suction off.

3. **Repeat Step 2 for each of the suctions until you identify the source of your problem.**

   When you notice a difference in how the pump looks — either less or more air — then you can narrow down at least to the pipe leading from one of your suction lines that's causing the issue. So, if you have a skimmer and a main drain, and you turn the skimmer off and the air goes away, that identifies your skimmer line as causing the issue.

As far as fixing it goes, that's something I would leave up to the professionals unless you want to dig up the whole line. If you have a crack in a pipe underground, pool service professionals who handle that type of service will have leak detection equipment that will pinpoint where in the underground line you are leaking from. Without that equipment, you are going in blind and would have to dig up the entire pipe to find the problem section and replace it.

Your water level is too low

If your pump starts to run okay, and then all of a sudden, it goes empty and starts a cycle of slowly filling back up, running, and emptying again, that's a sign that your water level is too low. To double check your water level, open your skimmer lid and watch. If your water level is too low, you'll see the water pull in and empty the skimmer because the water can't get into the mouth of the skimmer faster than it's being pulled down. This problem has an easy fix — just add water! If you can, turn off the skimmer in the meantime so that your pump isn't pulling in the air from a dry skimmer while you fill the pool.

Back pressure

From time to time, back pressure, which is when the pump is pushing water, but something in its path is not allowing the water to move forward in its path, is mistaken for air in the lid (which I talk about in the section "Air in the lid," earlier in this chapter). If you see a bubble in the pump, your initial thought is to assume it's being drawn in from somewhere. This isn't always the case! The way to tell the difference between pulling air and a bubble from back pressure is that the back-pressure bubble doesn't slosh or move much at all, really. It's just a bubble that stays in place, maybe vibrating a little. A bubble without much movement is an indication of back pressure because the pump is attempting to push the water at a certain speed, but an issue within the pressure side is causing restriction. Two potential causes for this are

>> Your filter is dirty.

>> The impeller is clogged.

Your filter is dirty

Back-pressure air in the lid mainly happens when your filter is too dirty. Look at your pressure gauge to see whether you're reaching a point where you need to clean the filter (which would be 7 to 10 psi higher than what your pressure reads right after being cleaned).

If you don't have a pressure gauge to check, you can place your multiport valve on Recirculate if you have that setting. If the bubble breaks up and goes away over a few seconds, your filter needs to be backwashed or cleaned.

If you don't have the Recirculate option, then unfortunately you need to take your filter apart and clean it out without verifying that a lack of cleanliness is definitely the problem. Sometimes with these kinds of filter with no recirculate option, you can also remove the internal element (whether it is a cartridge or a DE element) and reassemble the filter without the element inside. If you turn on the pump and the water pressure going back into the pool has improved dramatically, it tells you right away that the part you removed was your problem. You can start by spraying off that filter element and chemically clean it with a filter cleaner from your local pool store and then put it back into the filter.

The impeller is clogged

A more uncommon cause of back pressure than a dirty filter (see the preceding section) is that your pump's *impeller* (the spinning fanlike piece in your filter that moves the water around) is clogged with debris. A clogged impeller is equivalent to a standing fan filled with clothes — it doesn't work very well!

For most pumps, you can reach the impeller with your hand, but you have to do it very carefully! To check the impeller, follow these steps:

WARNING

1. **Turn off the pump.**

   This is the most important part. Do not attempt to reach in to touch the impeller with the pump on, or with the possibility of it being turned on. The power from the impeller is enough to break of a finger.

2. **Remove the lid and basket from the pump housing.**

   Inside the pump housing, towards the bottom on the motor side, there's a hole.

3. **Reach into the hole with your hand and feel for twigs, pine needles, leaves, or any other debris.**

   Bark mulch is a huge culprit of impeller clogging!

4. **If there's debris, try to clean it out by hand.**

5. **If you can't get the debris out by hand, partially disassemble the pump.**

   Accessing the impeller is slightly different for every pump, but usually it involves removing the screws that attach the front half of the housing to the back half. Check out Figure 4-6 for a few references.

6. **With the impeller exposed, clean it out by hand, removing any debris.**

Capacitor problems

A capacitor works to turn on a pool's pump much like a car's battery gives the engine energy so that you can start the car. Your pump has a capacitor that stores enough energy to jump-start the pump and get it going until the pump can switch over to an alternative power source.

FIGURE 4-6:
Some pumps
have proper bolts
that you have to
remove to get to
the impeller.

Without the capacitor functioning, your pump motor can't complete its startup on its own, which is what causes it to hum. After the motor attempts to start to no avail, your electrical circuit's safety feature of the breaker kicks in to stop the attempt.

Your capacitor will be a small cylinder that has two wires connected to it. Pumps can have their capacitors in two places externally:

>> On the top of the motor in a small metal covering

>> In the back of the motor, underneath the cap where the cord goes in

The more common of the two capacitor locations is shown in Figure 4-7.

WARNING

If you don't see the capacitor in either of these places, unfortunately, that means yours is internal. That's not a fix I recommend doing on your own. It's best to bring it to either a pool professional or a local motor repair company because it requires a complete disassembly of your pump motor. This is not an easy task, and you can easily break a component on the inside of the motor in the process, rendering the motor useless.

To replace the external capacitor, follow these steps:

1. **Turn off all power to your pump.**

2. **Remove the capacitor from its spot on the pump.**

   Your capacitor will be attached to two wires. Those wires will have quick disconnecting metal ends for easy removal. The capacitor will often be held in place by a metal arm that has one screw keeping it in place. Unthread that screw to loosen the arm and the capacitor will easily slide out of its spot.

3. **Undo the two wires.**

   Be sure to check which wire connects to which side of the capacitor — like sides of a battery, there's a positive wire and a negative wire.

   REMEMBER

4. **Bring your capacitor to a local pool, electrical, or hardware store and have them get you a new capacitor.**

   If you don't bring the capacitor with you to the store, you need to get all the numbers and information on the capacitor. To be sure you are getting all the right information, take a photo or write down any number or word you see. Don't forget any numbers, or you may not get the correct capacitor. Not all pool supply stores will know what capacitor goes with what motor, so make sure you provide all the information that you can.

   REMEMBER

5. **Attach the new capacitor to the motor and reintroduce power.**

   Your pump should turn on normally now.

If changing out your capacitor doesn't solve your issue, it's possible that your motor is causing the problem. Instead of getting into the internals of the motor, I suggest taking it to a professional repair shop.

Leaking from the bottom

As normal wear and tear goes, a leaky pump is a really common occurrence. When your pump starts leaking from the bottom or sprays water from the shaft of the motor, you need to replace your mechanical ceramic seal. This replacement is a relatively easy fix if you haven't let the leak continue for a long period of time.

If the leak has been a problem for quite some time, it'll cause swelling and corrosion of the shaft and bolts, making disassembly very difficult.

The following sections walk you through performing a proper seal change.

Work slow, work clean, and watch videos on the internet if you need more than just words to guide you.

Collecting needed items

First things first: You'll need a new seal. You can get such a seal individually or in a kit that includes all other O-rings and gaskets for your diffuser, lid, and housing. I highly recommend getting the kit. That way, you change everything all at the same time, which saves you time and money. For tools, you'll want

- » 7/16-inch wrench
- » Phillips screwdriver and flathead screwdriver
- » Needle nose pliers
- » Socket set

You may not need all of these tools, but have them around, just in case.

You may also want

- » O-ring lubricant
- » Paper towels
- » Metal-bristled brush

Exposing the impeller

To start, be sure all power to the pump is off. If you can disconnect your pump from the pipes and raise it up onto a bench, this process is much easier. If you can't, don't worry — you can still access the parts that you need to from where your pump is located at the filter system.

Expose the impeller by undoing the bolts that separate the front housing from the seal plate. Reference Figure 4-6 to see an example pump with its bolts removed.

After those pieces are separated from each other, you'll have the impeller basically exposed. In some types of pumps, the diffuser will be covering the impeller, and in other types of pumps, it won't. There are also some pump styles that have the diffuser screwed into place, so make sure to look for those to avoid the frustration of trying to remove something that's screwed in. For diffusers that are not screwed in, they will just pull off of the front of the pump. Figure 4-8 shows an opened Hayward pump.

FIGURE 4-8:
A Hayward pump that has the side open to show internals. Arrows point to the diffuser.

Kristine Blanchard (Book Author)

Replacing gaskets

By this step you've exposed two gaskets that you want to replace:

» **Housing gasket:** Around the center of the two parts that came apart after removing the bolts to expose the impeller. It is pressed inside the housing of the pump.

» **Diffuser gasket:** On the end of the diffuser.

Remove the old gaskets, clean the surface of where they were removed from with a clean rag or paper towel and put the new gasket in place. You can also lubricate those gaskets with O-ring lube that you can get at a local pool store.

Removing the impeller

The impeller is threaded onto the shaft of the motor, which are threaded together and will spin together. To remove the impeller, you must hold the shaft in place to unthread the impeller from the shaft. In most cases, the easiest way to hold the shaft still is from the back of the motor, where the cord goes in because the shaft goes the entire length of the motor.

In the back of the motor there are two common layouts. Here are some tips for both types:

» **For the kind with a large black cap and two screws:** Taking the cover off can sometimes be tricky, but it's held on by only two screws. Once those are loose, you can simply slide it off or use a flathead screwdriver to pry the cover off of its spot and expose the internals of the electrical portion of the motor as seen in Figure 4-7. In the back of the motor, the shaft is in the center, sometimes behind an A-shaped piece called a *switch*. You can see it in the center of Figure 4-7 to the right of the capacitor which is identified by the arrow. To better identify what part the shaft is, you can spin the impeller and see where the shaft spins in the back.

On shafts that are accessible in this fashion, there will be a flat spot that the wrench will fit right over. It may be easier to move the capacitor out of the way by detaching it (see the earlier section "Capacitor problems," for more steps on removing your capacitor). Slide the wrench onto the shaft and spin the impeller until the wrench becomes wedged in place on the shaft. There are protruding pieces of plastic in the back of the motor that will prohibit the wrench from moving once it is spun up against one. Spin the impeller counterclockwise, and after the shaft is locked in place, you can now unthread the impeller from the shaft.

>> **If you have the half dollar sized cap:** These pry off easily with a flathead screwdriver and the shaft is the metal circle with the slit in it. You can use the flathead screwdriver in that slit to keep the shaft from spinning while you unthread the impeller from the shaft.

REMEMBER

It's possible that some impellers will have a screw holding them to the shaft. It's not as common as it once was but be sure your impeller does not have a screw in the center of it. That means the screw is threaded into the shaft from the impeller and you have to undo the screw in order to remove the impeller.

Removing the old seal

After you remove the impeller from the shaft (see the preceding section), remove all the old ceramic seal. Half of the seal is located on the impeller, and the other half is in the seal plate. On the impeller, it will almost look like a spring coiled up with a black shiny ceramic part on the end, and in the seal plate it will be a white circle of ceramic surrounded by a rubber gasket.

The piece on the impeller can be removed by hand or with a pair of pliers. For the piece inside of the seal plate, which consists of a rubber gasket and a white ceramic circle in the middle, you can either grab the ceramic piece with needle nose pliers or by prying it out with a flathead screwdriver.

When you take these seal halves out, make sure that you get all the old rubber pieces as well. If you leave something behind (including any dirt), the new seal won't fit as it should and will leak right away. After the seal is out, I usually take a clean rag or paper towels to clean off the impeller and in the seal plate.

Replacing the seal

When you remove the old pieces of seal off of the impeller and seal plate, your new seal will look exactly the same as the old one, just clean and shiny! The spring-looking half will go on the impeller, and the white ceramic part with the gasket will go into the seal plate. The part that goes on the impeller should slide on easily, but if you need to lubricate it to make it easier, be careful not to get the lubricant on the ceramic shiny end. The best way I have found is to put a small amount of lubricant on the impeller itself and slide that part of the seal on.

This goes for the seal plate half of the seal as well, only add small amounts of lubrication inside the seal plate to make inserting that part of the seal into place easy. Nothing should have to be forced; if it is not fitting, something is wrong. Recheck all your pieces to make sure remaining pieces from the old seal are not still in the way of the new seal. Your new seal on both the impeller and in the seal plate will be nice and flush against surfaces when they are in their spots properly.

Work clean; a small amount of dirt between the two pieces of ceramic after the pump is reinstalled could cause a leak quickly.

Putting things back together

Putting everything back together is the easy part. Just follow these steps:

1. **Thread the impeller back on the shaft.**

2. **Put the diffuser with its new gasket over the impeller.**

3. **Put the whole assembly back together with the housing.**

    The housing also has a new gasket.

4. **Screw the bolts back into the housing securely.**

    Do not over-tighten; you could crack the housing. The new gaskets and O-rings you replaced will do the work of sealing things well without having them be super tight.

5. **Remove the wrench from the back of the motor and replace the cover.**

6. **You did it! Turn the pump back on and start it up.**

If you run into any issues, it will be one of two things:

>> **It still leaks, even after you replaced the seal.** It's not impossible that it was a bad mechanical seal, but more likely something went wrong in the seal replacement process.

>> **The impeller is making a loud grinding or squealing noise when spinning.** Although it's unlikely your bearings started to go bad during the seal replacement process, bad bearings are a cause for a squealing sound. But, more likely, the impeller wasn't threaded all the way down or is cross-threaded, which is causing it to rub against the diffuser.

Unfortunately, both of these situations require you to start over, and you will need to go back to beginning of this section of "Leaking from the bottom" and repeat at least the steps up to "Removing the impeller" if it's a grinding noise and all of the steps if you need to replace the seal again.

Getting a new motor or a whole new pump

It's a common misconception that when your motor burns out, you have to buy a whole new pump. Luckily, this isn't the case. Sometimes, it ends up just making more sense to get a whole new pump, like if you want to upgrade to a new variable speed pump (see Chapter 3) or if your pump is very old.

This mini-table breaks down the cost of replacing a 1.5-horsepower (hp) inground pool pump versus replacing just the motor.

Pump	$600–$1,000	Motor	$350–$400
		Seal Kit	$20
Replumbing	$200–$300	Replumbing	$200–$300
Total	$800–$1,300	Total	$570–$720

If you get a new pump and you don't have unions (nuts in the plumbing that come undone to remove large pool equipment easily) that allow for a quick swap, you're stuck replumbing the new one in (the cost of which is factored into the values in the mini-table). You can also have the pros install your new motor at about the same cost. So you're looking at a $570-to-$720 job for a motor swap versus a $800-to-$1,300 job for a whole new pump.

But on the other hand, if you have an above ground pool that has a 1.5-hp pump, I break down the potential costs in the following mini-table.

Pump	$375	Motor	$200
		Seal Kit	$20
Replumbing	$200–$300	Replumbing	$200–$300
Total	$575–$675	Total	$420–$520

Swapping an above ground pool pump is much more pool owner-friendly than changing out an inground pool pump. Because the costs of replacing the whole pump versus only the motor are so close, you might as well replace the whole thing.

I think deciding whether to replace only the motor or the whole pump boils down to cost effectiveness. If it's an inground pool, you're saving some money by doing just a motor swap, but with above ground pools, replacing only the motor usually doesn't save you that much. For inground pumps, if the front plastic pieces are still in good working order, a motor replacement is more cost effective.

TIP

If you're going to get a whole new pump, look into one that's energy efficient. Variable-speed pumps are slowly becoming a requirement in many states, so consider making that change while you're in the market. For more information on variable-speed versus regular pumps, check out Chapter 3.

My Light Won't Turn On

I don't encourage pool owners to work on their pool light unless they're confident in their abilities to do it safely, because you are working with electrical cords and water, which can be a deadly mix if done incorrectly.

WARNING

Always remember to shut off all power going to your light before doing any work on it.

For the most part, only one thing goes wrong with the pool light — it won't turn on. There are two very different causes:

>> **A burned-out bulb:** A simple problem that can be handled by a regular pool owner

>> **An electrical issue:** Should be handled by a professional

Checking the bulb

If you have a light that uses just a standard light bulb, then (just like every other light fixture) the bulb will burn out eventually. Replacing the bulb is something I feel most pool owners can handle. If you feel comfortable doing so, go for it!

Note: If your light is LED, it is not going to be a bulb problem if it burns out or stops working. It will be an electrical issue. LED pool lights are known for lasting decades; if it burns out, it's either really old and the whole light is most likely due for a replacement, or there is something electrical causing the issue.

Replacing the bulb is a fairly easy procedure. Your light is a separate fixture from the hole in the wall that it sits in, and you can actually pull the light and about 10 feet of cord out of the hole in the wall and bring it up on top of your pool deck. To do so, follow these steps:

1. **Identify how the light is secured to the niche.**

   The majority of lights are held into the *niche,* which is the hole in the pool wall, with one single screw. The light will fit into a small notch at the bottom of the niche, and then a screw at the top will hold it in place.

2. **Undo the screw to separate the light from the niche.**

3. **Pull the light up onto the deck.**

   The water does go behind the light; it just doesn't go beyond the niche. The inside of the light should be nice and dry.

If you have water inside the light itself, then unfortunately that's most likely where your issues arise. Sometimes, the light is still savable, but not always. Try drying out the light as much as possible, then replace the bulb and gasket and see if it burns out again or gets water inside. If it does, the light is likely due to be replaced as a whole. If it doesn't, then the seal of the gasket may have broken down and the water getting in was a fluke.

4. **Remove the gasket.**

   Your light will have a metal band clamp around the rim to keep the pieces together and keep the gasket sealing. If you undo the clamp, the gasket comes off.

5. **Give the gasket a quick once-over.**

   Inspect the gasket, especially if it hasn't been checked in a long time. The gasket can break down from long-term chemical damage and may be stretched out or cracking.

TIP

6. **(Optional) Replace the gasket if you can, just to be safe.**

   They're usually inexpensive, and most pool stores will carry common parts for common brands and equipment.

7. **Separate the lens from the body of the light; it will pry apart easily.**

   You can now see the bulb.

8. **Remove the old bulb and screw in the new bulb.**

9. **Check to be sure the new bulb works while you still have the light up on the deck.**

   Turn the power to the light on. If it works, turn the power off and continue to the next step. If it doesn't turn on, unfortunately you either have a bad bulb or another underlying electrical issue.

10. **If the new bulb lights up, reassemble everything and secure the light back in the pool niche.**

Replacement bulbs can be purchased anywhere, from your local pool store to an electrical supply or hardware store. Bring the bulb with you, wherever you go for a replacement, to ensure you're getting the correct one.

If there's no writing on the bulb itself about volts or amps, make sure you look at the light fixture; it will have a tag or stamp from the manufacturer that gives you all the information that you need to get the correct bulb.

Asking for lighting help

Lights are one of those things that you want to be careful with. If the problem isn't a simple bulb swap, I really do encourage you to seek out a professional. The first place to start is with an electrician to check out the conduit, the breaker, and the cord. They can identify where the problem may be, and most of the time, they can fix it while they're there. If they identify it's a problem with the light itself or the cord, that's when you want a pool company to put a new light in.

To replace the light, you need to drop the pool water level down below the niche and make sure you snake the new cord through the hole where the old one was. This process isn't overly complicated, but it's something that I've seen a pool-owner try, and they didn't use the old cord to snake the new cord through, so there was no easy way to get the new light cord through the ground to the junction box. Getting the new cord into the old hole can be tricky so it's better to leave it to a professional.

My Multiport Valve Isn't Working

The *multiport valve* is the valve either on the top or side of your sand or DE filter that allows you to select one of numerous settings, such as Filter, Backwash, and Waste. The water from your pump enters the valve, and depending on the setting it can go through the filter and back to the pool, bypass the filter and go back to the pool, or exit through the waste port. It's the main focal point of proper filtration and circulation outside of the filter itself. If your valve is misbehaving, the water can travel to places it shouldn't, which is going to lead to either water loss or inefficient filtration.

Water going to waste

Water coming out of the waste line is a very noticeable issue. If you're losing inches of water a day — especially when the filter system is running — the multiport valve is the first thing you want to check. It is the easiest fix and most likely culprit. If it's the issue, you have two ways that you can fix it:

>> **Replace the failing gasket.** Open up the multiport valve by undoing the screws on the top and pull on the handle until the internal assembly comes out. Inside, you'll see multiple chambers where the water can be directed, and usually there's a wagon wheel–looking gasket pressed in between those chambers. (See Figure 4-2 for a reference.) In some cases, the gasket is actually on the *diverter* (which is the part of the valve that moves inside to

separate one chamber from another on the different settings), which is on the assembly you removed.

Look for lifting, swelling, or defects in the rubber gasket. If there's even a little bit of a problem, it'll cause the seal of the diverter to waver, which causes leaking. The gasket that's in the bottom half of the valve is replaceable with a little bit of elbow grease. It is glued in, and the easiest way is to grab it with needle nose pliers and use a flathead screwdriver to pry it up as you go. The glue used is very strong, and sometimes the gasket will be difficult to remove. Keep working at it until it is removed from the slot it's in. Be careful not to damage the plastic groove the gasket is setting in, or it may not seal well after you replace it with the new one.

If the gasket is not in the valve and it is on the diverter, unfortunately the company that made the valve doesn't sell that particular gasket separately. They recommend replacing the whole diverter, which comes with a new gasket. If you do some research online, you may be able to find an aftermarket company that sells a replacement for that gasket, but it won't be brand name.

>> **Put a shut-off valve on your waste line.** If you decide that you don't want to replace the gaskets on the inside of the valve, the simpler option is to put a shut-off valve on your waste line, such as a ball or gate valve. Adding this valve allows you to manually shut the waste line so that no water can escape and to manually open it when you need to use it. Learn more about these valves in Chapter 3.

TIP

I've found adding a shut-off valve ends up being the easier of the two options, even if a small amount of plumbing is needed, because those gaskets really can be a pain to remove.

Dealing with a stubborn handle

The handle is the only piece that you need to touch on the valve, and if it's giving you a hard time, then it really isn't helpful, is it? Your valve should be easy to push down and easy to swivel from one selection to another. If it's not easy to move, then it's due for a little TLC.

Loosening your valve handle isn't at all a simple task — in fact, it can end up being a two-person job unless you have proper tools. Read through the steps in this section before deciding whether it's worth doing on your own.

TIP

Before starting this process, be sure to note the orientation of the handle and the diverter so that when you put the pin back into the valve, you have those components together correctly.

Before you start work on your multiport valve handle, get your tools ready. You'll need

>> A small hammer

>> A chisel or small flathead screwdriver

>> Silicone lubricant

>> A rag

>> Water or isopropyl alcohol

After you have your tools, follow these steps to loosen your valve handle:

1. **Remove the screws on the top of the valve and pull the internal assembly out of the body of the valve.**

   This internal assembly is called a *key assembly* and consists of the handle, the diverter, gaskets and washers, and the top half of the valve (the part of the valve that has the sticker label on it identifying the different settings).

2. **Compress the spring inside the key assembly on the shaft of the diverter so that you have full access to the pin in the handle with no obstruction.**

   You can compress the spring by using a set of vices or clamps, or you can do what I do and stand on either side of the top and press down to compress the spring.

3. **Use the small hammer, and either the chisel or flathead screwdriver, to slowly tap the pin out from the handle.**

   If you need to stop to regain your balance, you can. Take your time! This is where a second person comes in handy — one to press and the other to remove the pin.

4. **After the pin is out, disassemble the key assembly.**

   Keep track of what parts go where for when you have to put it back together. You'll have gaskets, plastic and metal washers, and a spring.

   In Figure 4-9, you can see the whole assembly with all the parts labeled.

5. **Clean and lubricate all the parts of the assembly.**

   All the parts should be cleaned thoroughly with the alcohol and rag, and then well lubricated with the silicone-based lubricant.

   WARNING

   Don't use Vaseline or any other petroleum-based grease. It will dry out and ruin rubber O-rings.

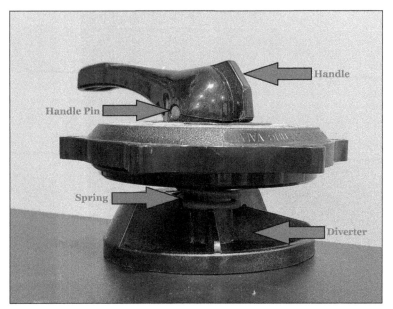

6. **Inspect all the parts of the assembly.**

   Make sure that there are no cracks or chips and that all the pieces still fit snugly in their spots.

7. **Reassemble the key.**

   Putting the key assembly back together is pretty simple. Just place all the pieces back together in the reverse order in which you removed them.

8. **After it's all together, recompress the spring by following the instructions in Step 2.**

9. **Lubricate the pin and reinsert it through the handle.**

   REMEMBER

   Make sure the orientation of the handle and the diverter is the way it was when you took it apart or the settings won't line up, or the cover may not screw down flush, and it will leak from the top of the valve.

TIP

The pin may have small rivets on one end of it. Those rivets allow for a more snug fit so that it's difficult for the pin to come back out. When you're tapping the pin back in, have the end with the rivets be the last part that goes into the handle to avoid a more complicated insert process.

After the pin is back in, the assembly should feel much easier to use, and it'll be that way for a long time. Before placing the key assembly back into the valve, make sure that the large O-ring that seals the key assembly to the body is clean and well lubricated as well.

IN THIS CHAPTER

» **Making the area around your pool safe for everyone**

» **Laying down the law with pool rules**

» **Keeping kids safe at your pool**

Chapter **5**

Staying Safe, Having Fun: Pool Safety

P ools offer days of fun in the sun, but they come with a big responsibility. As a pool owner, it's up to you to make sure not only that invited guests are safe while spending time in and around your pool, but that your pool area is secure from any outside persons.

This chapter can give you information on how to secure your pool and pool area, as well as the importance of developing a set of rules for all swimmers to follow.

TIP

For more information, check out the National Drowning Prevention Alliance's website at www.ndpa.org. This organization helps to educate pool owners on how to prevent drownings. It's a good resource to have.

Making Your Pool Area Safe

To prevent a tragedy, you want to make the area around your pool as safe as possible. There are quite a few options available that you can put in place to protect the people who are there to enjoy your pool. From fencing to safety covers to cameras, you have the ability to create a safe environment for everyone to enjoy.

Erecting barriers around the pool

Putting a fence around your pool, whether you have an above ground or inground pool, is a good step to help prevent accidents from occurring. Fencing comes in many styles and prices. The important thing to remember is that securing your pool area will protect your friends and family and pets as well as you, the pool owner.

Different states, cities, and towns have different pool fencing laws. Contact the Building Department for your area to find out just what your area's specific requirements are.

Securing an above ground pool

In some areas, a fence may not be a legal requirement for your above ground pool (always check with your local authority); however, if you choose to enclose your pool, here are some options:

>> **Fence in the area around your pool.** Having a barrier to prevent people from even entering the area in which your pool is set up will be the safest way for protection. A fence around the yard/pool area is a little more aesthetically pleasing than having the fence on the railing, and this type of fence won't be in the way when you are using the pool, vacuuming or brushing the pool, or putting on any type of cover.

>> **Add a fence to the pool railing itself.** This type of fencing attaches directly to your pool railing and stands around 24 inches tall. There are universal fencing options and also some that are made for specific pool brands. If you have a deck, the fence can either wrap around the whole pool with a gate that opens for access to the pool, or it will end where the deck and the deck railings begin. The biggest downside to adding the fencing to the railing of the pool, rather than fencing around the pool, is when it comes to winterization, the rail fencing is really hard to work around.

>> **Install a gate at the top of the stairs.** An above ground pool that has a deck attached to it should have self-latching spring-loaded gates at the top of the steps that lead from ground level to the pool. This safety measure focuses on preventing an unattended child from having access to your pool (which can happen when you least expect it).

>> **Eliminate access to the ladder.** If you have an above ground pool with no deck and no fence, you must have some sort of safety precautions in place, so your ladder is not accessible when the pool is not in use. All above ground ladders will have some style of safety feature; with most, the ladder that is outside of the pool will flip up and lock in place. This will make it so little ones

can't pull it down to use. In most cases, there is a spot for a padlock to ensure it won't be flipped down. Another style is either a plastic roll-out guard that covers the steps so you can't use them, or a small latching door that is attached to the ladder frame and swings over the steps and locks in place.

Securing an inground pool

Even if your yard is fenced in, it's a good idea to install safety fencing. *Safety fencing* is a durable removable fencing that gets installed sort of like a safety cover does. (You can read about safety covers in the following section.) After getting holes drilled into the surrounding concrete, you insert the fencing into those holes. Each panel is connected, and you can surround the pool with them.

A safety fence is an excellent option if you have dogs or small children, so they can enjoy the yard without having access to the pool. It's fairly inexpensive and works very well.

TIP

The space between the safety fence and the pool's edge is typically 24 inches, which makes it difficult to move around for weekly maintenance, such as vacuuming or skimming, and it makes it difficult to cover the pool for the winter. For those tasks it is a good idea to remove the fence and replace it when the tasks are done. This fencing can get damaged in the winter from the snow, so if you are using a safety cover, it is best to leave it removed for the duration of the winter.

Utilizing safety covers

Safety covers are a must-have for inground pools or any type of pool with a wrap-around deck. The purpose of a safety cover is to fully cover your pool to prevent children, adults, and animals from accidentally gaining access. They're fitted to your specific pool and securely attached. The three types of safety covers are mesh, solid, and automated:

» **Mesh safety covers:** Resemble a trampoline and have springs that tightly attach to anchors drilled into the concrete surrounding your pool. They can hold a serious amount of weight and can easily be walked across (although you'll get wet), even with a pool that hasn't frozen yet.

For safety purposes, these are the only type of cover I recommend for a pool owner who has young children or pets, especially if the pool is not surrounded by a fence.

You can use a mesh safety cover to winterize a pool (see Chapter 8) and also during times when you go on vacation and won't be around to check on the pool. Not only does the safety cover protect you from the possibility of any living thing entering your pool, but it will also help keep dirt, leaves, and the majority of sunlight out.

>> **Solid safety covers:** These are made the same way as a mesh safety cover and are used in the same fashion. The difference is that the material is not porous and will prevent sunlight and dirt from entering into the pool, except for a small strip of mesh that allows water to drain into the pool. They are safe and customizable. However, the solid material is heavy and can be difficult to handle and store.

>> **Automatic safety covers:** Installed at one end of the pool, these covers sit in a track along the wall. When you turn them on, they slide along the track to distribute a heavy-duty cover over the pool's surface. And you can use that same switch to have the cover retract and roll up inside the compartment at the end, which is specially designed to store it. The switch can either be a remote that you can hang up out of reach, or you can have it installed on the wall with a locking cover over it to prevent children from accessing the power and opening up the pool. An automatic cover has a complicated setup and should be installed by a professional.

REMEMBER

While not meant to be walked or played on, these covers will prevent debris, pets, and people from falling into the water. Automatic covers can be used as safety covers if you take the proper steps to prevent damage to the cover or the track it sits in. You must keep the water level higher than you normally would for a mesh or solid safety cover and you want to prevent the buildup of excessive snow or water on top of it. I recommend this only as an option for areas that get inches of snow versus feet in their winters.

REMEMBER

Have your mesh or solid safety cover professionally installed. A safety cover requires a certain amount of tension on the springs to give the correct tautness that makes a safety cover a *safety* cover. If you don't have the correct tautness, or if you don't install the anchors in a straight line, you could put unnecessary stress in certain sections of the cover or on the anchors drilled into the ground, which could lead to a premature collapse of the cover.

After you have a safety cover installed, if the cover ever needs to be replaced in the future, you must be sure to get another cover that matches the same anchor hole pattern. Even if your pool is a standard rectangle, the strap pattern on the new cover may not match the original cover and your anchor pattern in the ground won't line up. That means you would lay out the new cover and either need to drill new holes in the deck, or your straps won't be straight, which significantly lessens its safety abilities.

LOOKING AT LIABILITY INSURANCE

If you're the homeowner and you have a pool, you may be wondering how or if that affects your insurance. Now, homeowners insurance will cover your pool in regards to damages. So if there's damage to your pool, such as a tree falling on it during a windstorm, that's typically covered under your homeowners insurance policy.

But you need to consider liability insurance when you own a pool. The liability portion of your insurance will cover anything that may happen in or around your pool, but that typically covers only around $100,000 worth of protection. Because liability insurance is intended to cover lawsuits or medical bills for the individual or individuals who sustained injuries or lost their life in your pool, the recommendation is to actually get $500,000 worth of coverage.

Insurance companies will work with you on what they require, as far as fencing or other safety features, and they'll go over their rates and coverage. It's definitely something to look into if you're looking to put a pool on your property, just had one installed, or just got a property that has a pool.

Using cameras to keep an eye on your pool

At-home security cameras are becoming more commonly used at homes all around. (I have a doorbell camera at my own home.) They give a sense of security and assurance that if something goes wrong, you can either stop it or have an answer to what happened. Installing a security camera around your pool can alert you to potential dangers.

Certain security cameras can notify you if there's movement around your pool. If you happen to be away from your pool area and get a notification, you can check the footage from your smartphone to see what's happening. If need be, you can call for emergency services, even if you aren't at home.

Monitoring with an alarm

An effective item in your safety arsenal is a pool alarm. Pool alarms come in many styles, but I believe the best model is one that goes off when it senses a disturbance in the water.

What happens is the alarm attaches to the pool deck or a ladder and is set on the surface of the water. Any time there is a major disturbance while the alarm is armed, it will let out a siren, which will alert anyone within earshot. It is highly effective and very loud. Now, with today's technology, you can purchase pool alarms that will send a notification to your cellphone with any alerts.

TIP

Be sure it is set loud and test it at least once a month by manually setting it off.

Installing drain-related safety features

Before safety measures were put in place for drains and suctions, a number of pool-related tragedies occurred. Now there are systems available to help stop accidents from happening.

Anti-entrapment drain covers are specially designed main drain covers that have lots of slits and holes in them to allow water to flow through while preventing dangerous suction. They are used to prevent entrapment and are the industry standard on all pools. All new pools are required to use these drain covers. Check to see whether your current pool has them and, if it doesn't, discuss with a pool professional how to have them installed.

Another safety feature available is a *safety vacuum release system*, known as SVRS. This feature is required to be installed on all commercial pools that have a single drain since the Pool & Spa Safety Act of 2007 as a secondary anti-entrapment protection. The SVRS helps prevent entrapment by monitoring the pressure on the pool pump. If there's a blockage on the pool drain, the SVRS will detect the change in pressure and automatically open a vent on the SVRS device, which will allow whatever caused the blockage to immediately be released. You can add an SVRS onto existing residential pool systems, or it's a feature on some pumps if you're looking to upgrade that part of the system.

Keeping rescue devices nearby

Having the tools that you need on hand in the case of an emergency can be the difference between life and death. Here are a few simple things to keep near your pool, all of which can be purchased for very little money:

>> **Life ring:** A *life ring* is a donut-shaped flotation device, like the ones you see on boats. If you have a life ring nearby, you can easily toss it to the person in trouble so that they can stabilize until you can safely get them out. When someone is panicking in the water, it's not uncommon for them to unintentionally create a dangerous situation for a person who's trying to rescue them, so having a life ring on hand will help both you and the person in trouble.

>> **Safety line:** A *safety line* is a line of rope that floats on top of the water to mark where the shallow end of the pool ends and the deep end of the pool begins. These lines come in multiple lengths, so you can get one that fits your pool properly. And you can buy them premade from many different companies. A safety line not only indicates the drop-off to swimmers who aren't ready for that part of the pool, but these lines also provide something that a bather can grab onto in case they accidentally go too deep.

>> **Safety hook:** A *safety hook,* also known as a shepherd's crook, is a device that has a large hook at the end of a pole, which allows someone standing at the edge of the pool to reach a person who's in danger in the water. A safety hook provides a good way to reach a person in need without possibly putting yourself at risk. It can also be used as an aid for beginning swimmers by allowing you to help hold them out of the water by the waist using the hook to keep them afloat.

>> **First aid kit:** Pool-related injuries happen all the time, even from just slipping on the pool deck. It's always best to have the necessary tools to deal with a situation like that close by so that the person who's hurt isn't left untreated for too long. Keep your kit nearby and be sure it includes the following items:

- Bandages, including band-aids, rolled bandages, and absorbent pads

- Gauze

- Antibacterial ointment

- Butterfly stitches

- Gloves

Establishing Rules of Use for Your Pool

Having a party by the pool is a lot of fun — and kids tend to enjoy it the most! But, one thing I've learned is that kids love to play hard. A pool is one of those places where playing hard can lead to serious injuries. If you're going to have people use your pool, you want to be sure there are clear boundaries set in place. These rules help keep people safe and hopefully prevent anyone from getting hurt.

Everyone has seen the Pool Rules signs at public pools, and they're there for good reason. You want everyone to have fun, but establishing a set of rules for everyone to follow is a must. Don't think of rules as being a party spoiler. If you're careless and allow your guests to be, too, accidents will happen. Here are three main rules to enforce:

TIP

>> **No running.** Surfaces surrounding pools usually get wet and can be slippery. In fact, I've slipped and hurt myself from running by the pool. I was lucky and only bruised my ego, but not everyone is that lucky. Running can also cause tripping, which may make someone unintentionally fall into the pool or hit their head.

To help with slippery surfaces, you can place mats around the pool for better traction.

>> **No horseplay.** Something as simple as a small shove could lead a person to fall into the shallow end of the pool just right and cause a neck injury.

>> **No diving.** I know there are some pools out there that are designed to be safe to dive into — they might even have a diving board. The big problem with that is everyone's ability to dive is very different. I can still remember, when I was a kid, diving into my friend's huge inground pool off of the diving board and hitting my chin on the ledge where the shallow end and deep end meet. Diving is not worth the risk, in my opinion. It's too easy to make a deadly mistake.

Have your pool rules made into a sign and hang them where everyone can see them. Be sure to read them out loud to every person who uses your pool because their mistake is still your responsibility.

Keeping Kids Safe in and around Your Pool

If you have a pool or plan to get a pool, and you have young children, you'll want to make sure you do everything you can to keep them safe.

Signing up for swim lessons

I highly encourage you to have your kids learn to swim if they don't already know — and I mean kids of all ages. There are amazing swim teachers out there teaching children as young as 1 year old how to handle being submerged in water. I wasn't a strong swimmer growing up, and I'm still not, and there was a time I had a close call when I slipped into the deep end from the shallow end. Thankfully, the rope float was in place, and I had that in my hand at the time, so I used it to help me up. But not every child is that lucky. If you can teach your child to swim, or at least how to float on their back, it will give you a lot of peace of mind.

Providing life jackets

Make sure that you have properly fitted life jackets available to any children who can't reach the bottom of the pool. Any child who is not able to swim should be wearing some sort of floatation device like a life jacket or even floaties. Pool stores or aquatic sport stores will usually have a good selection of adult and children life jackets, where you can try them on and size them properly. You want life jackets to be comfortably snug and the sizes are based on chest size, not so much your weight.

Watching Out for Waterborne Illnesses

Providing clean water for your guests to swim in is a pool owner's responsibility. Swimming in unsanitary water can make people very sick. (Turn to Chapter 10 for details on proper sanitation.)

Here are three waterborne illnesses that can occur, which is why you never want to have a dirty pool:

>> **Legionnaires disease:** A serious lung infection caused by the bacteria Legionella. You get this type of disease from breathing in droplets of water or drinking it "down the wrong pipe" and into your lungs. Legionnaires is easily killed with normal sanitation levels (for chlorine that is ideally between 2-4 ppm), so all you have to do to prevent this is to keep your pool sanitized.

Although this illness can be treated with antibiotics, it can be fatal to people who have weak immune systems, have heavily used tobacco products, or are just over the age of 50. At a fair in North Carolina, 136 people got sick from a vendor's hot tub display. The spas weren't sanitized because they were filled for only a few days. But during that time, all the people who got into the hot tub display were exposed to Legionella bacteria. Out of that 136 people who became ill, 96 of them were hospitalized, and 4 of them actually died.

>> **Pseudomonas Aeruginosa:** A bacteria more commonly found in hot tubs but on rare occasions can be found in swimming pools. It will live in a dirty waterline and is a bacteria that affects the skin, causing puss-filled pimples and rashes. The bacteria enter a person's pores when the skin is exposed to contaminated warm water, get trapped in those pores, and begin to grow in your skin. This type of bacteria can live in chlorine at 1ppm, which is still technically an acceptable range on the chlorine ppm scale, so it could happen to anyone. If you shock your pool weekly as recommended, this is completely preventable as chlorine levels higher than 1ppm will kill it. See Chapter 10 for more information on shocking your pool.

>> **Cryptosporidium:** Also called the crypto parasite, this is the grossest one, so I'm warning you now! More commonly found in public pools, crypto is a parasite that's transmitted through the accidental ingestion of water that has fecal matter that contains the cryptosporidium germ cell. Yes, you read that correctly. It's from someone having diarrhea in the pool and you accidentally drinking that water. The symptoms you get from it are similar to a stomach flu: stomach cramps, diarrhea, vomiting, fever, and so on. And this parasite is also extremely resistant to chlorine, so even a perfectly sanitized pool couldn't definitely prevent you from getting it.

The safest way to prevent this parasite from entering your pool is to do your best to not have people who are sick swim in the water. Make it a pool rule to not swim when feeling ill!

WARNING

Make sure to wash your bathing suits well after using them! Damp bathing suits can harbor enough bacteria to cause urinary tract infections, yeast infections, or even bacterial vaginosis.

BEING CAUTIOUS ABOUT COMMERCIAL SWIMMING POOLS

Public swimming pools can be a breeding ground for bacteria. It's hard to say just how clean the water you're swimming in is.

If you decide to take the plunge and go to a public swimming area, take a hot shower and wash yourself thoroughly after every use. Never ever, ever, ever drink the water — like EVER. And if you're a crazy person like me, you can keep a bottle of test strips with you at all times, so that you can test the water before using it. I've been doing this for years, and yes, I'm sure I look very paranoid doing it. But it's the only way to be sure the pH, cyanuric acid, and chlorine levels are all where they need to be for me to comfortably enter. Even if you confirm the pool's sanitizing chemical levels are in the right ranges, I don't recommend putting your head underwater because there is always the possibility that a swimmer near you could introduce the bacteria that creates a waterborne illness. By putting your head underwater, there is more of a chance for that possible contaminate to enter your body through your mouth or nose. Also, avoid overly crowded pools or water parks because no matter how sanitary that water was at the beginning of the day, there is no way for it to be that sanitary with an excessive amount of bathers.

2

Hiring Yourself as a Pool Pro

Get your pool open and ready for the spring season.

Maintain that perfect, clear pool by cleaning, cleaning, cleaning.

Discover the wonderful world of winterization, with tips and tricks for closing everything up for the cold and info for people who aren't used to a freeze.

Chapter **6**

Opening Your Pool for the Season

O pening your pool signifies the beginning of summer fun for many, and if you live in an area where you had snow for the previous five months, you're ready to start swimming! Opening your pool doesn't have to be a scary or complicated experience — it's actually fairly easy. I'm here to guide you through the opening process — whether you have an above ground or inground pool — to ease your mind and start your summer.

After your pool is up and running, you'll want to begin cleaning and treating the pool chemically right away. Check out Chapters 7 and 9 for further pool-setup steps.

Opening an Above Ground Pool

When it comes to opening an above ground pool, there are very few mistakes you can make that are life or death for your pool. In the following sections, I go over the do's and don'ts of this whole process. And I promise to make it as simple as I can. Above ground pools have significantly fewer parts and complications than inground pools, which makes it much harder for things to go wrong.

Choosing when to open your above ground pool

Opening season varies based on your location (and whether you're ready to see water instead of a cover on your pool). I know that, in New Hampshire (or maybe even most northern locations), people say that pool season typically starts on Memorial Day. Now, that's just a suggestion. You could open your pool as soon as the snow or ice has melted. It's completely up to you.

My recommendation is to open it any time in April, May, or June. In April, the water may still be very cold, but the temperature will prevent algae growth, and this will give you plenty of time to perfect your chemicals before it warms up enough to want to use the pool. And hopefully by then, it's done snowing and the temperature stays consistently above freezing. In May, you are looking at similar benefits as in April, but the temperature is a little warmer and the pool season is set to begin with Memorial Day right around the corner. Once you get into June, you are starting to risk opening the pool up with algae in it because it has sat in warm temperatures, which is a great breeding ground for algae. The benefit to waiting this long is that you may have kept the pool covered long enough to get through pollen season and that saves you a lot of possibly hassles.

REMEMBER

Another perk of opening any pool early is you don't need to run the filter for as many hours a day as you would in the summer because there is less use, and less hot sun. That means the pool will stay clean with very little effort. That cold temperature also helps prevent you from going through as many sanitizing chemicals to keep it from growing algae.

A couple of things come into play when deciding when to open your above ground pool:

>> **Your type of cover and the outside temperature:** These two things go hand in hand. If the weather is consistently warm, say getting toward 80-degree days, you don't want to open too late and have your pool water baking under a cover.

If you have a mesh cover or one that has tiny holes in it, sunlight can get through the cover and promote algae growth. If you have a solid tarp pool cover, you can delay opening your pool for a little longer.

See Chapter 8 for more information on picking a good winter cover.

TIP

>> **Your desired start date:** It takes a few days of circulation and chemicals to get your pool in a clean and usable condition. So, don't wait until a day or two before you think you'll want to swim before you open your pool.

Think ahead for when you want your pool to be ready, and then plan to open your pool at least two weeks before you may want to use it.

Removing the above ground pool cover

When it comes to opening an above ground pool, actually removing the cover is one of the more time-consuming and complicated steps. No matter what precautions you take when putting the cover on to winterize your pool, your cover will get a lot of water on top of it. See Chapter 8 to learn how to properly cover your pool. Follow these steps to take the cover off your pool:

1. **Remove the water on top of the cover.**

    Siphoning the water from the top of the cover can be done a couple of ways:

    - *Start a siphon by using a garden hose.* The easiest way to do this is to place one end of the hose into the water on top of the cover, then have the other end of the hose where you want the water to drain; ideally this will be downhill. To start the siphon, the easiest way is to draw the water into the hose by sucking on the end of the hose where the water is going to be draining out.

    - *Use a submersible pump thrown on top of the cover.*

TIP

      If there are a lot of leaves on the pool cover, I recommend taking a 5-gallon bucket and drilling 1-inch holes into it to place your sub-pump into before putting it on the cover. This will prevent the leaves from getting sucked into the submersible pump and clogging it. If you need to make the bucket heavier to bow the cover and therefore draw the water towards the bucket, you can place a brick or rock in the bottom of the bucket to weigh it down. (I use a zip-tie to prevent the pump from falling out of the bucket.)

2. **Remove excess folds in the cover.**

    While the cover is draining, pull the cover down the wall of the pool, removing the excess folds on top of the pool and pulling the cover taut. This allows the water to drain faster and to get fewer deep spots.

3. **Remove any leaves and debris from the cover.**

    The easiest way to remove leaves from the cover is to scoop them off using your leaf net (the skimmer head attachment that has a big bag on it) on your telescopic pole. For more information on cleaning equipment, see Chapter 7.

WORKING WITH MESH TARPS

If you're dealing with a mesh-style tarp cover, you can't drain the water off prior to removal because the water from inside the pool will just seep through the cover and you will drain the pool at the same time. And the water doesn't drain from the mesh like water going through a pasta strainer; it drains like water passing through a t-shirt. That means you can't just pull it taut from the water in the pool and the cover will just drain out. You can remove leaves and debris, and then fill the pool under the cover (if it isn't already full) to make the removal more of a slipping-off process. Also, keep in mind that if you're in a climate where the water freezes, a mesh cover likely won't last more than one season. Because the water is going in between the fibers of the mesh, when it freezes and expands, the water causes the fibers to separate, and you can end up with tears and holes. These holes will allow large debris like leaves or pine needles to get into the pool, which is what the cover is meant to keep out to begin with.

4. **Fill your pool.**

   You'll want your pool higher than normal, about 3 inches from the top of the wall when removing your pool cover. If your water level is very low from displacement over time, make sure you fill the pool first using a garden hose under the cover.

TIP

If you're using a submersible pump to drain the water off of your pool cover before it starts to grow algae, you can pump the water into the pool (to conserve water) by putting the hose attached to your submersible pump underneath the cover. Two birds with one stone!

5. **Detach the cover.**

   Remove whatever anchors you have securing the cover to the pool.

6. **Pull the cover down evenly all the way around the pool.**

   You want the excess cover hanging down the outside of the pool and be sure the cover is taut on top. You will most likely still have an ice equalizer pillow (covered in Chapter 8) that was added in for ice expansion during winterization, leave that until the cover is off.

TIP

   This step is much easier with a second person to help you.

7. **Fold one end of the cover on top of itself.**

   With a helper, pull the cover over itself until the cover is about halfway across the pool, as shown in Figure 6-1.

   You're folding the cover to create a pouch so that while you pull the rest of the cover off, any debris or water left on top won't fall into the pool.

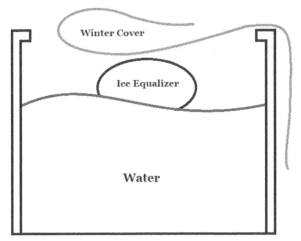

FIGURE 6-1:
Diagram of folding the pool cover over itself.

Courtesy of Kristine Blanchard

8. **Grab the end of the cover that's hanging down and drag the cover down to the ground, pulling the folded half towards you.**

9. **After the folded portion of the cover reaches you and the cover is mostly off of the pool, grab the folded half and start to pull it over the edge.**

   Start with the two ends and work your way towards the middle. Your main focus now is to take the cover off of the pool without the leaves or water that may be in the pouch you created falling in.

10. **Clean the cover.**

    After you've gotten the cover off of the pool, it's best to lay it out somewhere and spray it down thoroughly so that it doesn't grow mold or get really stinky.

    There are cover-cleaning chemicals that you can use as well, to prevent a gross layer forming while the cover is in storage. You can find these chemicals at your local pool store, it is typically a liquid sold in a quart sized bottle.

    On hot days, don't leave the cover laying out on grassy areas for extended periods of time — it can kill the grass under it.

WARNING

11. **Store the cover.**

    After it's clean and mostly dry, roll the cover up and store it in a container that rodents can't get into — preferably a hard plastic container or an aluminum trash can.

Getting your above ground pool filter up and running

After the cover is off of the pool (which I talk about in the preceding section), make sure that you get your filter system up and running right away. If you leave the water for too long not circulating, it'll start to grow algae, which will make spring startup more complicated because you will have to treat an algae bloom while also trying to balance your pool chemistry.

REMEMBER

You can't get an accurate water sample done until the pool has been circulating for at least two days, especially if you added water when you removed the cover. The pool needs time to properly mix all of your chemicals back up because a lot of dissolved solids settle towards the bottom of the pool after you close it down for the cold season.

Connecting your filter

Getting your filter hooked up is a pretty straightforward process. For this discussion, I walk you through hooking up a sand filter, like the one in Figure 6-2. (For more information on sand filters, refer to Chapters 1 and 3.) Although some above ground pools use a diatomaceous earth (DE) or cartridge filter, the setup is basically the same.

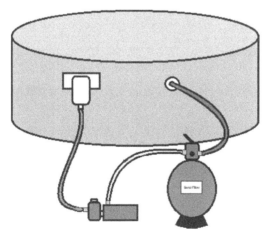

FIGURE 6-2:
The proper hookup for a sand filter.

Courtesy of Kristine Blanchard

Here's the flow that Figure 6-2 shows:

>> One hose comes off of the skimmer and hooks up to the front of the pump (on the left).

>> A hose connects your pump to your filter (in the middle).

>> A hose connects your filter back to the pool (on the right).

REMEMBER

When you're attaching your hose from the pump to the filter, be sure to have the hose going into the correct port on the valve. These ports are usually marked Pump and Return, as shown in Figure 6-3.

FIGURE 6-3:
Pump and Return
identifications on
a multiport
valve's ports.

There are a few different kinds of DE filters for above ground pools, but the difference really lies in the appearance. They all have only one port in and one port out. This setup goes for cartridge filters, as well, but just like with your sand filter, you want to make sure you have your ins and outs correct before attaching hoses.

WARNING

A filter hooked up backward could result in cloudy water, a quickly clogged filter, low flow, or even damage to the internals of your filter.

TIP

When you're hooking the hoses onto the hose adapters, be sure they don't slide on super easily. You want them to be fairly snug and secured with a metal hose clamp. If your hose slides onto the adapter very easily, it probably won't create a great seal, which could lead to leaks or air in the pump. For tips and tricks for repairing your pump, see Chapter 4.

Ensure that all of your pieces of equipment have their plugs in place. In the fall, you pull all of the drain plugs and stash them somewhere safe, such as in the pump basket. Make sure you thread all of your plugs back in when you're opening your pool — otherwise, you'll have water coming out of those holes when you start your pump up.

Most plugs will have some form of an O-ring or gasket. Make sure it's in place, and not cracked or broken. If a plug is missing its O-ring, sometimes you can get away with using plumber's tape to seal around the threads. If not, you'll have to take a trip to your local pool store for a replacement O-ring, or a whole new plug.

Almost all plumbed-in pool equipment will have some sort of a drain plug, so here's a quick reference of how many plugs to look for, depending on the piece of equipment:

Equipment Type	Number of Plugs
Pump	2
Filter	1
Heater	1
Chlorinator	1
Salt generator	None

If your filter area has equipment in addition to your pump and filter (such as a salt generator, a heater, or an ozone system), they will all be plumbed in after your filter. Some of these items like a heater or chlorinator will have drain plugs as well, so make sure you thread them in. With above ground pools, a lot of the filter area is disassembled and brought inside (more information on proper winterization is in Chapter 8). When you put all of these components back together, they all hook together either by hoses or by hard PVC plumbing that was installed when the filter system was built. If you are unsure how your system reassembles, asking your local pool professional for help will save you lots of time. If you are confident that you can reassemble on your own, just remember that your filter system goes in a certain order:

> Pump connects to filter, filter goes either back to the pool or into the next piece of extra equipment you may have such as a heater, and then into a chlorinator (if you have both).

REMEMBER

Always make sure that any type of inline sanitation system such as a chlorinator or salt to chlorine generator is plumbed in last. If you have a salt generator or inline chlorinator before a heater, you'll ruin the internals of the heater very quickly because the high concentration of chlorine on the output will deteriorate the metal inside the heater.

Before starting up your filter, remove any winter hardware that's in place. Read the following section to find out what to look for.

Removing winter hardware

When closing an above ground pool, there are recommended steps to take to ensure the safety of your pool wall. (In Chapter 8, I go over the suggested closing techniques and winterizing equipment.) So, when you open your pool, you have to remove that equipment. The things you need to remove usually consist of a plate on your skimmer, a plug in your return, and an ice equalizer pillow in the water.

Ensure that your filter equipment is hooked up (which I talk about in the preceding section) prior to removing your winterizing equipment. If you don't, the water in your pool will dump onto the ground through the holes on your pool from the skimmer and the return where your hoses normally attach.

Here's how to handle each piece of hardware:

>> **Skimmer plate:** If you're using a winter skimmer plate that gets screwed into your existing skimmer face plate, carefully remove the screws so that you don't drop them into the pool. If you drop one and your pool is green or cloudy, it will make them much harder to find at the bottom. If you lose them, you'll have to get replacements right away so that the skimmer doesn't leak. Also, be cautious removing the winter skimmer plate, especially if it's made with stainless steel. If you drop that skimmer plate in the pool, it could land on the corner first and possibly puncture the liner.

>> **Return plug:** Your return outlet should have some form of a plug or cap in it. Remove that plug and store it somewhere safe for next fall. Place your return eyeball (see Chapter 3 for a description of an eyeball) back into the threaded hole on the inside of the pool to make sure you get optimal circulation after the filter is running.

>> **Ice equalizer pillows:** There's a possibility of the ice equalizer pillows left in the pool being deflated from the pressure of the ice, but I go over how to try to prevent that in Chapter 8. If the pillows are still inflated, gently remove them from the pool and deflate them. If the pillows are slimy from algae, you can use the same cleaner that you would for your winter cover to scrub it down before storing it. If it's already deflated when you open the pool cover, just remove it from the pool and throw it away.

Turning on your above ground pool filter system

After your system is all hooked up, which you can read about in the section "Getting your above ground pool filter up and running," earlier in this chapter, it's time to turn the pump on. Because the filter had no water in it over the winter, it will take some time to fill up. Different pumps will turn on in different ways. Some are simply plugged in and start working; others need to be plugged in and then a switch turned on. The switch can be on the pump or at the outlet, depending on the setup.

Cartridge and DE filters

Cartridge and diatomaceous earth (DE) filters have a manual air relief valve on the top of the tank that you'll open while the pump is on. The filter tank will fill with water from the bottom, and the air will escape from the top. This air relief valve usually looks like a small plastic knob that unthreads. (For a visual of this component, see Chapter 3, which has some parts breakdowns.) After water begins spraying from the air relief on the top, you know the tank is full; you can close the air relief valve.

REMEMBER

If you have a DE filter, make sure that you add your DE in right away. You add the DE through the skimmer while the pump is running. For further instructions, you can check out Chapter 3.

Sand filters

On a sand filter, you probably don't have a manual air relief valve that you can unthread to bleed the air. Some sand filters have an internal air escape in the tank. It's a long skinny tube that has a screen on the top. It connects from the bottom of the lateral assembly and reaches to the top of the tank on the inside. The air will travel through the screen, down the tube, and exit as small bubbles into your pool through the return. With this style, all you have to do is have the pump on and the filter's multiport valve (see Chapter 3) set to Filter. The tank will begin to fill with water on its own. Don't be surprised if you have air coming through your return for the first few hours. It will go away after the air is completely gone from inside the tank.

If you have a manual air relief, which will usually look like a small threaded knob on the side of the multiport valve, you can unthread that and open it up the same way you would for a cartridge or DE filter.

Checking for leaks in your above ground pool filter system

After you have the filter system running (see the section "Turning on your above ground pool filter system," earlier in this chapter), this is when you'll look for either water or air leaks. Check the following:

>> **Filter hoses:** If you're getting a leak where one of your filter hoses attaches to an adapter, sometimes you can wrap the adapter in some plumber's tape. If you notice that the hoses are really loose, it's usually worth just replacing the hoses. They may be at a point of no return.

>> **Pump lid and return jet:** If you're noticing air in your pump lid or bubbles in your return jet, there's a good chance you're dealing with an air/suction leak. Like I talk about in Chapter 4, your air leaks draw air only on the suction side of the pump. For an above ground pool, the suction side includes the skimmer, hose, adapters, and front of the pump. If you have any ball valves, your pump might also pull air from those.

Typical spots that you want to check are any threaded piece and any O-rings. I recommend going through and cleaning, lubricating, or even replacing O-rings, and retaping threaded adapters by using plumber's tape. For further details on air leaks, check out Chapter 4.

>> **Spraying or dripping water around the filter:** As far as leaks on the pressure side, which is where the water is going back into the pool through the return hose, those will present with water dripping or spraying out of cracks or unsealed areas. When the water is being forced through something, it seeks the easiest route.

It's not uncommon to have a leak or two when you first get your filter up and started, so be ready with some plumber's tape and O-ring lubricant.

TIP

There are thousands of O-rings in the swimming pool industry, and if you just ask for a 2-inch O-ring without explaining what it goes to, there's a very strong chance you won't get the correct one. If you ever need to replace a part on your filter because of cracking or from it being worn down from age, if you're not familiar with the parts, always bring the part with you — or at least take a photo.

Opening an Inground Pool

Having an inground pool in your backyard that needs to be opened up can be intimidating to the novice pool owner. While opening a pool can seem like something beyond your comfort zone, I want to assure you that it is one of the easier tasks to perform on inground pools.

Choosing when to open your inground pool

Similar to getting an above ground pool open for the season (flip back to the section "Opening an Above Ground Pool," earlier in this chapter), opening an inground pool can really be done at your leisure. Of course, there are some pros and cons to opening too early or late, so let me go over those.

If your pool has a solid tarp-style cover that doesn't let sunlight through, you can open your pool pretty late into the spring if the cover is in good shape. Those types of covers will prevent algae growth, which will make your initial startup in the spring a quicker and easier process, so you can open in late June and still be algae free.

If you closed your pool by using a safety cover (which attaches to pegs drilled into the concrete of the pool decking), that style does allow light through. There are solid safety covers that block a significant amount of sunlight, but these covers always have a mesh strip (or squares) that allow for algae growth. So if you have a safety cover, open your pool earlier in the spring, before the water warms up too much, creating probable algae growth and headaches. Memorial Day would be the latest I would wait — but, in reality, the earlier you open the pool, the clearer your pool water will be to start. I recommend shooting for mid-April if the weather is beginning to warm.

Essentially, it comes down to how much initial cleanup you want to deal with, but I suggest that you open early and get the water circulating. If you leave the pool stagnant while the temperatures rise, you're more likely to open up to a green pool, which means more elbow grease and money to get your pool into swimming quality.

Removing your inground pool cover

Taking the cover off of your inground pool is usually the first step in your pool opening process. Inground pools have one of two kinds of covers you could be using:

>> Solid tarp-style cover

>> Safety cover

You remove each type of cover by using different methods. In the following sections, I give you tips and tricks on the best methods for removal of your particular type of cover.

Taking off a safety cover

This style of cover doesn't require being drained, and it's super simple to remove. In Figure 6-3, you can see that a safety cover is suspended over the pool by using springs that attach to anchors in the surrounding decking. In Chapter 5, I go into further details on the perks of this style of cover for safety reasons.

When you decide it's time to remove the cover, follow these steps:

1. **Remove debris from the top of the cover.**

   Either brush or spray off any debris on the top of the cover so that the debris doesn't fall into the water during removal.

2. **Attach the notch of your safety cover removal tool to the head of an anchor.**

   As shown in Figure 6-4, a safety cover removal tool consists of a long rod that has a notch cut in the end.

3. **Spin the tool around the head of the anchor between the anchor head and the spring.**

4. **Bend the removal tool towards the pool.**

   The spring will slide up the rod, releasing from the anchor. Once it is off, move onto the next spring until the whole cover is loose.

5. **Repeat Steps 2 through 4 for each anchor.**

TIP

   If you're dealing with a non-rectangular pool, I recommend marking one spring with a zip-tie and marking the corresponding anchor with paint. These reminders will ensure that you have a definite starting point in the fall when you go to put the cover back on.

6. **With a partner on the opposite side of the pool from you, pull the cover onto the deck from the shallow end — bring it onto the deck about 5 feet from the edge of the pool.**

   As soon as the last of the springs are removed, the cover will start to sink into the pool, so work somewhat quickly.

   Starting the folding process is most easily done on the shallow end for the majority of pools but work with whatever side makes the most sense for you. Remember the side from which you start taking the cover off because it will be much easier to roll out and install for winterization.

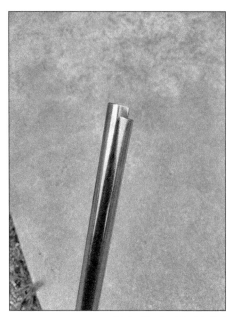

FIGURE 6-4:
A safety cover
removal tool.

Kristine Blanchard (Book Author)

7. **Both you and your partner grab straps that are straight across from each other and pull tight like you would a rope to create a straight line.**

   Keep the cover as flat as possible.

8. **Fold the cover fold it up accordion style.**

   Grab the cover 3 feet from the end and move towards the center. Take that piece of the cover and line it up with the free end of the cover. Repeat this step to create an accordion-style pleated fold. See Figure 6-5 for how to start this fold.

   Folding the cover like an accordion will make it easy to put back on in the fall.

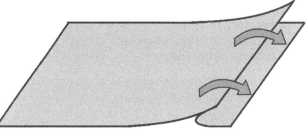

FIGURE 6-5:
Folding a cover
accordion style
for the spring.

Courtesy of Kristine Blanchard

9. **Pull the rest of the cover out of the pool, one strap at a time, folding the cover onto itself like an accordion.**

10. **After the cover is completely removed and folded on the ground, fold the cover in half, end to end.**

11. **From the folded end, roll the cover up like a sleeping bag.**

   You want it nice and tight so that it can fit into its bag or container. If your cover is wet when it's folded up, you can leave it standing up, rolls on the top and bottom, to allow excess water to drain out for a few days before putting it away for the summer.

Removing a solid cover

To remove a tarp-style cover, follow these steps:

1. **Fill the pool with water using your garden hose under the cover.**

2. **Remove any leaves and water from the pool cover.**

   Removing leaves and water from the top will make the cover lighter and easier to remove.

3. **Remove the weights on the edges of the cover.**

   These covers are weighted down along the edges, instead of being attached by anchors like safety covers are (see the preceding section).

   It's discussed further in Chapter 8, but your weights can be anything, from water tubes that are specifically designed to be a cover weight to large wood boards cut into 6-inch pieces.

4. **Prepare your weights for storage.**

   If you're using water tubes, pop open the tabs where they were filled and lift the tube from the opposite end to dump the water out. Then roll from the end that doesn't have tabs towards the tabs in a tightly bound roll for easy storage. If you are using wood, simply roll them off of the cover and out of the way or begin stacking them wherever you plan to store them.

5. **Pull the cover out of the pool evenly around all edges.**

   You don't want to have folds in your cover.

6. **On the side that you plan to fold the cover from, pull the cover up onto the deck until it almost starts to fall into the pool on the other end.**

   I typically recommend starting on the shallow end because it is the least likely spot to have obstructions like diving boards and it usually has the most amount of deck space.

7. **Go to the opposite end of the cover and fold that part of the cover up onto itself to create a pocket.**

   You make this pocket so that debris doesn't fall into the pool.

8. **With a partner on the opposite side of the pool from you, pull the cover onto the deck from the shallow end, about 5 feet from the edge of the pool.**

9. **Both you and your partner grab straps that are straight across from each other and pull tight like you would a rope to create a straight line.**

   Keep the cover as flat as possible.

10. **Pull the rest of the cover out of the pool folding the cover onto itself like an accordion.**

11. **After the cover is completely removed and folded on the ground, fold the cover in half, end to end.**

    This is going to be a "messy fold" because if you want to clean it off with a hose or cover cleaning chemical, you will need to unfold the cover in a different location.

12. **Spray off any algae or remaining debris from your cover by using a regular garden hose or pressure washer.**

    If the cover is not on grass for this process, you can leave it out to dry for a few minutes before folding it back up.

13. **(Optional) Clean the cover by using a liquid chemical called cover cleaner and then spray it off with a hose.**

14. **Refold the cover neatly for fall.**

    You want to try and follow the same folding technique as you did when you took it off the pool, folded accordion style, then in half, then rolled up like a sleeping bag. This will make your cover easy to store and easy to open back up come fall when you need to winterize.

Removing winter hardware and replacing summer hardware on an inground pool

REMEMBER

If your filter system is lower than your pool's water level, make sure that you're not removing winterizing items before getting your filter hooked up first. When the filter system is down gravity from the pool, the water will begin to pour out of all the disconnected and unplugged areas you had created for winterizing. Jump to "Hooking up your inground pool filter" and then return to this section for proper setup of this style of system.

After you remove the cover (flip to "Removing your inground pool cover," earlier in this chapter), it's time to remove the winter equipment. On inground pools, there are two places in the pool to look out for winterizing equipment:

>> **On the pool wall — returns and side suctions:** The two most common kinds of winterizing equipment used for return and side suction ports will be rubber expansion plugs and threaded plastic caps. You can see an image of them in Figure 6-6. Rubber expansion plugs have a wing nut on them that needs to be unthreaded to loosen it from the hole, then it can be pulled out. With the threaded caps, those need to be unthreaded and removed from the hole they are in.

>> **Outside of the pool's interior — skimmer(s):** For your skimmers, they can be plugged by rubber expansion plugs or threaded caps. But, the majority of the time, they are winterized with something called a skimmer guard. *Skimmer guards* are cylindrical hollow tubes with threads on the bottom. They thread into the hole at the bottom of your skimmer after the pool is winterized to not only plug the hole to prevent water from getting in the pipe, but to also give you protection from ice expansion for water that may accumulate in the skimmer housing. To remove them, they can just be unthreaded from the hole they are in.

TIP

Figure 6-6 shows examples of a plug, cap, and skimmer guard. Remember to store these items in a location where they won't get lost. If you have a bag or container your winter cover is stored in, I recommend putting any plugs into a plastic baggie and placing them along with the skimmer guard in the container with the cover.

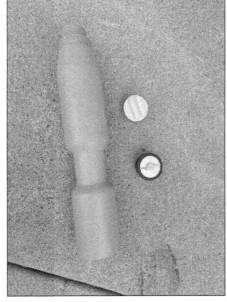

FIGURE 6-6:
Winter hardware includes a skimmer guard (left), plastic cap (middle), and rubber expansion plug (right).

Kristine Blanchard (Book Author)

Replacing hand railings and ladders

One of the things that you do at the time of closing is remove all ladders and hand railings, which are usually located near steps. There are some pools that have exceptions to this, but for the majority of inground pools that have railings, you remove those railings at the time of closing. (You can read about the process of closing your pool in Chapter 8.)

Clean your deck by using a hose after you remove the cover. A deck spray-down will give you a chance to rinse off the anchors, along with spraying out the sockets (the device your railings and ladders slide into in the deck), removing any debris that gets trapped inside. If you don't clean out the sockets or anchors, you may not be able to get your railings or ladders all the way into the holes or your anchors threaded all the way down, making them much more difficult to remove in the fall.

Reattaching the railings is pretty straightforward. Just follow these steps:

1. **Slide the railing/ladder into place.**

    You want to place the railing/ladder into the designated sockets in the deck where they were removed in the fall for winterizing.

    You may have 5-inch-wide circular plates with a hole in them — sometimes they are white, chrome, or match the deck color. These flat donut-looking pieces are called *escutcheon plates.* They are used as a decorative cover, and they slide onto the pipe of the ladder or railing on the open end where it will be going into the sockets in the deck. After the ladder/railing is secured in place, the escutcheon plates slide down and lay flat on the ground to cover the socket and leave a more finished look.

2. **Tighten the wedge in the anchor socket by using a wrench.**

    The wedge is a triangular piece in the socket that is attached to a bolt. Once the ladder/railing is in the socket, you tighten the bolt, which will raise the wedge up, pressing it against the pipe of the railing/ladder and anchoring it in place. You want these fairly tight, so there is no wiggle to the railing or ladder. These are what keep your railings and ladders locked in place while they're being used.

    REMEMBER

    If the ladder or railing does not seem to fit into the socket, that can sometimes be from the wedge being in the way. Be sure to unthread the bolt from the wedge until it is towards the bottom of the bolt (that is considered loose) and then make sure the wedge is tucked against the side of the socket and not sticking out in the way of your railing/ladder.

3. **Repeat Step 2 for each railing and ladder you install.**

    There is a socket with a wedge for every "leg" of the railing or ladder that mounts to the deck.

The railings are a safety feature, so be sure they're nice and tight in their anchors. If not, you could easily pull a railing out without even meaning to if you put enough weight on it. If you can't get the railings tight into their anchors, it's safer to not use the railings at all.

When you install a ladder, be sure that it has protective bumpers on the bottom where the ladder sits against the liner (see Figure 6-7). If you put your ladder into the pool without bumpers, it can easily put two circular cuts into your liner the first time you use it.

FIGURE 6-7:
Ladder bumpers
in place.

Kristine Blanchard (Book Author)

Putting down the pegs

If you remove a safety cover (which I describe in the section "Taking off a safety cover," earlier in this chapter), you'll have pegs sticking up all around your deck. Be cautious while you walk around. And put the pegs down as soon as you can by following these steps:

1. **If you spray off the deck with water, spray directly onto the anchors to ensure no dirt or debris gets trapped in the threads.**

2. **Screw the pegs down into the deck.**

   The pegs have a slot at the top meant to fit either an Allen wrench or a flathead screwdriver.

Make sure you put the pegs all the way down and flush with the concrete so that no one trips. Do not tighten them down too tight. Over the summer they can almost cement in place and come fall when you need to pull them up again, they can be very hard to remove.

3. **If there's an anchor that you can't get to go down all the way, mark it obviously with a rope or caution tape.**

   You can easily break a toe on these anchors, so be careful.

Some safety covers that have small surrounding decks or landscaping on one side may not use standard anchors all the way around the pool. Safety covers can also be secured by

WARNING

>> Cables that snap into eyelets around the pool.

>> 12-inch to 18-inch stakes that get driven into the ground for the springs to hook onto.

   Always triple check and remove all stakes when you remove the pool cover. They can be a tripping hazard if left in the ground.

>> Anchors hiding in bushes or landscaping.

WARNING

If you decide to get crafty and use a power drill to put the anchors down flush to the deck, don't overtighten them. If you hear a click when they hit flush, you went too far. If you leave it like that, it'll be locked in place come fall. Unthread the anchor slightly to undo the "click" then be sure to thread the anchor back down until it's flush, but not tight down like it was.

Hooking up your inground pool filter

One thing that's slightly easier with inground pools than above ground pools is that, most of the time, the filter system doesn't come apart. You leave it assembled and just winterize it by blowing it out (the process of emptying the pipes of water for the winter) and removing drain plugs.

In Chapter 8, I go over removing your drain plugs and placing them inside your pump basket. That's a very common place for them to be stored, and most pool professionals will put them in there. So, if you're looking for your drain plugs, I would start there.

After you find them, put all of the drain plugs back into their respective locations.

Almost all plumbed-in pool equipment will have some sort of a drain plug, so here's a quick list of how many plugs to look for:

Equipment	Number of Plugs
Pump	2
Filter	1
Chlorinator	1
Heater	1
Salt generator	None

If your drain plug or cap has an O-ring, be sure that the O-ring is in good shape and lubricated to ensure that you don't get any leaks. If it only threads in and doesn't have an O-ring, use plumber's tape to create a good seal on the threads. If you disassembled your filter and brought it inside (which is not a common or necessary practice), the hook-ups should all be quick-connect unions, so reassembly will be simple!

Starting up your inground pool filter system

Inground pools have a slightly more complicated startup process than above ground pools. (Flip to the section "Getting your above ground pool filter up and running," earlier in this chapter, to see how to start an above ground pool for the season.)

For the most part, inground pools don't get help from gravity to feed the water into the system. Your filter system is usually higher than the water level, so it has to pull the water through the pipes.

Follow these steps to start up your inground pool filter system:

1. **Fill your pump with a bucket of water to help prime it.**

    The water will give the impeller its first gust of power and start the priming process after all other steps are completed.

2. **If your filter has a multiport valve, put it on the Recirculate setting.**

    This will give the water the path of least resistance and will help the pump prime and get water circulating through the system faster and easier.

If you do not have a multiport valve, as some cartridge or DE filters do not, you will ignore this step for your filter and you will want to open the manual air relief on your filter (for better identification of that, see Chapter 3). Because your filter will have water entering it during the start-up process, you want to prevent as little restriction (air in the tank) as possible and opening the air relief will do that.

REMEMBER

Sometimes, during the start-up process, priming can take a little while, which is normal. But you want to ensure there are no restrictions on the pressure side that would complicate things. So be sure you have followed all other steps in the preceding section on taking out plugs that were in place for winter.

It is also possible your return lines have valves by the filter system so you can shut off your returns if ever needed in the future. Be sure all shut-off valves are open on the pressure side of the filter system (after the filter) so that water can flow back to the pool.

3. **Close the pump lid back up by threading it in place or tightening it with the proper clamps/knobs.**

   Seal it well by making sure the lid is nice and snug. There will be some form of a rubber seal where the lid of the pump meets the pump housing and that seals the lid and makes it airtight. Be sure the O-ring or gasket is wiped clean and lubricated with O-ring lubricant (you can get this at any hardware or pool store).

WARNING

Do not use petroleum-based lubricants on rubber components. It will break down the rubber and dry them out, leading to cracks that will require the O-ring or gasket to be replaced.

4. **Open one line at a time, starting with the main drain.**

   I like to start with a main drain first because it is the easiest for the pump to pull from due to the force of the water going into the main drain pipe and trying to reach its own level.

TIP

Most inground pools have multiple suction pipes like a main drain or a side suction, along with a skimmer pipe. Your suction pipes should all have some sort of a shut-off valve plumbed on it, and they are likely all closed from when it was winterized. Be sure to only open one line at a time, because if you open all of them, it is way too many places for the pump to pull from at once, and all of them have air in them.

5. **Turn your pump on and let the pump clear all of the air from that first pipe.**

   Most inground pools will have an On/Off switch like a light switch or a switch in the timer.

6. **Check to see that the first line has primed and water is moving through the pool and filter system at full speed.**

7. **Open the next suction pipe to remove the air from that line.**

TIP

When opening the second pipe, open the shut-off valve slowly. Air is much easier for the pump to pull in than the water is, so if you were to just open the pipe immediately, the pump would suck in all the air in that pipe in one big gulp, and most likely cause the pump to lose its momentum. You will have to wait for the pump to regain its prime and get the water moving again. If you open the valve a quarter turn at a time, the pump will suck in the air a little at a time and should still allow the water flow to keep the pump moving.

8. **Repeat Step 7 for any additional suction lines you may have, until all valves are open, and the water is flowing strong through the filter system.**

9. **Inspect the filter system and all above ground plumbing for leaks.**

Take a thorough look and address any leaks that are more than a drip every five seconds. Sometimes it is as simple as tightening a nut that was loose or maybe there is an O-ring that is not sealing properly. It all depends on where the leak is! For some common repairs, check out Chapter 4.

10. **If you have a multiport valve and it's set to Recirculate, shut the pump off and change the valve to Filter.**

When the multiport valve was on Recirculate, it was bypassing your filter, which means your filter still has no water in it. By switching it to Filter, you are not allowing the water to enter the filter tank. The majority of filters have the water enter in through the bottom port on the tank, which means the filter is filling from the bottom up.

11. **Open the manual air relief on the top of your filter if it has this valve.**

Opening the manual air relief on the filter (if it has one) allows the air to escape while the filter is filling. Not all sand filters will have a manual air relief because they have a way to allow the air to escape into the pool internally. To better identify the air relief and how it works, see Chapter 3.

12. **Start your pump up again.**

Chapter **7**

Time to Get Cleaning!

I f there's one part to this whole owning-a-pool thing that you can totally handle, it's cleaning. Trust me when I tell you it's one of the most relaxing and rewarding parts. One thing you have to keep in mind, though, is that cleaning a pool is sort of like cleaning your house: You do it at your own pace and to your own liking. There's no real weekly schedule; it's all based on when the pool needs it and when you have time to do it. But, it typically ends up that weekly maintenance on routine cleaning is the way to go. A tidy pool is a more enjoyable experience.

WARNING

If you leave some things on the pool floor, such as leaves or dead animals, they can cause staining. Remove those items quickly to prevent that possibility. You want to remove them for safety and cleanliness reasons too.

There are times and environments where you should, or may need to, clean more often. Yards that have a lot of trees, neighbors who have a lot of trees, well-manicured lawns, a yard of mostly dirt with a few patches of lawn trying to survive — you get it. All of these things can end up playing a part in your regular cleaning regimen.

In this chapter, I explain how to do all of those fun cleaning procedures and the best ways of completing them in an efficient and effective manner. I also go over all of the sweet robots that you can buy that can clean the pool for you while you lounge on the deck drinking an ice cold lemonade.

Cleaning Your Pool by Hand

When it comes to cleaning your pool by hand, there are three major parts you want to pay attention to:

» Bottom

» Walls

» Water's surface

Some tools can take care of more than one cleaning need; other tools are more useful for certain types of cleaning; and some tools you can use on only certain surfaces. The best strategy for cleaning your pool involves starting with the floor and working your way up, so that's how I organize the following sections.

Manually vacuuming

Manually vacuuming is typically done by using your pool's pump for suction and having the dirt, leaves, and dead worms go into your pump basket or filter. For the most part, manually vacuuming is done very similarly in all types of pools, whether it's above the ground, below the ground, or just a blow-up pool.

In the section "Vacuuming to waste," later in this chapter, I also go over what vacuuming to waste means, and when that would need to be done and why.

Gathering your equipment

Before I walk you through how to vacuum (which I go over in the section "Getting the vacuum process started," later in this chapter), you need to know what to vacuum with. Following is a list of the items involved in this whole process (and you can see examples of them in Figure 7-1):

» **Vacuum head:** This is part of the vacuuming equipment that you actually push around on your pole. It serves as a guide to where you're trying to vacuum, as well as a brush in some cases, such as vacuuming up algae on the floor.

» **Telescopic pole:** The item you use for all manual cleaning procedures. It's an extending pole, typically made of aluminum or fiberglass, that allows you to reach the bottom of the pool without having to dive down there yourself.

>> **Properly sized vacuum hose:** A vacuum hose is pretty key in manually vacuuming. It's what actually gets the suction of your pump to the bottom of the pool where you need it.

>> **Vacuum plate:** Also known as skimmer plates, these flat plastic dishes with a hose adapter ensure you're not causing possible underground or in-line clogs (which are a big uh-oh).

FIGURE 7-1:
Tools needed to vacuum your pool: A vacuum head, telescopic pole, vacuum hose, and vacuum plate.

Choosing the vacuum pieces that best fit your pool type and size is key to an optimal vacuuming experience. The following sections go over the most commonly used options and which options may work best for you.

VACUUM HEADS

There are three different types of vacuum heads, so you have some options. The most commonly used type is the triangular brush vacuum head (as shown in Figure 7-1); then there's the wheeled flexible vacuum head and the leaf bagger vacuum head.

TIP

I always highly recommend that you use a brush vacuum on all vinyl surfaces and wheeled vacuum heads for gunite-plaster or fiberglass surfaces. Of course, that doesn't mean there aren't gunite-plaster pools that use brush heads and vinyl that use wheeled heads. You just want to make sure you pick a head that benefits you long term and is safe for your surface type:

>> **Brush vacuum heads:** Do just what their name suggests — brushing! The downside to using them on gunite-plaster surfaces is that they wear down much faster and are harder to move because of the rough texture of the surface.

>> **Wheeled vacuum heads:** Can vacuum much faster than a brush and roll over leaves, instead of possibly pushing them away. But if you buy one that's too low to the ground and use it on a vinyl surface, it can get stuck to the floor and might tear the liner.

>> **Leaf bagger vacuum head:** Doesn't use the suction of your pump to work; it actually hooks up to a garden hose. This kind of vacuum head has small spouts on the inside that are angled upwards and create a reverse suction up into the center of a bag. These aren't used as commonly, but they're great if you have really good water pressure and a bunch of large debris or leaves.

TELESCOPIC POLE

TIP

Telescopic poles typically come in two lengths: 6 feet extending to 12 feet or 8 feet extending to 16 feet. I personally prefer an 8-foot-to-16-foot pole because you can extend it to your desired length. If you have an inground pool or an above ground that's over 15 feet long, I definitely recommend getting the 8-foot-to-16-foot pole because shorter poles won't be able to reach the deepest parts of an inground pool or the middle of large above ground pool. Or you can have a longer pole for vacuuming and a shorter one for skimming to cut down on the weight.

Telescopic poles come in a large variety of colors and materials. Pick one that suits you, price- and weight-wise. Go to your local pool store and see which you like best.

VACUUM HOSES

If your vacuum hose isn't the right size, you'll never get your pool properly cleaned. When it comes to the length, your hose should be

>> 3 feet longer than the longest part of a single-level pool.

>> Long enough to extend to the farthest distance in your pool from the skimmer, also accounting for the depth of the deepest part.

If you have 30 feet for the long distance with an 8-foot deep-end, get at a minimum a 38-foot hose (or just round up to 40 feet).

There are two different size diameters for vacuum hoses: 1.5-inch and 1.25-inch. If you have either an inground or above ground pool that has a 1.5-horsepower (hp) pump or larger, I usually recommend just getting a 1.5-inch-diameter hose. Of course, you can use an 1.25-inch-diameter hose for your inground pool, but those pumps are so strong that you either cause the hose to collapse or cause strain on the pump, which can lead to long-term damage on the hose and the pump.

TIP

Most 1.5-inch-diameter hoses come with one end that swivels. The swivel end is typically indicated by a color, or it has a distinct two-part look to it. The swivel end helps prevent the hose from tangling when you vacuum, so make sure to put the swivel end on your vacuum head.

VACUUM PLATES

Vacuum plates are designed to fit over your skimmer basket so that while you're vacuuming, large debris gets caught there instead of in your pump basket. Why is that important, you ask? Well, let me tell you!

Let's say you suck up something you think is harmless, such as a small twig the length of your hand. It goes into your pipe that leads to the front of the pump and gets caught somewhere in the line. While you continue vacuuming, leaves, pine needles, or whatever else may be on the bottom of the pool get stuck on that original twig and clog your line underground. Now, you have an issue that may require calling a service company — and that's never fun or cheap. (And yes, this oddly specific example comes from personal experience — even as a professional, I had to make mistakes, like this one, so that I can show you how to avoid them.) To prevent this kind of clog situation, use the handy-dandy vacuum plate.

REMEMBER

Vacuum plates are designed to fit onto certain types of skimmer baskets. And no, they're not universal. That's a trend in the pool industry — almost nothing is universal. Check the skimmer basket and/or the skimmer cover for part numbers, which can help you identify the correct plate for your skimmer basket.

Preparing to vacuum

Before you begin the vacuuming process, make sure you're using the optimal vacuum port. You probably vacuum from the skimmer, but not necessarily. You may have a designated vacuum line, which I talk about in Chapter 3. If you have a designated vacuum line, you can attach your vacuum hose directly into that suction on the pool. Alternatively, you can use a vacuum leaf canister or leaf trap that can catch what you vacuum before that debris goes into the suction port on the pool. A leaf trap is a very helpful tool that essentially gives you the effects of a vacuum plate (see the preceding section) without using the skimmer.

No matter whether you're using your skimmer or a suction port, you can get optimal suction by adjusting the valves in front of your pump to close all lines except the one you're vacuuming from. You may need to adjust the power of the suction; if your pump is too strong for one line (which might collapse your hose or cause your vacuum head to suction to the floor), you may need to keep other suction ports open to allow proper water flow.

TIP

Consult your local pool professionals to figure out the best vacuuming method for your pool setup if you're not sure.

Things to check before hooking up your vacuum hose:

>> All baskets (for the pump and skimmer) are empty and have optimal flow.

>> Your filter isn't due for a backwash. (Flip to Chapter 3 for the details on backwashing.)

Getting the vacuum process started

After you identify the ideal vacuuming port and settings, prep your pool, and get all of the proper equipment ready (discussed in the preceding sections), you're ready to manually vacuum. Be sure your pump is running, and the filter is on the proper setting for the type of vacuuming you plan to do. Maintenance vacuuming is done on the Filter setting of your multiport valve; see Chapter 3 for more details. Follow these steps to manually vacuum your pool:

1. **Attach your vacuum head to your telescopic pole.**

   Figure 7-2 shows how the handle of the vacuum head inserts into your vacuum pole and uses the pins in the handle to hold the two parts together.

2. **Attach your vacuum hose to your vacuum head.**

   In Figure 7-3, you can see how the vacuum head slides over the adapter on your vacuum head.

3. **Submerge your vacuum head under water.**

   Figure 7-4 shows the depth your vacuum head should be submerged under water.

TIP

If you have fine sediment on the floor of your pool, don't position your vacuum head all the way to the floor until you actually turn on the suction (see Step 7). Otherwise, you disturb all the fine sediment, which can make the water cloudy, or cause sediment to be suspended and drop after you have finished vacuuming. Holding the vacuum head up off the pool's floor while it's submerged while also trying to complete the next step may require a second person. If you are trying to do it alone, it is easy for the vacuum head to fall all the way down to the floor, which can cause that agitation to the floor you are trying to prevent.

FIGURE 7-2:
A vacuum head
attached to a
telescopic pole.

FIGURE 7-3:
Attach the
vacuum hose
securely to the
vacuum head.

FIGURE 7-4:
A vacuum head, pole, and hose submerged under water.

Kristine Blanchard (Book Author)

4. **Take the end of your vacuum hose opposite the one that has the pole and head attached, and place that end over your pool's closest return jet.**

   The flow of the water from this jet shoots down the hose and causes the air to escape from the hole in the vacuum head.

5. **Maintain your hose in this position until all air has been removed from the hose.**

   After the air has been completely pushed out of the hose and the bubbles stop coming out, you know the vacuum hose is full of water.

TIP

When bringing the end of the vacuum hose over to the skimmer, either keep the end of the hose you removed from the return submerged or cover it with your hand so that you don't end up getting air into the hose that could lead to an air pocket getting sucked into the pump and causing it to lose its prime from lack of water.

6. **Attach your vacuum plate to the hose by pressing the end of the hose you carried over from the return and sliding it onto the adapter on the vacuum plate.**

7. **Place your vacuum plate onto your skimmer basket (see Figure 7-5) and allow the draw of the pump to seat the plate in place.**

FIGURE 7-5:
Place a vacuum plate attached to the vacuum hose into the skimmer.

Kristine Blanchard (Book Author)

If the pump suddenly stops sucking water when you attach the vacuum plate to the skimmer basket, or the pump sounds like it emptied and has a higher pitch to it, it may have lost its prime because of an air pocket. Don't remove anything — just give it a moment; it regains its prime quickly if it was just a small amount of air.

If there was a lot of air, you may need to remove the vacuum hose and plate from the skimmer and allow the pump to reprime before trying it again.

REMEMBER

8. **Now that you're up and running, just take your time, relax, and enjoy the satisfaction of cleaning the bottom of your pool.**

   I personally like to start from the end farthest from your skimmer and work my way back, to prevent the hose from tangling too much.

9. **After you get the pool looking the way you want, check the pressure of your filter to make sure it doesn't need to be backwashed.**

   See Chapter 3 for details on backwashing. It never hurts to backwash after vacuuming, so if you're ever unsure, just do it.

Vacuuming to waste

Manually vacuuming to waste is a trick you have up your sleeve for some specific situations when vacuuming on the Filter setting of your multiport valve just isn't going to work. *Vacuuming to waste* is when you manually vacuum, but instead of having the debris enter your filter, it goes out your backwash/waste line and is emptied onto the ground. This process saves your filter a lot of wear and tear — and you a lot of time and labor.

Why would you need to vacuum to waste? Great question! Vacuuming to waste allows you to take the sediment or algae that may be on the bottom of the pool and vacuum it directly out of your backwash line. This is an incredibly helpful tool to have if you're dealing with particles on the floor that are finer than your filter may be able to handle. It can also help when what you're vacuuming isn't really something you feel like clogging up your filter with. The following list gives you some very common situations in which you may vacuum to waste:

>> **First Scenario:** A severe algae bloom has occurred, where algae is covering the entirety of the surface of your pool.

This particular situation can be treated in two different ways:

- Brushing, shocking, algaecide, and filtering.

- Vacuuming the majority of the algae to waste, and then completing the steps in the preceding bullet, just with a lot less algae to treat. Vacuuming to waste first puts you so much further ahead before you even really start treating the algae.

WARNING

Green algae is sticky and slimy, and it ruins filter media very quickly. I never recommend vacuuming on filter (which I talk about in the section "Manually vacuuming," earlier in this chapter) for severe algae blooms.

>> **Second Scenario:** You've killed all the green algae or yellow mustard algae by shocking and adding algaecide (see Chapter 12 for more steps of treating algae), and you're just left with the floating dead remnants.

These remnants are usually a very fine consistency, and if you have a sand filter, it may not be physically capable of trapping that fine of a particulate. Even with a cartridge or DE filter, you just may not want that stuff inside your filter — it may be easier to waste it.

>> **Third Scenario:** After the winter is over, you open your pool by removing the mesh tarp or mesh safety cover on it.

When you remove your mesh winter cover, it's not uncommon to have a fine layer of dust and sediment on the bottom of the pool. Usually, if you turn the filter on when you have this type of sediment in your pool, it kicks up that sediment and causes a very cloudy pool. Vacuuming to waste in the beginning saves you time and gets you swimming faster.

>> **Fourth Scenario:** You had a severe cloudy-water issue that lead you to a floc treatment. (See Chapter 12 for how to floc.)

You usually floc a pool because the water has been consistently cloudy with no change, indicating the particles in your water may be too fine for your filter to handle.

If that's the case, after you floc your pool and end up with a lovely layer of sediment on the floor of the pool, you definitely don't want to vacuum that up through the filter because it'll just end up circulated back into the pool again. Get that stuff out of the pool the easiest way possible — through the waste line.

Vacuuming to waste is easiest if you have a multiport valve on your sand or DE filter (you can read about types of filters in Chapter 3) that includes a Waste setting (see Figure 7-6). The only other easy way to vacuum to waste is if your filter is plumbed with a 3-way valve. This valve is different from a multiport valve and allows you to adjust the flow of water to go to a waste line. It is mostly seen on cartridge filters. See Chapter 3 for a reference photo.

FIGURE 7-6:
Multiport valve's settings include Waste.

Kristine Blanchard (Book Author)

WARNING

Vacuuming with the multiport valve set to Waste is not the same as vacuuming with the valve set to Backwash. Never vacuum on Backwash because it causes dirt and debris to enter into areas it is not supposed to, such as inside of the DE grids or inside laterals at the bottom of the sand filter, which can ruin filters very quickly.

Vacuuming to waste causes you to lose water from the pool fairly quickly. It's not uncommon to lose 6-plus inches of water after just 30 minutes. Make sure your pool is overfilled before starting. If you can't spare the water, this procedure may not work for you.

When vacuuming to waste, go slowly enough that you do not kick up the fine debris but quickly enough to vacuum out as much in one session as you can. You need to be conscious of the water loss, so you can't go too slowly. So, take your time — but hurry up!

If you're using a brushed vacuum head when you vacuum to waste, remove the brushes that are in front of the suction hole. That way, the sediment doesn't get pushed out of the way during vacuuming; it gets properly sucked up the hose.

Brushing it off

When it comes to brushing a pool, I have to say, it's kind of, well, lame. This isn't a complex procedure, but it is one of the more labor-intensive chores. Brushing a pool is a necessity in keeping up with algae growth, and it's particularly important in a pool that doesn't get a lot of use or in gunite-plaster pools:

>> **Unused pools:** When you brush the surface of a pool that hasn't been used for awhile, you break away anything that may be settling in and trying to grow.

>> **Gunite-plaster pools:** Brushing the surface helps prevent the buildup of scale on the walls and floor in these pools.

The general rule on brushing is: Do it weekly. This process is never a super fun one, but it's worth the effort if you can do it because the prevention of algae buildup is easier and less expensive than dealing with it if you have a bloom.

There are three kinds of brush bristles: nylon, stainless steel, and hybrid (nylon and stainless steel); check out some brush options in Figure 7-7. Nylon bristle brushes are safe on all surface types. They're non-abrasive on vinyl liners, but they're tough enough to clean fiberglass and gunite-plaster pools.

The stainless steel and hybrid options are for gunite-plaster pools only. If you use a stainless bristled brush on any other surface, that brush can scratch or even tear your pool's surface.

FIGURE 7-7:
An example 360°
nylon bristled
brush and a
standard nylon
bristled brush.

Kristine Blanchard (Book Author)

TIP

Want to keep the bristles in your brush from falling out or rusting? Keep a foot bath or small trash can of fresh non-chlorinated water by your pool to rinse your brush with after use. Then, store your brush in a place that doesn't receive direct sunlight. (The mixture of chlorine on the bristles and sunlight can deteriorate the nylon or stainless steel and ruin your brush quickly.) Follow this same tip for vacuum heads that have brushes as well!

Just skimming the surface

Skimming is an easy part of pool cleaning. Manually skimming the pool's surface uses an attachment that goes on the end of your telescopic pole like your vacuum head does. Skimming is just another part of the cleaning process. If you have a lot of trees around your pool, buckle up because skimming is your time to shine!

When I talk about *skimming*, I mean removing debris such as leaves, pine needles, bugs, and frogs from the pool's surface. You definitely need to do it more often if you have a lot of trees in the surrounding area that drop stuff into the pool. It is very important to skim your pool manually during the spring and fall when a large amount of debris is falling from the trees.

There are two distinctly different types of skimmer heads. There's a regular skimmer head and a leaf rake.

>> **Regular skimmer heads:** Easier to use than leaf rakes if you have minimal items on the surface and just want to do quick touchups.

>> **Leaf rakes:** Have a large bag behind them to hold a lot of debris at a time. A leaf rake is ideal when you're getting all the springtime pollen or fall leaves out of the pool. It holds a lot more stuff, so you will make fewer trips from having to empty out the skimmer head over and over.

I always recommend having both types of skimmer heads on hand, but you may find you prefer using one or the other under all circumstances. There are different qualities of skimmer heads out there. If you find one that has a plastic or rubber-coated metal frame, those types of skimmer heads can really hold a lot of debris and are very durable!

Turning to Automatic Cleaners

The world of automatic pool cleaners is where the party gets started — nothing better than not having to clean but reaping all of the cleanly benefits! There are three different types of automatic pool cleaning vacuums (also referred to as APCs):

>> Suction-side cleaners (see the following section)

>> Pressure-side cleaners (discussed in "Pressure-side pool vacuums," later in this chapter)

>> The ever-so-popular robotic cleaners, including solar skimming robots (flip to the section "Robotic pool cleaners," later in this chapter)

REMEMBER

All pool cleaners, regardless of type, are meant to keep a clean pool clean. They're not designed to carry heavy loads or clean algae blooms. Do all initial vacuuming by hand when opening the pool. And after the pool is pretty clear and clean, you can use your automatic cleaners to maintain it that way.

Suction-side pool vacuums

When it comes to pool vacuums, the suction-side pool cleaner is most commonly used on above ground pools. Suction-side cleaners are inexpensive and easy to use.

As you can probably guess from the name, these vacuums use the suction of your pump to vacuum the pool, similar to your manual set up (which you can read about in the section "Manually vacuuming," earlier in this chapter). That means the setup for these cleaners is also similar to manual vacuums. You need to fill the hose with water, get your valves in the proper settings, and make sure your pool is running.

Suction-side pool vacuums come in all sorts of fun and adorable styles, such as Wanda Whale and Scuba Sam. They also have some more traditional-looking ones for some of the more traditional-style people. After this cleaner is hooked up to your skimmer, it starts working right away and works until the filter gets too dirty or the pump turns off. The actual way in which they move isn't programmed and has no logic behind it. With the suction pulling from behind the cleaner, a small check valve style flap (or a diaphragm) suctions shut and quickly releases, causing the cleaner to move in quick forward jerking motions. That's how the vacuum chugs along doing its thing.

Suction cleaners have a few downsides:

>> They're not smart, so to speak. They don't understand and can't correct things if they're stuck on the ladder or fell over on their side. Also, these cleaners just click along the pool floor randomly cleaning, so it's not uncommon for them to miss spots.

>> The pool pump and filter must be running efficiently for the cleaner to be working. It doesn't work well if the filter gets dirty or the pump or skimmer baskets get full because it restricts the flow and suction of the water.

But suction cleaners have their upsides, too:

>> Inexpensive in the APC world, so they're a great starter tool.

>> Help increase circulation in the pool quite a lot. Having the cleaner suck water from the bottom of the pool and having that water return to the top through the returns is an excellent way to keep the pool circulating more efficiently.

Pressure-side pool vacuums

Much like the suction-side vacuums discussed in the preceding section, pressure-side vacuums are exactly what they sound like. They're automatic pool cleaners that use the strong flow of the water on the output of a return line or a designated pressure side pipe in the pool to shoot through small spouts that move the unit along and create a current to catch debris in a bag. (It's a very similar concept to a leaf bagger, which I talk about in the section "Vacuum heads," earlier in this chapter.)

A suction-side vacuum either connects into one of your returns or into its own special vacuum port, and it has a long multi-section hose that allows the cleaner to move around the pool. Most of these cleaners use a gear-and-belt setup internally, which is powered by using the pressure of the water against a fan wheel. While the water flows down the long hose and through the small spouts, the gears begin to spin, the belts start to turn — and before you know it, the cleaner is off and running. These cleaners also depend on the pump and filter systems to be working efficiently to function.

These cleaners are also like the suction cleaners in the sense that they're very random and not smart. They'll be on and running, but they might still have the possibility of getting stuck or missing spots. But they do tend to do a better job than suction cleaners because they not only vacuum up debris, but kick up anything it misses, which allows those particles to get filtered out.

WARNING

Not all pressure-side cleaners can be used on all pools. There are styles made specifically for certain types of pools that come set up with a designated return line and separate pump to run them. Consult your local pool professional to ensure you buy a cleaner that works for your setup.

There are some downsides to pressure cleaners:

>> The good ones require a separate pump to make them work, but those pumps don't turn on without the main pump also being on. That means these cleaners need two pumps to be running the whole time. That also means if that secondary pump dies, you have to replace it before using the cleaner again.

>> Because of the gear mechanism and small spouts, these cleaners are known for not working properly for very small reasons. They're known for having more annual maintenance needed, which has annual costs to it.

And there are upsides to pressure cleaners:

>> Although they're more expensive than most suction cleaners, they are less expensive than robots (see the following section) and do a better job than suction cleaners (discussed in the preceding section).

>> If your pool comes ready for a pressure cleaner, they're an easy setup.

>> If you're mechanically inclined at all, they're pretty easy to repair. Just be sure to keep track of your pieces!

Robotic pool cleaners

Robotic cleaners are exactly that — they're adorable little robots that you can name Wally, or Herman, or whatever your heart desires. They're sort of like one of those household vacuum cleaner robots for your pool; the only difference is the cord. Pool cleaning robots are usually corded, but there are some cordless models out there. Cordless models are almost always for above ground or small inground pools, but the motors aren't strong enough for the steep inclines of the deep end of inground pools.

Robotic cleaners come in a vast array of brands, options, colors, sizes and price points. I highly recommend doing your research. There are two major kinds of robots:

>> One type uses a very high-tech mapping system that strategically plans out a set cleaning cycle. They clean your pool specifically by mapping it out and cleaning every surface in the selected timed cycle.

>> Belt-driven robots follow timed movements to attempt to clean the entire pool. Essentially, that means they move forward for a certain amount of time, and then they reverse at an angle to clean another path. Then they go forward straight for a few seconds, and then backward at an angle. They follow this pattern until their timed cycle is complete.

Both kinds of robots get hooked up and used in the same way. You have your robot and its very long cord, and then you have a power supply that's also a transformer. The cord plugs into the power supply, and the power supply plugs into your closest outlet. Some are Bluetooth compatible, so you can remotely program it. With others, you select your cycles on the power supply itself.

Then you toss (okay, maybe ever-so-gently place) the robot into the pool, along with its cord, and push Turn on the power supply of the robot. The robot starts its cycle immediately, and you get to sit and watch. After it's done, you very gently pull the robot to the pool's edge by the cord and remove it from the water by using its provided handle. Some of the fancier ones have a recall feature, where you can make it actually meet you up at the waterline.

WARNING

Never pull your robot out of the water by the cord — the cord isn't designed to hold that much weight, so you can end up causing damage to the cord, which can lead to a disconnect internally preventing the connection from powering the robot. It would end up dead in the water! And for safety reasons, never use an extension cord with these robots because there is the risk of the cord falling in and possibly electrocuting someone swimming.

When choosing your robot, be sure to identify what you want the cleaner to do. There are so many options for you to choose from that I highly recommend doing a decent amount of research online or ask your local pool professional. They will be a great resource to cover all the options and what may be best for you.

Features/options to look out for include

>> **What the robot can clean:**

- **Floors only:** It will not be designed to brush the walls, which means it typically doesn't have the motor strength to climb slopes of deep ends either.

- **Floors and walls:** It will vacuum the floor and brush most of the wall but will not break the waterline.

- **Floors, walls, and waterline:** It will scrub your pool from top to bottom, including that pesky white waterline at the tile.

>> **Multiple timing cycles:** This allows you to choose how long or deep of a clean you want the cleaner to do. Sometimes there are quick cleaning cycles where the robot will only vacuum the bottom and it does it in an hour; this is great right before a party while you're still running around getting decorations put up!

>> **Bluetooth capabilities:** This allows you to control your robot from your phone, setting timers, selecting cleaning cycles, or even driving it.

>> **A caddy:** This is a cart where you can store and wheel your robot around for easy storage.

>> **Warranty:** This can vary depending on where you buy the robot (online versus in store) and what level in the series of robots you get.

>> **Internal bag versus internal cartridges:** The bag style compartment is becoming less common, but you are talking the difference of rinsing out a diaper (bag) versus rinsing out a pleated box (cartridges).

I recommend Maytronics Dolphin robots more than any other brand. Maytronics keeps up with changes, alters designs to make their robots more user friendly, and has an abundance of models to choose from (for one example, see Figure 7-8).

Robotic cleaners possess their own set of drawbacks:

>> They can become pretty expensive, with some price tags being upwards of $2,000.

>> If they do malfunction, repairs are generally more expensive because of how few small, inexpensive parts they contain. They're largely made up of major components such as the cord, motor, and power supply, and those range between $250 and $600 to replace.

Kristine Blanchard (Book Author)

TIP

>> Some models out there are fairly heavy and hefting them around may not be possible for some people. Even though I'm able bodied, even I can have a hard time pulling robots from the pool.

Always kneel on the pool edge to remove a robot from the pool because the weight of the cleaner coming out of the water is significantly heavier than when it went in, and you could pull a muscle pulling it from the pool.

But robotic cleaners have their good points, too:

>> Completely separate from your pump and filter system. That means they cost just pennies to run because they use only 24 volts of electricity, as compared to the full 115/230 volts it takes to run your pool pump.

>> The most thorough and quick pool vacuums that you can get. After you see the ability of these units, you'll be itching to get one for your pool.

REMEMBER

Keep your robot stored in a dry, cool location — don't leave it out in the sun. Constant exposure to sunlight wears on the components and plastics, causing premature deterioration.

For safety reasons, remove your robot from the pool before swimming. It isn't so much the electricity (because it's only 24 volts) as it is the danger of getting tangled in the cord.

Solar skimming robots

When solar skimmers hit the market, they exploded! It's one of the fastest growing add-ons in the industry. After you experience one of these in your life, you'll never want to go back. But like with the vacuums discussed in the preceding sections, these robots are meant to maintain an already cleaned pool, not clean up a spring or fall mess.

The item itself is pretty self-explanatory: It's a robotic pool skimmer that runs off of solar panels (genius!). The brand I recommend is Solar Breeze. Check out their bestselling model, the Ariel (see Figure 7-9). This little robot uses a cylindrical paddle to chug along and sweep surface debris into a small basket. They're priced around $600 — and many clients have told me they're worth every penny. They don't have size restrictions or specific requirements for them to work; just buy it, plug it in, and plop it in the water.

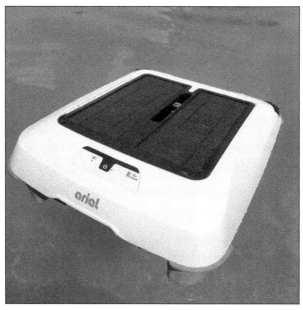

FIGURE 7-9:
The Solar Breeze Ariel solar skimmer.

Kristine Blanchard (Book Author)

Here are some of the best features of solar skimmers:

>> Don't have cords that could get in the way

>> Have small eyes on the front of them to prevent them from getting caught on obstacles in the pool

>> Come from the box completely charged, so there's no waiting time

They have two large solar panels on the back of them that start charging the second that they're in sufficient sunlight. As long as it has sun, it's doing its thing. It does have a power switch if you do not want it running, or if it is removed from the pool.

A solar skimmer can hold a substantial amount of debris in its basket, whether that debris is leaves and pine needles, or pollen that may have accumulated on the surface in the spring.

Of course, there are several brands and models available to consumers. Do your research online or by asking a pool professional and read the reviews to find the best solar skimmer for you.

IN THIS CHAPTER

» **Figuring out what wintering means for you**

» **Preparing to winterize your pool**

» **Covering your pool for the winter**

» **Removing all the water from unground pipes**

» **Dealing with short bouts of below-freezing temperatures**

Chapter **8**

Winterizing Your Pool

Winterizing a pool is one of those things that I wasn't sure I could properly cover in a book. There are so many variables, and there's no one right way to do it. Just like most pool-related activities, there are different routes that you can take to reach the same solution when winterizing your pool. But over the years, I've figured out a lot of ways to do things — and, in this chapter, I share the most common and easiest ways to winterize your pool.

REMEMBER

Winterizing is one of those things that, if you're not 100 percent confident in what you're doing, I don't recommend doing it at all. Or only take on the steps that you feel comfortable with and have a professional take care of the rest. In the case of above ground pools, there aren't as many things that can go wrong to cause major damage, as compared to inground pools.

Pools that have underground lines are much more likely to have things go wrong if they're not properly taken care of prior to a freeze. I strongly urge you to have a professional at least blow out (force water out of pipes using the force of air) your pool lines if you're not positive that you can do it with no mistakes.

TIP

You can have a professional winterize your pool for you the first time around so that you can see firsthand how to do it.

I believe everyone has the ability to do this part of pool ownership, but just remember that it's where expensive mistakes can be made. If you're not confident in your process, don't try it.

Winterizing: What and When

Winterizing your pool is the process of preparing your pool for freezing temperatures. You are ensuring that while the pool is still full of water and completely stagnant that it will be useable once springtime rolls around. For areas where you have defined four seasons with freezing temperatures and snow in winter, winterizing will typically take place once you hit the time of the year where leaves start falling and nighttime temperatures start to dip below 50 degrees. If you have a pool heater and you can prolong your season before the water is uncomfortably cold, then you can wait longer, but for the other half who do not have heaters, it is best to start considering closing your pool down when temps start dropping. The main purpose of all the precautions you are taking is to prevent damage from happening to your pool or pool equipment.

If you live in an area where you do not have snow or freezing temperatures, winterizing your pool is optional. If you never have freezing temperatures but come fall you stop using the pool because it is too cold for your liking, you can still take the steps to winterize if you want.

For areas like where I am in the northeast, winterizing is considered starting in September and can be pushed off until end of October. But the longer you wait and the closer you are to freezing temperatures, the more at risk you are of ice damage from flash freezes or early snowstorms.

Do I need to winterize?

If you are in an area where the ground freezes and you get ice and snow, winterizing is a must to protect your pool. If you are not in an area like that, but you don't find that you use your pool November through March, then winterizing can save you a lot of time and money. If you don't winterize a pool in an area that may not freeze, but the pool isn't used, you still have to run and maintain that pool in the meantime, so it doesn't become a swampy hazard. If you winterize your pool, you will be giving yourself a break from pool care until you decide it's time to open up and start using the pool again.

When should I close?

There isn't a hard and fast time in the year when you need to close your pool. The type of cover you're using makes a difference in deciding on the best time to close:

>> **If you're using a solid cover:** If your cover isn't porous and doesn't allow any sunlight or dirt through, then you can really close the pool whenever you feel like it. Of course, industry standards recommend ideal times being once the water temperature is below 50 degrees. But if the water is clean, you can put your cover on at any time without having to worry about algae growth, even if it's warm out.

>> **If you have a mesh cover:** The later you can wait to close your pool, the better. You're susceptible to algae blooms before the temperatures drop to the freezing range. I would say as close as you can get to the water temperature being 55 degrees or cooler, but before freezing temperatures and snow.

TIP

If you have a lot of trees around your pool and need to close earlier than what is recommended, you certainly can. If you need to cover the pool early because of an excessive amount of leaves falling into the pool, I'd leave the filter system attached and running until the temperature gets a little cooler. That way, you're not letting leaves in, but you're also keeping the water circulating, which will help prevent algae growth by not letting the water be stagnant. It also allows you to still add chemicals like shock and algaecide as needed, too.

Taking the Steps to Winterize

Closing an above ground pool and an inground pool have a lot of similarities and a lot of differences:

>> **Similarities:** What you do to prepare the pool and to winterize the equipment above the water level, such as the pump and filter system.

>> **Differences:** A lot of the important work for your inground pool happens underground, and that's where it is easy to run into trouble (see the section "Blowing Out Underground Lines," later in this chapter).

In the following sections, I cover the preparation for closing a pool and the ways to winterize your filter system, cover it up, and keep your pool equipment safe.

Getting it clean

This tip may seem obvious, but cleaning your pool as well as you can before closing it is just as important as any other part of the winterizing procedure. If you close your pool down with leaves or algae in it, you're going to give yourself a lot of work in the spring because all of the debris or algae that was left behind in the fall will still be there in the spring. Sometimes it actually gets worse; the algae grows more, and the leaves begin to disintegrate and fall apart. Follow these steps to clean your pool and get it ready to be winterized:

1. **Scoop out all the leaves on the surface of the water.**

   Those leaves will eventually fall to the bottom of the pool and start to disintegrate and possibly lead to staining.

2. **Vacuum the pool floor.**

   If you leave dirt, leaves, or dead animals on the floor of the pool, they will increase the chance of algae growth and you will have a mess come spring.

3. **Treat any present algae.**

   If you have algae now, you will have it in the spring, and sometimes the blooms get worse over time.

Adding chemicals

One of the most important steps you can take to prepare your pool for winterization is to add in the correct chemicals. The following sections can help you to figure out how and when to add in the appropriate chemicals.

Getting your water tested

Get your water tested about a week or two before you plan to close your pool so that you have plenty of time to add the chemicals that you may need to get it properly balanced before adding in winterizing chemicals. In areas where the water freezes, balancing your pool water before closing is especially important. To start all of this, you want to make sure your water is tested at a local pool store or with an at-home testing kit that you trust (for more information on testing equipment, see Chapter 9).

Balancing your pool water

Balancing your pool water in the spring in preparation for warm temperatures is different than balancing for the winter's harsh cold temperatures. Your water's condition becomes much more corrosive as the water temperature drops down. In

Chapter 9, I cover the importance of using your LSI (Langelier Saturation Index) to properly balance your pool water. One of the factors in your LSI is temperature, so you must adjust your equation accordingly.

REMEMBER

Testing your pool at a pool store is the easiest way to get proper balancing recommendations because their computer programs have a setting to select different environments and can automatically adjust the recommendations based on the date. If you plan to test and balance at home, follow these steps:

1. **Find the average winter temperature that your pool will be experiencing.**

   Here in New Hampshire, that would be around 39 degrees Fahrenheit from December through March. I was able to find out that information on a weather tracking website.

2. **Use your at-home test kit to get the levels of your pool's water balance and enter them in the LSI equation.**

   pH + Temperature Factor + Calcium Factor + Alkalinity Factor – TDS Factor = LSI

3. **Make adjustments to your water's chemical balance to reach the ideal level of negative 0.3 to positive 0.3.**

Basically, because your water becomes more corrosive to your pool's surface the colder the temperature is, you want to balance your total alkalinity and your calcium hardness slightly on the higher end of the scale. For more details on how to properly balance your water using the LSI, see Chapter 9.

Adding in winterizing chemicals

After your pool is properly balanced (see the preceding section), it's time to add in your winterizing chemicals. Add these chemicals two to three days prior to closing.

For a chlorine or bromine pool (see Chapter 10), you'll add in

TIP

>> Winter algaecide.

>> Double dose of your maintenance shock.

   Be sure to use a chlorine-based shock, not potassium monopersulfate. Although potassium monopersulfate won't hurt the pool if you use it, it's not as aggressive on organic material as a chlorine-based shock.

>> Clarifier or stain preventer (not necessary products to add but are an excellent way to help ensure a clear and stain free pool!).

For biguanide systems:

>> A winter algaecide (poly or quat based only)

>> Hydrogen peroxide at a dose of 2 gallons per 10,000 gallons of water

>> Clarifier (optional, will help settle any suspended particles that your pool contains or may get over the course of the winter)

Running your filter

The reason that you want to begin the chemical-adding process two to three days prior to closing is because your chemicals will need time to circulate through the water thoroughly to be as effective as possible. If you add the chemicals to the top of the water only an hour before closing (and therefore shutting off your filter), you're not really mixing it in.

If you're using chlorine shock for winterizing, your pool water will have really high chlorine levels at first, and those chlorine gasses can ruin your winter cover if you put it on right after adding the shock. Another reason to plan ahead and give your filter time to circulate the water.

Lowering the water level

When winterizing your pool, you need to lower the water to protect the pool walls or structure and equipment. You also need to do this if you are going to be blowing out any lines.

The following sections discuss how to lower the water in above ground and an inground pools.

TIP

Set an alarm on your phone to check the water every 20 to 30 minutes while it's draining. It will drain much faster than you think, so make sure you're home and paying close attention.

Removing some water from an above ground pool

For above ground pools, lower your water to just below the return jet before closing the pool to protect the structure of the pool during ice expansion. After the pool is drained, you cover your return jet and skimmer with a plate and a plug (which I cover later in this chapter) to protect your pool wall even more.

WARNING

If, for some reason, you decided to not drain your pool prior to putting on the plate and plug, don't be surprised if you still end up with a much lower water level in the spring. As the cover gathers weight on top from rain and snow, it will push down and force the water from inside the pool up the sides and eventually out over the wall. This displacement will happen whether you prep the pool for winter by draining or not. But if you don't drain, you are putting your pool at high risk of ice damage.

The easiest way to drain an above ground pool is to either

>> Remove the hose attached to your return and have the water drain out.

>> If you have a sand filter with a Waste setting, use that to drain the pool (see Chapter 3 on using the Waste setting).

Your above ground pool can't be drained completely unless you plan to disassemble the pool. An above ground pool gets most of its structural integrity from the pressure of the water pushing on the walls, keeping them in place. If you drain the water too far and there's a large gust of wind, it could actually blow the pool over.

WARNING

Never drain your above ground pool down to less than 24 inches of water unless you plan to immediately fill it back up. The pool and the liner can pull from the wall and wrinkle along with the possibility of the pool collapsing.

Reducing the water in an inground pool

For inground pools, drain the pool to just below your return lines so that it's easier to blow them out (which I talk about in the section "Blowing Out Undergrounds Lines," later in this chapter). You don't want to go more than 20 inches down from the top of your pool before closing because your cover uses the water in the pool to sit on so it doesn't fall in. This is also very important if you live in an area with a high water table because there is the possibility of the pool being pushed from the ground by hydrostatic pressure. Learn more about that in Chapter 15.

If your returns are deeper than 20 inches but you want to drain your water below them so that they're easy to blow out, just fill the pool back up to the 20-inch mark after you blow out the lines.

WARNING

If you use a safety cover, that type of cover rests on the water in the pool while weight builds up on top of it from snow and ice. If you drain your water too far down before closing, you could cause damage to your cover, or it could fall into the pool.

Here are a few options to lower the water level in your inground pool:

>> If you have a Waste setting on your multiport valve, just put the valve on that setting and drain the pool down. See Chapter 3 for more information on using the Waste setting.

REMEMBER

As the pool drains, your water will eventually go low enough that it will be below your main suction, which is your skimmer. At that point, you can use the shut-off valve in front of your pump or plug your skimmer to eliminate it as a suction. Then you can open up a secondary suction line like your main drain or side suction to continue to bring the water down below the returns.

>> If you don't have a Waste setting or a main drain/side suction, you're best off either starting a siphon with a hose or purchasing a submersible pump.

Removing the summer parts

You take out items from your pool when winterizing to protect the pool, protect the part, and to make way for a winterizing part (see the following section).

Here are the most common parts you'll want to remove before closing up your pool, for both above ground and inground pools:

>> **Ladder or steps:** Remove all steps, including large wedding cake steps, which can sometimes be a two- or three-person job, depending on the style of steps. If you need to get into the pool to remove any stairs or ladders, you want to take them out before it gets too cold.

WARNING

Ladders and steps should never be left in the pool for winter because they can shift with the ice and cause damage to the liner, or the steps themselves can be damaged by the ice.

TIP

To prevent ice expansion damage in the ladder sockets after the ladder is removed, fill the sockets with pieces of pool noodle.

>> **Return eyeball(s):** The piece referred to as an eyeball in your return pipe is threaded in and meant to help be a directional for your water flow. It needs to be removed because the plugs that fit in your return pipe go in place of the eyeball.

TIP

Any pool that has a return newer than 2007 should have an eyeball that's made up of three pieces, so be sure you remove all three. People often accidentally remove only the directional ball and the front ring, leaving the internally threaded part behind. If that does happen, there's a special tool called a *seat removal tool* that can help you gain some leverage on the last piece. Figure 8-1 shows the return eyeball broken down into its three pieces and the winterizing plugs that fit in its place.

FIGURE 8-1:
A disassembled
return eyeball, a
threaded winter
plug, and an
expansion plug.

Kristine Blanchard (Book Author)

>> **Toys or floats:** Having them in the pool over winter can cause damage to the items themselves or to the pool if they are on the pool floor.

>> **Skimmer basket:** You need to remove the basket for two reasons: It can easily be damaged from ice expansion, and it will be in the way of the skimmer guard that is used when winterizing a skimmer.

Your basket will give you a safe place to store your return eyeballs and other things without losing them.

TIP

For above ground pools, specifically, remove your hoses. Here are some tips for proper hose removal and storage:

>> Detach your pool hoses either from the filter or pool, and then allow the water to drain that way.

Alternatively, you can remove the hoses after the water is already drained. See the preceding section "Lowering the water level."

>> Save your hose clamps so that you can find them come spring.

>> Store your hoses somewhere that little critters won't get inside and make nests. The easiest place to store your hose clamps is in your skimmer basket with the other parts.

TIP

Installing winter parts

In all of the places that you remove a part (see the preceding section), there's a winterizing part meant to fit in its place. In the following sections, I go over the different parts and practices, depending on what type of pool you have.

Winter parts for an above ground pool

The items you need to insert in an above ground pool are

>> **A skimmer winter plate:** The skimmer winter plates are designed to work as a dam for the mouth of the skimmer, preventing water from entering the body of it where the basket is and freezing. It can come in a variety of designs: Some have holes and get screwed in, others look like a reusable container lid, and some are just a foam square that inserts into the hole of the skimmer mouth.

The different kinds offer styles that may be easier to install for different customers. Here's how each type gets inserted:

- *Screw-in:* On the skimmer faceplate the inside of the pool (to see what plate I am referring to, see Figure 3-1 in Chapter 3), remove the corresponding screws that line up to the holes in the skimmer winter plate, place the plate over the skimmer face plate, and put the screws back in. The winter plate will have a gasket that seals while you tighten the screws, and it won't budge.

  This type of plate can come in either stainless steel or plastic. If you use a stainless-steel version, it's thin enough to put the original screws back in. The plastic ones come with longer screws that you have to use because the plastic plate is too thick for the original skimmer plate screws. The best place to store your summer skimmer plate screws is right in your skimmer basket with the other small pieces you have removed so far.

- *Snap-on:* This style of cover is meant to fit a skimmer that has a certain style of face plate that has a small lip all the way around the perimeter. It snaps into place just like a reusable kitchen container does.

- *Plug-in:* This style is a flat plastic plate with a foam backing on it about an inch thick. The foam backing is cut to size to fit inside the mouth of the skimmer, so there are varying sizes depending on what size your skimmer is. Simply press it into the mouth of the skimmer firmly and you're done!

  A lot of the time, this type of plate can end up falling out in the middle of the winter — or they don't seal at all. Not my recommendation.

>> **Plugs:** These go in the other outlets you have in your pool like returns. For your returns, you can either thread in the standard threaded 1.5-inch plug that a vast majority of pools use, or you can put in a rubber expansion plug.

The purpose of plugs that go into any open hole is to create the effect of a seamless wall internally and to prevent any water from getting into the fittings and pipes. On above ground pools, while the water rises from the displacement of the weight on the cover, that water will seek out the easiest route of escape. If you have your return hole and skimmer open, the water will dump out of those spots first. This water overflow will not only lead to a lot more water loss, but in some climates, that water can freeze inside those two ports. If that happens, you'll end up with a block of ice inside your skimmer and return, which can lead to ice damage.

I've seen situations where the ice alone expanded enough to break the skimmer housing. I've also seen a pool where the very large piece of ice floating in the pool shifted, and because it was also attached to the skimmer in the wall, it took the skimmer with it and destroyed both the skimmer housing and the wall of the pool. This happens on pools that do not have a skimmer plate to block the ice.

Winter parts for an inground pool

Inground pools are a little different from above grounds. Because they have the weight of the world holding them in place, their plastic components like the skimmer are more durable against ice. That being said, there is still always the possibility of ice damage, so different parts are used to protect them:

>> **Skimmer guard:** This protects the inside of the skimmer from the water that enters by using something for ice expansion.

>> **Plugs:** If you have eyeballs in your returns, you can replace them with a standard 1.5-inch plug. If you do not have eyeballs, which is possible with gunite-plaster pools, you may just have a hole in the wall with nothing in it. In that case, you would use the rubber expansion plugs and use one that fits in the size hole you have in your pool.

REMEMBER

None of these parts are put in place until after your underground lines have been blown out of water.

Prepping the area around the pool

Getting your pool area ready for winter just makes your life a little easier, both when you're actually closing the pool and come springtime, when you open your pool (which I talk about in Chapter 6). Here are some points to keep in mind:

>> **For above ground pools that have a deck:** Clean the deck off as much as possible. Clear it of dirt, leaves, and patio furniture. All of those things can accumulate mold in and on them, which can cause permanent staining to the deck or furniture.

>> **For inground pools:** Clean away all the leaves and dirt from the area surrounding the pool as much as you can to help prevent staining and keep the pool clean while you put the cover on.

>> **For inground pools that have safety covers:** With these trampoline-looking covers, you have brass peg anchors drilled into the concrete surrounding your pool. Those anchors have to be raised up so that you can fit your springs onto them. You can raise them by using a pool anchor key or an Allen wrench. Bring the anchors up about the width of your pinky finger. Don't raise them too high, or they could rip out of the ground after the cover has weight on it. I like to completely expose the smooth part of the peg but not expose the threads at all (see Figure 8-2).

FIGURE 8-2:
The height to which you want to raise safety cover anchors.

Winterizing the pump

All pumps should be winterized the same way, and luckily, all of them are set up basically the same way, too. (If you have a very uncommon pump, you may want to work with a pool professional.)

REMEMBER

If you have an above ground pool, you can winterize your pump right away. If you have a pool that has lines that you need to blow out, this part can wait. (See the section "Blowing Out Underground Lines," later in this chapter.)

Follow these steps to winterize your pool pump:

1. **Empty your pump basket of any debris.**

   You don't want to deal with that smell in the spring, trust me!

2. **Drain your pump basket of any water by removing the pump's two drain plugs.**

   If you don't properly drain all of the water, it can freeze and cause cracks or shattered pieces. Here's where to find each plug:

   - *Hair and lint trap housing:* Where your basket is. It'll be towards the bottom, either on the front or on the side. It's small and threaded. (Refer to Chapter 3 to get the details on this housing.)

   - *Volute:* The volute, also called the pump housing, houses the impeller. This area has the second plug, which can sometimes be a little trickier to find. It will be either on the bottom or towards one side of the volute.

3. **Place the plugs inside the pump basket for safe keeping.**

4. **Leave the pump attached if you do not have quick disconnection unions for easy removal.**

   The pump, once empty of water, is completely safe to be outside in the elements. If you want to cover the pump up with a tarp you can, but it is not required.

   Or you can bring the pump to a dry indoor location if you have the ability to through quick disconnecting unions. While this isn't necessary, it doesn't hurt to protect it when you can.

If you can't get the plugs out of your pump, another way you can empty the pump is to remove it from the base, and from any hoses or pipes, and then dump the water out of both ports, going back and forth until no more water comes out. Obviously, this approach isn't always possible, especially if you have an inground pump that's hard plumbed with no quick disconnects.

Winterizing the filter

Prep your filter system to be winterized by cleaning anything that can be cleaned and then allowing those parts to drain of water. (I go into what parts should be cleaned for different types of filters in the following sections.)

After the filter parts are drained, you have two options:

> ›› Leave them outside by the pool, covered by a tarp.

> ›› Bring them into an indoor storage location, such as a shed or basement.

Both options are perfectly fine. Of course, it's better to put them in an indoor storage spot because not only does it protected them from the sun and snow, but it also will help prevent rodents from making homes inside them. But, if you don't have that available as an option, winterizing your filter parts properly by draining them and covering them with a tarp is more than enough.

REMEMBER

For inground pools or pools that have underground lines that need to be winterized, wait to pull any drain plugs until after you complete blowing out the lines. The section "Blowing Out Underground Lines," later in this chapter, goes over clearing your lines.

The following sections discuss how to winterize a filter based on which type of filter you have.

Winterizing sand filters

Follow these steps to winterize your sand filter:

1. **Do a chemical wash while the pool is still full.**

   A backwash filter cleaner is used by pouring the filter cleaning chemical into the skimmer while the pump is running and the valve on the filter is set to Backwash. (For full details on cleaning your sand, see Chapter 4.)

2. **For above ground pools, remove all hoses from your filter and store them.**

3. **Remove the drain cap from the bottom of your sand tank and allow it to start draining.**

   In Chapter 3 there is a photo of your drain cap, so flip back there for reference.

WARNING

   After you remove the cap, you should have a fairly steady stream of water coming out, not just dripping. If your filter is only dripping, there's a chance your sand may be too far gone to properly drain, so the sand could stand to be replaced. You can read about all your sand draining needs in Chapter 4.

4. **Put your multiport valve on the Winter setting.**

   If your multiport valve doesn't have a Winter setting, put the valve in between any two other settings so the valve is half open.

   Leaving the valve partly open will prevent any water from getting trapped in any ports and causing ice damage.

5. **Allow the filter to drain completely of water.**

   Don't put the drain cap back on after the filter is empty. Place the cap inside your pump basket, which you can see how to identify in Chapter 3, to prevent it from getting lost.

6. **Store the filter.**

   Your sand filter can be left outside covered or uncovered. Or you can put it on a dolly and bring it inside somewhere, like a shed or basement. Just like garaging your car in bad weather, it's best to bring the filter inside if you have the ability because it will cut back on wear and tear, giving your filter a longer life.

Common advice that I read around the internet is that, every year, you must replace the sand in your sand filter. Although yearly sand replacement certainly doesn't hurt anything, it really doesn't need to be done if the water has stayed fairly clean all season.

In Chapter 3, I talk about how sand filters should have their sand replaced every three to five years, depending on the quality of the water throughout the seasons. If you don't want to replace the sand every year or bring the empty sand tank inside, you don't have to.

TIP

If you use a backwash filter cleaner (which you can read about in Chapter 4), you can put off changing your sand until the five-year mark. This type of cleaner makes a huge difference when it comes to removing oils and grease from the sand.

Winterizing DE or cartridge filters

Diatomaceous earth (DE) and cartridge types of filters are easy to winterize because most of the time, you're familiar with the draining and disassembling process from having to clean the filter during the summer. It's pretty straightforward, so I'll keep it simple. Just follow these steps:

1. **Drain the tank of water through the drain cap.**

   This is the same process as if you were cleaning the inside filter. Chapter 4 goes into detail about cleaning your filter.

2. **Open up the tank and remove the DE element or cartridge.**

3. **Spray down the DE element or cartridge thoroughly with water.**

   At the same time, spray the inside of the tank to remove any old diatomaceous earth or dirt.

4. **Chemically clean your filter element by using an acidic filter cleaner.**

   The cleaners that you can find at your local pool store have instructions for soaking the filter element in a bucket with water or spraying and rinsing the element. Be sure to do something to properly degrease and clean your filter element.

5. **Prepare your filter for storage.**

This can be done in two ways:

- Put the filter assembly back together with the drain plug loosely placed back in its spot so that the filter is set, assembled, and ready to go for spring.

- Leave the DE or cartridge element out of the filter tank and store it separately in a tote or trash bin.

REMEMBER

When you prep your DE or cartridge filter for storage, make sure that your fabric pieces won't become rodent bedding — keep them away from mice or chipmunks (store with mouse repellents for extra help).

6. **Store your filter system.**

For above ground pools, how you store it depends on a number of factors:

- *Indoor storage:* If you have everything emptied and disassembled, the filter system is much lighter and easier to store than a sand filter is, so storing it inside is ideal.

- *Outdoor storage:* If you can't store it indoors, it can be left outside just like the sand filter (discussed in the preceding section).

For inground pools, I suggest just leaving the filter assembled and outside, because it's difficult to disconnect and move that large of a tank. If you have a multiport valve, it will be set to Winter after you finished winterizing. If you have to blow out the lines before the filter is disassembled, place the multiport valve to Recirculate for now, and set it to Winter after blowing out the lines is complete.

Winterizing other filter parts

If you have additional parts to your filter system, such as a chlorinator, heater, or salt cell, you'll want to properly winterize those things as well. Here are some details for winterizing these extra components:

- ❯❯ **Chlorine tablet dispensers:** Let the tablets inside the dispenser dissolve completely so that you don't have a bunch of wet and stinky chlorine to deal with at the end of the season. Letting the tablets run out can take a week or two, so it's best to not add any chlorine tablets a week or two before you plan to winterize the pool.

WARNING

If you don't let the tablets run out, be very careful emptying them because the gas buildup can be extremely potent and dangerous. Remove any leftover tablets by using a gloved hand and place them somewhere that they can safely dry out with plenty of ventilation.

After they're dry, you can put the chlorine tablets in a reusable container for the spring. Most tablet chlorinators or brominators will have a small ¼-inch drain plug that needs to be removed after removing the tablets.

>> **Salt cells:** Keep them attached if you're blowing out lines because, if not, you will have a large gap in your pipes. But if you're not, remove the salt cell from the hoses or pipes that it's attached to and bring it inside.

Clean the salt cell with an acidic salt cleaner before storing it. The calcification buildup can cause more damage the longer it sits on the platelets on the inside, so clean the cells right away.

>> **Heaters:** Blow them out. Even if you have an above ground pool, I highly recommend blowing out any excess water inside your heater before removing the drain plug (yes, your heater will have a drain plug, just like your pump and filter). The only issue with heaters: Some of them don't have an easily accessible drain plug, which is why blowing them out is so important.

REMEMBER

On pools that need to have all the lines blown out, you don't need to blow out the heater separately. It gets emptied in the process of blowing out everything else. (Flip to "Blowing Out Underground Lines," later in this chapter, for a how-to on this winterizing activity.)

All additional components to your filter system will need to be emptied of water, and most will have a drain plug. If a component doesn't have a drain, always empty it however you need to before storing it for the winter. That may mean disconnecting it from the plumbing and dumping it out.

Using pillows for protection

This section is for you if you have an above ground pool. Above ground pools are a lot more susceptible to winter damage, mainly because they're freestanding and don't have the pressure of the ground holding them safe and steady. When you winterize an above ground pool, use ice equalizer pillow(s) to protect the walls of the pool from ice expansion. Ice equalizer pillows — also known as simply *pillows* or *bubbles* to some — are commonly misconstrued as a mechanism to prevent your cover from falling into the pool or to keep the cover taut. Although they're sometimes capable of helping out in those areas, pillows have a different purpose.

Your pillow is designed to cover a certain amount of square inches on the surface of the pool so that when the ice begins to form and expand, it will squeeze in against the vinyl pillows that you've added and not outwards onto the walls.

Because of that pressure from the ice, make sure the pillow isn't filled tight with air — you want them kind of squishy. Fill them only about two-thirds of the way full. If you fill them all the way up with air, they'll more than likely pop when the ice expands against them. If you lose your pillow every year (meaning it pops and deflates by the time you open the pool in the spring), there's a good chance that you need to fill it up less than you usually do.

A common misconception with pillows is that they need to be completely centered in the middle of the pool. Although it may be more aesthetically pleasing to have your pillows centered, they'll do their job as long as they're touching the surface of the pool water. The main thing is to make sure it's not up on the side of the rail of the pool — it doesn't work in that position because it's not touching the water's surface to help with ice expansion.

I don't recommend using a strong rope to tie them down or to tie them tightly in place. The pillow is made of vinyl, and it's possible it will tear if the rope has no give. If you want to tie your pillow in the center of your pool surface, use twine or thin rope — and make sure the pillow has the ability to shift and move with the ice; otherwise, it will tear.

Using the proper-size pillow is very important. If you don't have a pillow large enough to compensate for the size of the pool, you won't get the proper effect because it won't cover enough surface area to make a difference. See the following mini-table for tips on choosing a pillow size based on your pool's size.

Pool Size	Round Dimensions	Oval Dimensions	Pillows
Small	Smaller than 24 ft. round	Smaller than 12 ft. x 24 ft. oval	One 4 ft. x 5 ft.
Medium	24–30 ft. round	12 ft. x 24 ft. to 15 ft. x 30 ft.	Two 4 ft. x 5 ft. One 4 ft. x 8 ft.
Large	Larger than 30 ft. round	Larger than 15 ft. x 30 ft.	Three 4 ft. x 5 ft. One 4 ft. x 15 ft.

I personally prefer to have multiple smaller pillows, rather than one large one, because if a pillow does tear or deflate for any reason, at least you still have the other one(s) available to do the work.

If you fill the pool up with pillows and pull the cover tight, you'll likely still get water and ice buildup on the cover. It's nearly impossible to prevent that from happening if you're using a solid or mesh tarp, so I recommend just letting it do what it's going to do and stop trying to prevent it.

Covering Up Your Pool

The last step in closing any pool is covering it up. There are a lot of styles of cover, along with all different sizing recommendations and preferences on how to tie it down. Living in New England, I know that our winters aren't the same as winters in North Carolina, so our winter covers shouldn't be the same, either.

TIP

Any time you take advice on how to winterize your pool, get it from a source that understands what your winters are like. Far too often, I have customers whose pools are ruined because their cover is too small or the cover tears with the first real snow they get. It's all about getting what's best for you, based on all the particulars of your pool including size, type, and environment.

Properly sizing your pool cover

Above ground pools and inground pools are treated a little bit differently when it comes to sizing a pool cover because of the way they need to be covered.

Sizing an above ground pool

Above ground pools are mostly covered by using a tarp style cover that is solid and not porous or mesh. When you're sizing your cover for an above ground pool, remember that it has to go over the pillow in the middle, and then up and over the railings of your pool. For example, if your top rail on an above ground pool is 6 inches wide, that means you need a foot of excess on your cover just to cover the top rails of the pool. That excess doesn't include having to go over the pillow and around the edge of the top rail and still touch the water.

The standard sizing for winter covers is a 3-foot overlap. So a 24-foot round pool would use a cover that is 27 feet in diameter.

In most cases, your cover will have some taut spots, where the cover isn't touching anything and is suspended in the air. Figure 8-3 shows how the cover is lying flat with very little slack on all surrounding edges of the pool.

This cover application is a perfectly fine way to winterize your pool if you're in a climate where you get only inches of snow, not feet. If you're in an environment like I am in New England, where we get multiple feet of snow during an average winter, a tight cover will lead to damage somewhere:

» The cover might tear at the taut parts.

» The cover won't have any more slack to give because of the weight of the snow, and the cover will sink, bringing the top rails or walls down with it.

Kristine Blanchard (Book Author)

FIGURE 8-3:
A cover properly installed on a pool that doesn't get a lot of snow — it fits but with very little slack.

TIP

If you get multiple feet of snow in your area, size your cover up. Get a 5-foot to 7-foot overlap with your winter covers and put all of the excess slack inside the pool so that it can slowly release with the pressure. As shown in Figure 8-3, you want the cover to go just under the rails, and all of the rest of the cover sits in the pool, not hanging down on the sides. This setup will prevent the cover from sliding up towards the inside of the pool while it gets weight on top of it and possibly catching on the skimmer or return and breaking them off.

Sizing an inground pool cover

For inground pools, you have two main ways to cover your pool:

>> A solid tarp-style cover

>> A safety cover

The safety covers are much more popular now than they used to be, so if you have one of those, this particular section isn't very important for you. But, if you're using a tarp-style pool cover, you'll want to keep reading.

The standard overlap for inground pool covers is 5 feet, so a 20-foot-by-40-foot rectangle would have a 25-foot-by-45-foot cover. This sizing is perfectly fine if you're in an area where you don't get feet of snow. But if you do get a lot of snow, this sizing doesn't give you enough slack, and the cover is likely to fall in. Here's how the standard sizing breaks down:

>> **Lower water level:** You drain the pool at least 18 inches from the top of the pool (which I talk about in the section "Lowering the water level," earlier in this chapter), so you have 3 feet of overlap already used up out of the 5 feet standard overlap because the cover needs to go down the wall 18 inches on both sides.

>> **Tacking material:** You'll need an additional 18 inches of cover on the deck around the pool so that you can position your water bags or other tacking materials on the cover to prevent it from blowing away or falling in.

TIP

If your pool has steps that extend beyond the edge of your pool, you can either count that in with your measurements, or you can cover your stairs separately. I've found that if you have steps, you can cover them with a large piece of plywood and use a small tarp on top of that to prevent leaves from falling in on your steps. Setting up a separate cover for exterior steps is a great way to save your tarp from tearing on corners because then you're not causing the cover to be tight on the corners.

Looking at types of covers and leaf nets

In the following sections, I cover the differences in the kinds of covers that you have available and why you may choose one over the other. I also go over leaf nets, which can be added to any cover.

Solid covers

This kind of cover resembles a tarp (well, it is a tarp) and doesn't allow water through it. Solid covers are usually rated by their binding and weave count (*binding* is the edging of the cover and the *weave count* is the density of the cover material), and for the most part, rectangular covers don't have any special features to them.

Here are a couple of features you might find on solid covers:

>> **Loops:** Some inground solid pool covers have loops attached to them to help hold water bags in place.

>> **Eyelets:** Covers for above ground pools that are round or oval have eyelets and a cable with a winch. The cable threads through the eyelets, and the winch tightens the cable around the top of the pool.

>> **Grommets:** Solid covers are available that attach to grommets you install on the uprights of your above ground pool to keep the cover really tight. That's an excellent idea if you're in an area that has only a little bit of snow, but they won't hold up long term against a lot of weight on the cover from feet of snow.

There are other options for attaching your above ground pool cover like clips and wind wrap. I cover those in more depth further in the chapter.

A solid pool covers has its pros and cons:

>> **Positives:** It prevents anything from getting into the pool, even sunlight, which will keep your pool much cleaner for longer periods of time. If there is no sunlight for photosynthesis, you can open and close your pool at your convenience, even if the weather is still warm because it will prevent algae growth.

>> **Negatives:** The biggest downside to solid pool covers is that they will collect water and leaves on top that have to be removed. This removal can be a hassle if you don't keep up with it throughout the fall and spring by draining off rainwater and removing leaves when they fall. If you wait until before opening the pool to remove everything that's ended up on top of the cover, it can be a lot of work — and very frustrating.

REMEMBER

You will need to tack down your winter cover on inground pools using some sort of a weighted item. The safest way is to use a *water bag*, which is a vinyl tube 8 to 10 feet long that you fill up with water. They are heavy and are placed on top of the overlap of the cover on the deck. They're a safe item to use because if they fall into the pool they won't cause any damage.

Mesh tarp covers

Mesh tarp covers are just like solid tarp covers (see the preceding section), except they're porous. They allow water to flow through them, so fine dirt or silt, as well as sunlight, can go through, too. Because it's porous, this type of cover will make your pool much more susceptible to getting algae prior to opening, so prepare for that with the correct chemicals and make sure to wait until colder weather to close.

One not-exactly-accurate comment I commonly hear about mesh is that you don't drain it off in the spring in the same way that you would a solid cover; you can just pull it tight to drain it. The only issue with that approach is that the water doesn't drain through like a strainer; it's more like letting water drip through a t-shirt. It's not fast, and it really isn't easier to remove water from a mesh cover than from a solid cover.

I don't recommend mesh tarp covers if you're in a climate where your water freezes. If the cover is sitting in (or on) the water and that water freezes, the water will expand inside the fibers of the weave and break the cover down fairly quickly.

Overall, a mesh cover isn't my favorite type of pool cover because the misconceptions about them lead to upset customers with dirty pools in the spring, but I understand that some people want them for the fact you do not have to drain the water off of the cover. You can scoop the leaves and other debris and then pull the cover off in one swoop.

Safety covers

Safety covers are most commonly used on inground pools, but you can use a safety cover on any pool that has at least a 3-foot deck around it. Safety covers resemble a trampoline and attach to anchors in the ground.

They're by far the best type of cover that you can use — if you have the deck to set it up — because it is the easiest to put on and take off in the spring and fall and lasts the longest. It is a much simpler process for removal in the spring.

A safety cover also holds true to its name and is extremely safe if you have children or dogs (or clumsy adults) around your closed pool. It has the same tension that a trampoline does, so you can safely walk on a safety cover if you're less than a baby elephant (seriously, look up the pictures!). I don't recommend walking on it for no reason, of course — but you could if you wanted to!

Safety covers are super easy to put on and take off, and they're offered in a variety of thicknesses. You can have a thin mesh, a denser mesh that allows less light through, or a solid vinyl that has only one or two mesh spots to allow water through.

However, a safety cover is a much more expensive investment upfront than a classic tarp because of the install of it and the price of the cover itself. It lasts for years and years, so you want to make sure it fits properly. Have the cover professionally measured, ordered, and installed to make sure you're getting the right size, installed to the proper safety requirements.

Safety covers can be custom made to fit any shape pool, and they have special tubes and anchors that work on landscaping edges. They're also very aesthetically pleasing, in comparison to any kind of tarp. After an owner gets a safety cover, they very rarely ever go back to a tarp.

Leaf nets

A *leaf net* is exactly what it sounds like — it's a net that you place on top of your pool cover to catch leaves so that you can easily shake them off when they fall and prevent a large buildup on the cover. You do have to go out there and clear the leaves off of the leaf net somewhat frequently because, if the leaves on top of the net get wet, they're a lot harder to shake off.

TIP

After the leaves have stopped falling and the snow has begun, take the leaf net off to protect it from the damage ice can cause. They can also be used over the pool when it's the time of year when helicopter-type seeds start falling from the trees, especially if you're leaving on vacation during that time.

What happens to an uncovered pool

I get asked a lot what would happen if a customer didn't want to cover their pool for the winter. The real answer? Nothing at all.

Your cover has one main purpose, and that's to keep the water clean during the times it's just sitting there not filtering. If you didn't cover your pool for the winter, you would most likely

>> Have a little more cleanup to do in the spring (and possibly through the winter, if you want to keep up with it).

>> Want to add chemicals every few months if the water doesn't freeze. Although algae is much less likely if the water is below 55 degrees Fahrenheit, it isn't impossible. So adding chemicals to keep the water clean will just save you a bigger hassle in the spring.

I recommend at least using a leaf net until the snow begins falling, and then you can leave it uncovered for the rest of the winter. Putting on a leaf net while leaves are falling will at least help keep the pool mostly clean.

If you have an above ground pool, you may want to put your pillows into the pool, even if you don't cover it, because their job is still important in the winterization process. (I talk about the importance of pillows in the section "Using pillows for protection," earlier in this chapter.) Without a cover, it's just a little harder to keep them in place and keep the leaves it collects dry.

Putting on your pool cover

Getting your cover on your pool is easiest with two people, regardless of the size of the pool or the type of cover you're using.

Tarp cover

If you're covering your pool with a tarp, follow these steps:

1. **Begin with your cover folded in half, underside up.**

   The underside is typically black, but not all covers have that coloring.

2. **With one person holding each end of the straight edge, walk the cover onto the pool until you reach halfway.**

   If you have pillows for your pool, you can either put them in before you begin and tie them, or you can put them into the pool after the cover is mostly on, pushing them to the center with the soft end of your vacuum pole.

3. **Grab the top half of the cover and pull it the rest of the way over the pool.**

   Try to get it distributed as evenly as you can on all sides.

REMEMBER

   For inground pools or pools that have a deck, your cover needs to be only about 18 inches onto the deck, with the rest of the slack in the pool. The 18 inches will be enough space for the water bag to fit and hold the cover down.

Safety cover

For safety covers, when you opened the pool last season, it should have been removed and folded like an accordion. Follow these steps to un-accordion the cover onto your pool:

1. **Tack down the two corners on one end of the cover to keep it from falling in.**

2. **Grab the other end of the cover and start pulling it across the pool (this is much easier with two people).**

   Try not to allow the cover to fall into the water. It gets much heavier when that happens because the water will pool on top, and it doesn't pour out quite as easily as it goes on.

3. **Attach the cover to the anchors.**

   If you have a free-form cover, hopefully when you opened the pool at the start of the season, you marked one of your springs with its corresponding peg for easy match-up. If you didn't and you don't have obvious steps to use as a guide, just open the cover completely and find a place to start. That's never a fun process, but it happens all the time.

Securing the cover

When you cover up your pool, the cover doesn't stay on all by itself. It needs something to keep it in place and help keep the wind out.

Securing an above ground pool cover

After the cover is in place, follow these steps to secure the cover with the cable system:

1. **Weave the cable through the eyelets on the cover until the two ends meet.**

   Most new winter covers will come with a long cable and a metal winch.

2. **Thread the two ends of the cable through the ends of the winch, and then through the center of the winch.**

   Pull all the excess cable through. See Figure 8-4.

3. **Start cranking the handle on the winch to tighten the cable on the pool.**

   Be sure that the cable is where you want it to end up (just below the top rail). Also, check that it's not caught underneath the skimmer or return.

FIGURE 8-4:
A cable threaded through a winch for an above ground pool cover.

Kristine Blanchard (Book Author)

ADDING WIND WRAP

Along with the clips or the cable that you use to secure your pool cover, you can also use cover wind wrap. It looks a lot like plastic wrap, but it's a little more heavy duty than the plastic wrap you use in your kitchen, and it's better against UV light because it won't break down in the sun, helping protect the cover itself from sun damage. You can wrap the wind wrap around the rim of the pool so that it goes about 6 to 8 inches above the edge of the cover and about 1 foot below the cover. I recommend doing at least three layers of the wrap to make sure you get a good seal. This wrap helps keep the cover tight against the pool so that it doesn't let as much, if any, wind under the cover. It's a very helpful tool for sealing your pool, but it really isn't enough to keep the cover in place on its own, so be sure to secure your cover as well as wrapping it.

If your pool cover doesn't come with a cable and winch, you might use one of these options to secure your cover:

>> **Plastic cover clips:** These clips are about 6 inches long, and they snap on over the cover and onto the edge of your top rail. They're an excellent alternative to the cable and winch because they won't allow as much air under the cover.

Also, clips will break in a situation where the cover has too much tension on it. Broken clips may not sound appealing, but the reality is that if your cover needs to fall into the pool and the cable won't allow it, you're possibly looking at damaging the rails of the pool. The clips can't handle a ton of strain and will end up breaking off, sparing your rails.

>> **Jugs of water or sand:** Gallon jugs full of water or sand can be tied to the cover to hold it down. You can use jugs if your goal is to keep the cover as tight as possible to prevent water or snow buildup.

WARNING

Not only do jugs not work a lot of the time, particularly in areas that have a lot of snow because they end up getting pulled into the pool, but using them also will void the warranty of the majority of winter covers. I really am an advocate for just allowing the cover to get water on it and sink a little.

Securing an inground pool cover

For inground pools, here are your options for securing the different types of covers:

>> **Tarp covers:** *Water bags* are long vinyl tubes that you fill with water and use as weights to hold your solid pool cover down. Put them no more than a foot apart so that they can keep the wind out and place them around the whole perimeter of the pool on top of the cover.

WARNING

Vinyl water bags are used because if the cover falls in and the water bags fall in with it, they won't cause any damage to the surface of the pool. If you use something like cinderblocks, bricks, rocks, or large pieces of wood, they can inflict some serious damage if they fall in your pool.

>> **Safety covers:** Use the pegs or stakes that came with the cover when it was installed. You don't need to do anything, outside of attaching the cover to those stakes.

Placing an above ground pool cover if you have a deck

Having a deck or fencing around your above ground pool makes placing a cover a little more complicated. Because of the deck, you usually can't easily put the cable around the pool or add wind wrap. If you're covering a pool that has a deck on it, there are two ways to do it:

>> **Cover only the pool and not the deck.** Try to shimmy the cover between the pool and the deck and treat the pool-covering process like the deck isn't there. Use your cable or clips to hold the cover down (which I talk about in the section "Securing an above ground pool cover," earlier in this chapter) and just work around (and under) the deck.

>> **Cover the pool and part of the deck.** Where no deck encroaches on the pool, attach the cover like normal using the cable or clips. But for the parts of the pool that is surrounded by deck, flip the cover up onto the deck and tack it down with water bags in the same way you would for an inground pool (flip back to the preceding section). It's easiest to use the clips in this situation, rather than the cable system, so that you don't have to get the cable Jerry-rigged to create tension. Rigging it is not recommended; it may not hold and if the cover falls in full of leaves you will have quite the cleanup come spring!

So, basically your cover is either on like normal and jammed between the pool and the deck, or you have the cover go up onto the deck where it needs to and have it held down by the same water bags that inground pools use.

Blowing Out Underground Lines

When it comes to blowing out lines, things can get tricky. Because all pools are different, the following sections give you only a very generic discussion of how to do a pool line blowout. It's not something I recommend you take on with no help.

If you are unfamiliar with your pool and are unsure the operations of any valves or components attached to your pool or filter system, please do not attempt to winterize your pool without help from someone who will know how to work the proper pieces of equipment on your pool.

Have a professional do the blowout for you at least once, and watch how it's done for your pool. There are a lot of moving pieces, and it's easy for things to get missed.

The following sections don't tell you how to blow out the underground lines of your pool; they tell you why your pool may have them blown out a certain way.

Identifying where your lines are

Before you can even start, identify all of the lines that you need to have blown out. Those lines include anything that has water in it that won't drain with gravity alone — and you may want to empty even those that do drain by gravity because if there is a low spot, water can accumulate and still become damaged from ice. Look for

>> **Suctions:** Start with figuring out how many suctions you have. If you have two skimmers, do they both have a pipe that comes up in front of the pump individually? Or do they connect underground, so you see only one pipe at the pump? If you have a main drain, make sure that it also has a pipe coming up in front of the pump. If it doesn't, your main drain may connect into a hole in the bottom of your deep-end skimmer.

>> **Return lines:** Check your return lines. How many return lines do you have, and how many pipes do you have above the ground at the filter? If you have four returns and four pipes going back into the ground after your filter, you know where those pipes start. But if you have four returns and only one or two pipes going underground, that means your returns T underground and are connected.

If you can't identify these parts, don't blow out your own lines. If you're in a climate where the ground freezes, you must blow out your lines correctly; otherwise you'll get cracked lines. I want you to be comfortable with your system before trying this process. If, in the following sections, I state that you should switch the valve to be skimmer only and you're not sure what that means, you may not be familiar enough with your system to effectively and safely blow out your pool's lines.

You can see whether your local pool professional can walk you through the process in the store based on pictures alone. I've walked people through blowing out their pipes in the past, so you may have that available to you.

If you decide to take on blowing out your lines alone, look at the filter system and pipes as sections. Categorize your lines and think of them all individually. If you have two skimmers and they connect in front of the pump, refer to them as skimmer #1 and skimmer #2, and do the same with your returns. If you focus solely on one pipe at a time, then there will be no confusion as to where water will be coming out. This isn't a project that you want to rush or get overwhelmed by, so take your time and make it easy for yourself.

Knowing what you need

To blow out your underground lines, you're going to need a few things:

>> **A compressor or blower:** The best thing to use to blow out your lines is either a 5-horsepower compressor or a 3-horsepower air blower. Both of these tools will give you the power that you need to clear out every drop of water in the lines.

A leaf blower or a shop vac isn't strong enough to do this job efficiently. They do not have the power to empty pool lines of long stretches.

You need to adapt your compressor or blower to fit into the opening through which you plan to be blowing:

- *Compressors:* I personally find that compressors that have brass fittings are easy to work with because you can use a rubber expansion plug with the bolt taken out of the middle as your adapter. If you can get sizes that will work in all the ports you need to blow through, it's easy.

- *3 hp air blowers:* Adapt them by using above ground filter hoses. But you'll need someone to hold the hose in place while you plug the area being blown out.

>> **A non-toxic anti-freeze:** The anti-freeze that you use has to be non-toxic because, in the spring, it will pour into your pool — and you don't want to poison the bathers. You can pour in anywhere from a half to a full gallon of anti-freeze into any line you blow out.

>> **Plugs:** Plugs for any holes inside the pool, such as returns or side suctions. A 1.5-inch male pipe thread plug fits most standard returns. But there are many kinds of returns, and not all of them have threads. You can purchase rubber expansion plugs of all sizes and use them to plug any hole in the pool. These expansion plugs range from a #000 (which is ⅜ inch) all the way to a #16 (which will plug a 4-inch pipe). Consult with a pool professional to figure out the sizes you need.

If you have a main drain line that leads up into your skimmer, you'll need something called a *purge plug,* which is a rubber expansion plug that has a blow-through valve in the center. That valve allows you to blow air through and then prevents the water from coming back up the pipe.

>> **A skimmer guard:** Something to protect your skimmer if you have an inground pool. The product is called a *skimmer guard,* a hollow cylinder that you thread into the bottom of the skimmer. It works to plug the hole at the bottom, while also protecting the inside of the skimmer from ice expansion.

If you don't have a skimmer guard, you can plug the hole in the bottom of the skimmer with a rubber expansion plug. And then, in the skimmer, you can either

- Place a coiled pool noodle.

- Wedge in an empty gallon bottle with a smaller bottle. They have to wedge in place so that if water pours in, they don't just float to the top.

Blowing out your skimmers

If your main drain line connects into the bottom of your skimmer, then skip down to the section "Blowing out the main drain and side suction," later in this chapter, and follow those instructions first. After that's done, you can start this process.

Blowing out one skimmer

To blow out your skimmer line, the safest way is to narrow it down to just that one pipe. You can either blow air from the front of your pump down towards your skimmer, or you can blow air from the bottom of your skimmer into your pump. Both directions work perfectly well when you have the right amount of pressure from your blower. The water will shoot out of the pipe with decent force; if it doesn't, then the air you are blowing in is too weak. This will happen with leaf blowers or shop vacs.

If you're blowing from the front of your pump to your skimmer, follow these steps:

1. **Close any other suctions that are still open.**

    These suctions can include a side suction or the main drain.

2. **Empty the skimmer of as much water as you can.**

    Your water level should already be drained 20 inches down (flip back the section "Lowering the water level," earlier in this chapter, for discussion of water removal), so this step is as simple as turning the pump on until the water gets sucked out.

If you don't want to turn your pump on because the power is already off, you can blow the water in the skimmer out; it just takes more time.

3. **Pull out your drain plugs in the pump until the housing empties of water.**

4. **Put the drain plugs back in.**

   Leave them in until you're done blowing out the lines completely.

5. **Remove the lid and basket from your skimmer.**

6. **Open up the lid of the pump, remove the pump basket, and blow from the hole where the water comes in.**

   Blowing air from this hole will force the water that leads from the skimmer to the pump to go up and out of the skimmer. At first, the water will geyser out of the skimmer, and then you'll have a steady stream of air.

7. **Shut off the blower for two seconds, and then turn it on again for five seconds.**

   You still have water left in the skimmer and in the pipe at this point, so this step helps you create some thrusting power to get the rest out.

8. **Repeat this process until you have very little to water coming out of the skimmer.**

TIP

If you feel you're not getting all the water out because it sounds like it's gurgling, try blowing from the skimmer to the pump. Sometimes, you just can't get the force needed to get the water high enough out of the skimmer. Blowing from the skimmer will be less of an incline to get the water out of the line; it will just pour out of the pump.

Another option is to blow from the bottom of the skimmer towards the pump and let the water exit from the pump. Follow these steps:

1. **Empty your skimmer of water by turning on the pump.**

2. **Remove the skimmer basket and lid.**

3. **Remove the pump basket, pump lid, and both drain plugs.**

4. **Hold the blower in the hole at the bottom of the skimmer.**

5. **Turn the blower on.**

   The water will shoot out of the pump housing. This should be a faster process.

6. **Shut off the blower when there is no more pressurized water coming out.**

7. **Repeat Steps 5 and 6 until the water seems completely gone.**

   If you see a little spittle of water coming out, that is normal. As long as it isn't enough to overflow your hands if they were made into a cup.

After it appears that the water is gone, fully winterize the skimmer by following these steps:

1. **Pour in half a gallon to a full gallon of anti-freeze into the skimmer.**

2. **Thread in your skimmer guard.**

3. **(Optional) Add plumber's tape to the threads of the skimmer guard, if needed.**

   You want to make sure the seal is good. You can test this by having a small amount of water in your skimmer after the skimmer guard is threaded in, and then blowing a small gust of air towards your skimmer from the pump. If you see bubbles, it is not sealing well, and you may have to use more plumbers tape or get a new skimmer guard.

4. **Place the lid of your skimmer back on top of your skimmer.**

Blowing out two skimmers

When you have two skimmers, blowing them out becomes a little more complicated, depending on how they're plumbed:

» **Your skimmers aren't connected.** You have two separate pipes coming into the front of the pump, so you can do the exact same process outlined in the preceding section, except you'll do it twice, once for each skimmer.

» **Your skimmers are connected.** Unfortunately, in some cases, your skimmers are connected to each other underground, and only one pipe comes up from the ground in front of the pump. The skimmer that's farther away from the pump is the one that you'll want to start with.

To blow out the lines of two skimmers that are connected, follow these steps:

1. **Make sure the water is emptied from the skimmers as much as possible, and then remove the skimmer baskets and lids.**

2. **Prep the pump by removing the lid, basket, and drain plugs.**

   You're going to be blowing from the skimmer to the pump, so having the plugs and lid off will allow the water to easily drain from the pump.

3. **Thread a skimmer guard or a rubber expansion plug into the drain of the skimmer closest to the pump.**

   The logical way to plumb a two-skimmer setup is to have the pipe underground travel the shortest distance. So the skimmer that's farthest from the pump will send water to the skimmer that's closest to the pump, and then the water will go on to the pump.

When you plug the closest skimmer's drain and then blow from the farthest skimmer, you'll clear the line that connects all the pieces together.

4. **Blow from the farthest skimmer towards the pump.**

   Repeat the same process you would if it was one skimmer (see the preceding section).

5. **Make sure the line is dry.**

   There should be very little water coming out, so if there's more than just spittle, repeat Steps 4 and 5.

6. **Switch the skimmer guard or plug to the farthest skimmer and now blow out the closest one to the pump.**

7. **Add in your anti-freeze and skimmer guards as normal and shut it down.**

Blowing out the returns

After you complete blowing out the skimmers (see the section "Blowing out your skimmers," earlier in this chapter), you want to move on to the pressure side of the pool. Your pool should be drained down below the level of the returns by now.

If your water level is at or covering your returns, just know that this process is much more difficult when the water is too high, especially if it's your first time blowing out the returns.

You can blow out your returns a few ways, based on what type of filter you have:

>> **Diatomaceous earth (DE) or cartridge filter:** The easiest way to blow out returns is to go directly into a pipe from a union or from the standpipe inside a DE or cartridge filter. Basically, you want a straight shot down a pipe, and on most filters, you have a way to do that.

>> **Sand filters:** With sand filters, sometimes a union is placed right next to the multiport specifically for this purpose. It can be disconnected and give you clear access to your return pipes.

>> **Salt generators:** Disconnect the generator and blow from the pipe where it was connected.

In the following sections, I cover a few different situations based on how your filter is set up.

Blowing out from a pipe inside your DE or cartridge filter

If you have a DE or cartridge filter, a main pipe inside your filter leads back the pool. On most DE filters and some cartridge filters, it's the stand pipe (which is the pipe inside the filter that guides the filtered water back to the pool; see more in Chapter 3). Other cartridge filters have a different-looking pipe that does the same thing as the stand pipe. In a worst-case scenario, if your pool doesn't have any unions or easily accessible pipes, you can blow the pool out from the inside of the pump. There's the hole you use to blow out the skimmers (flip back to the section "Blowing out your skimmers," earlier in this chapter), and then there's a hole towards the bottom of the pump on the opposite side that leads to the pressure side of the system, where the returns are.

Blowing out from a pipe outside your DE or cartridge filter

If you're blowing from a pipe that's in line after the filter, it's a fairly simple process. And if you have only one return, it's very easy. Blow out the pipe until the water stops, and then plug the hole — simple as that!

If you have two or more returns that are all connected, it gets a little more complicated. Narrow down the returns to one pipe at a time. You can approach this blowout a couple of ways:

>> **Plug all the returns except the farthest one.** Start blowing, and after the line seems dry (just a spittle of water coming out), close that return and open the next farthest one, working your way closer to the pump. Repeat that process until all the returns are done, and then plug them all up.

>> **Don't plug any of the returns.** Start blowing the lines and watch to see where the water comes from first. Plug that hole after it seems to be mostly empty. Then do the same process with the next return in line, and then do the next. When you're ready to start on the last return, plug it and open up the first one you plugged.

Make sure that no water got trapped in elbows anywhere in the lines by repeating blowing out the returns a second time. If some water refuses to leave, you can create some back pressure to get some additional force behind the air by partially plugging the return while the air is flowing, holding for a second or two, and then releasing it. You can do this back-pressure routine until there is very little spraying water coming out.

If you want to add anti-freeze to your return lines, pour a gallon or two into the pipe that you're blowing from, and then send a small burst of air into the pipe to shoot the anti-freeze through the pipes.

Blowing out from either inside your filter or pump

If you are going to be blowing from inside of the filter or going from inside of the pump, the concept between them is very similar. If you're working with a multi-port valve, you have to put it on the correct setting:

>> **Recirculate:** If you're blowing from the pump.

Don't forget to blow out your backwash line if you have one that goes underground. You can either

>> Detach the backwash pipe from the filter and blow directly down that pipe.

>> Put the valve on Waste and blow from inside the pump.

You don't need to put anti-freeze down the backwash line if you don't want to. That line has no water coming into it from the pool after it's been blown out so there is very little chance of ice damage. But, if you want to put anti-freeze down that pipe, there is no harm!

Blowing out returns that have separate valves

Some filter systems are plumbed where every return has a separate valve. If you have a setup like that, you have the ability to blow out only one line at a time. Plug the returns while you go because you don't want the agitated water splashing into the pipes of the return holes after they are empty. Be sure to properly winterize your filter, heater, salt generator, and anything else like that.

Blowing out the main drain and side suction

You can blow out these drains at any point in the process. But I like to wait until last to blow out the main drain or side suction because they're usually underwater, so when you blow them out it creates waves. If you do that before you blow out and plug your returns, sometimes the waves will cause water to go back into the return lines that you're trying to blow out. Also, after your skimmers are blown out, there are fewer valves to worry about identifying or adjusting when you blow out the main drain or side suction.

Blowing out the main drain

Your main drain is a pipe that either goes into the front of your pump or connects to the bottom of one of your skimmers.

COMING INTO THE FRONT OF THE PUMP

If your main drain comes into the front of your pump, follow these steps to blow it out:

1. **Connect your blower to the front of your pump.**

   If you're blowing out the main drain last, it should be the only line that air can blow through because your skimmers are closed.

2. **Open the valve to your main drain if it's closed.**

3. **Turn on your blower.**

   It shouldn't take more than a few seconds for you to see bubbles coming from the grates at the bottom of your deep end.

   After you see the bubbles, you know the main drain is blown out because the bubbles show that only air is escaping from the drain. It doesn't take long!

REMEMBER

4. **While the air is flowing through the main drain, shut the main drain off.**

   Shutting the main drain valve off creates an air lock at the bottom of the pool, so the water won't be able to come into the pipe.

REMEMBER

You don't need to put any anti-freeze in the main drain. As long as the valve isn't leaking, the main drain will be fine until spring.

CONNECTING TO THE SKIMMER

If you're blowing out a main drain that connects into the skimmer, you'll need a compressor that has an air compressor tire attachment for this part. With that equipment ready, follow these steps:

1. **Plug the hole for the main drain by using a purge plug and get it very snug.**

   See the section "Knowing what you need," earlier in this chapter, for information on a purge plug.

2. **Attach your compressor to the valve on the top of the purge plug using the tire attachment and blow air through.**

   After you see bubbles coming out of main drain, let the compressor run for a few seconds.

3. **Disconnect the compressor while the air is still blowing.**

   The plug will cause an air lock that will prevent water from coming back up the pipe.

Blowing out the side suction

When you blow out the side suction, you're going to treat it just like the main drain (see the preceding section), except it needs to be plugged like a return. You blow air from the front of the pump to the side suction line, making sure your skimmers are off or plugged.

Your side suction is likely still submerged in the water because it is lower than your standard return, so you'll need to plug it while the air is flowing and the water is bubbling. This is not a very fun process, especially if the water is cold. But, unfortunately, if you turn the air off and then plug the side suction, water will get back into the pipe in the pool.

TIP

A trick you can try is to have someone flicking the compressor off and on really quickly every 5 seconds or so, which will allow a small break in the air flow without letting water back in behind the plug.

After your side suction is plugged, you don't need to do anything else to it until you open your pool in the spring.

Preventing Damage to an Open Pool in Below-Freezing Weather

More and more, pools in climates that typically don't winterize or freeze are getting flash freezes that lead to some pretty extensive damage. Unfortunately, while the climate changes, this problem may become more common. So I have some tips on what to do if you're in a situation where freezing temperatures are heading your way and the pool is still running.

The steps you want to take become more extreme the longer that the temperature is below freezing. If it's going to be below freezing for only a day or two, you can get away with the basics. But any longer than that, and you're looking at a huge temperature drop in the pool water itself, which will lead to it freezing and possibly causing ice damage like broken pipes.

Freezing temperatures don't necessarily mean a freeze; they just mean there's the possibility of one. If your water temperature is 80 degrees Fahrenheit and the temperature around the pool is supposed to drop to 30 degrees Fahrenheit — but for only two days — you can prevent damage strictly by just letting your pool continually circulate. Moving water is much less likely to freeze, so keeping the pump and filter running 24 hours a day until the temperature comes back up will keep the possibility of damage very slim.

As for a real freeze, that's three-plus days of temperatures below 30 degrees Fahrenheit. In those temperatures for that long, even moving water may not be enough to prevent the pool water freezing and therefore expanding and cracking things like pipes or valves.

There really isn't a great way to prevent damage in these situations without doing a little bit of preventative work. I see all sorts of DIY anti-freeze protection setups, such as pool noodles duct taped around pipes and insulation taped around valves.

But the reality is that the pool should just be partially winterized. The good news is that typically even multiday freezes don't freeze the ground, so any underground pipes are likely going to be just fine. But anything above the ground should be emptied and maybe have some anti-freeze added.

Follow these tips based on what type of pool you have:

>> **For above ground pools:** Follow all of the tips for winterizing your pool that I talk about in this chapter, without using the pillows or the cover. Drain the water below the skimmer and returns (covered in the section "Lowering the water level," earlier in this chapter); remove and empty the hoses; remove the drain plugs on the pump, filter, and any other components (all discussed in the section "Removing the summer parts," earlier in this chapter); and make sure anything that could freeze doesn't have water in it (which you can read about in the section "Blowing Out Underground Lines," earlier in this chapter). All of these preventative actions will take about 30 minutes, but they could save you hundreds of dollars.

>> **For inground pools:** Follow the winterizing recommendations in this chapter but drain the water to only just below the skimmer, which lowers the point at which the water sits in the pipes. After you break the seal of the filter system by removing drain plugs and draining the water from the filter system, the water in the pipes will seek the same height as the water in the pool, which should be below the freeze line.

You could also dump a gallon of anti-freeze into your skimmer(s) so that any water that does end up in there won't freeze at all.

These flash-freeze preparations may seem like a lot of work, but the fact of the matter is that a frozen and broken valve is a lot more work and money to fix than just draining the water out of the valve to begin with.

TIP

If you're not sure what parts of the filter to winterize or how to do it because you haven't had to before, call a pool store in an area that has to fully winterize. They can guide you through it just fine.

3

Becoming a Chemist (Well, Sort Of)

IN THIS PART . . .

Get an overview of the importance of your pool water's chemistry and the role each chemical you add plays in the overall balance.

Review all the sanitation options that you have available and why one may be better for you over another.

Go beyond sanitation to consider oxidizers (also called shocks) and algaecides.

Identify the causes for your water problems, as well as some handy methods on how to reverse and prevent those problems.

IN THIS CHAPTER

» Using the right testing options

» Calculating perfect pool water with
the Langelier Saturation Index

» Measuring all the parts that make up
your pool water

» Keeping your chlorine stable with
cyanuric acid

Chapter **9**

The Perfect Balance

Welcome to the wonderful world of pool water chemistry! As someone who has been in the swimming pool industry for the majority of her life, chemistry is one of the topics I've had extensive training on. It's by far my favorite subject, and I promise it's not overly complicated after you understand the why's and the how's.

In this chapter, I take you on a journey to show you all the things you never knew about your pool water. Obviously, I don't really expect you to become a chemist — but I do hope, if you read through this chapter, you feel like one. Understanding this part of your pool can help you handle any issues that may arise so that you can come up with an understanding about why it happened and what actions you need to take to correct it. Becoming confident in the chemistry also helps you understand the advice given to you by local pool-store employees, making you feel less like you're being told what to do, and more like you're being guided. I also introduce you to the balance of your water and the importance it plays in clarity, equipment longevity, and bather comfort.

WARNING

Be sure to read the entirety of the label on any pool chemical you're handling. The label always has directions for use and safety guidelines that you should never stray from. These chemicals may be products that you can purchase at your local big box store, but remember that they are, in fact, chemicals. Some are dangerous to touch, and others are dangerous to inhale. Always keep safety in mind any time you handle a chemical that you plan to add to your pool.

Testing, Testing!

You need to know the ways in which you can test your water and how to make a judgement on what chemicals you need to adjust based on the results you get. Testing the water is necessary to keep your pool safe and balanced. If you let it slip for too long, bad things occur: You can cause premature breakdown of your equipment or pool wall or have an unfortunate instance of causing harm to bathers in the pool.

REMEMBER

Your pool isn't a natural water source that has an ecosystem helping to keep it balanced. This man-made body of water requires your intervention and effort to keep it in tip-top shape.

The main purpose for testing is so you can focus on the balance of the water, which includes the pH, total alkalinity, calcium hardness, total dissolved solids (TDS), and cyanuric acid (CYA). You also want to keep your sanitation levels in check as well, which will help keep your water clear and clean.

How much water are we talking?

To start, identify the amount of gallons you're treating. If your pool was just installed or you recently had the surface redone, the company that did the work should know the exact amount of gallons your pool contains. If you're just acquiring a pool through the purchase of a house or it recently became your responsibility, the following sections show you how to identify how many gallons your pool has, based on the type of pool.

The internet makes this part of the job fairly easy. You can just do a web search for "pool gallon calculators" to find websites that allow you to get your results with the click of a button. But, if you're old fashioned like me, then you'll love the helpful equations in the following sections.

Square or rectangular pools

If you have a square or rectangular pool that has the same depth throughout, use this formula:

Length x Width x Depth x 7.5 = Volume in Gallons

For example, say you have a 12-foot-by-24-foot rectangular above ground pool with a water depth of 4 feet. You'd calculate it like this:

24 x 12 x 4 x 7.5 = 8,640 gallons

Square or rectangular pools that have a gradual decline

If your pool has a gradual decline to your deep end, you want to use this equation:

Length x Width x Average Depth x 7.5 = Volume in Gallons

TIP

To get the average depth of your pool, add the shallow-end depth and the deep-end depth, then divide that total by 2.

Say that you have a 16-foot-by-32-foot inground pool that has a 3-foot shallow end and 8-foot deep end.

First, you need to calculate the average depth:

(3 + 8)/2 = 5.5 feet

Now, input the values you have into the volume formula:

32 x 16 x 5.5 x 7.5 = 21,120 gallons

Square or rectangular pools that have a drop-off

If your pool has two depths and they *drop off* (meaning that there is no gradual decline to the deeper water, it just, well, drops off!), then you treat the two pool depths as separate pools and add them together.

So you still use the standard rectangular pool formula, you just do it twice:

Length x Width x Depth x 7.5 = Volume in Gallons

For example, say that you have a 15-foot-by-30-foot inground rectangular pool that has a shallow end measuring 5 feet long by 15 feet wide by 3 feet deep and a deep end measuring 5 feet long by 15 feet wide by 8 feet deep. Here are the calculations you need to make:

Shallow End: 5 x 15 x 3 x 7.5 = 1,687.5 gallons

Deep End: 5 x 15 x 8 x 7.5 = 4,500 gallons

Total Pool: 1,687.5 + 4,500 = 6,187.5 gallons

Round pools

Calculating the volume of a round pool involves some higher math skills:

Pi [3.14] x Radius Squared x Average Depth x 7.5 = Volume in Gallons

REMEMBER

Radius is defined as half the *diameter* (a straight line that passes through the center of a circle), and *squared* is when a number is multiplied by itself.

To figure out the volume of a round pool that's 24 feet in diameter and has a 4-foot water depth, first figure out the radius squared:

Radius: 24/2 = 12 feet

Radius squared: 12 x 12 = 144 feet

Now, input all your numbers into the volume formula:

3.14 x 144 x 4 x 7.5 = 13,564.8 gallons

TIP

For above ground pools that have top rails, measure your lengths from inside wall to inside wall. Don't count the top rail for any measurements. For the depth, measure from the floor to the waterline. If the pool isn't full, use the screws on the face plate of your skimmer (see Chapter 3 for more information on your skimmer) and measure to the middle screw as your waterline.

Freeform or irregular-shaped pools

For these style pools, you're best off breaking the pool into multiple sections that are either rectangular or round, and then using the equations in the preceding sections and adding them together. Or you can reach out to the original pool builder for that information. If you don't know who the original builder was, sometimes you can ask local pool builders that make pools similar to yours whether they can give you an educated guess.

Kidney-shaped pools

For a kidney-shaped pool, you first find the surface area by measuring the length of the two widest points of the pool (see Figure 9-1) and plugging them into this equation:

(Length A + Length B) x 0.45 = Pool Surface Area

Then, you use this equation to calculate the volume:

Pool Surface Area x Length x Average Depth x 7.5 = Volume in Gallons

For example, say you have a 32-foot-long kidney-shaped pool where your Length A measurement is 16 feet, and your Length B measurement is 18 feet. Your shallow end is 3 feet, and your deep end is 7 feet. First, determine your pool's surface area and average depth:

Pool Surface Area: (16 + 18) x 0.45 = 15.3 square feet

Average Depth: (3 + 7)/2 = 5 feet

Now, input those numbers into the volume equation:

0.45 x 34 x 32 x 5 x 7.5 = 18,360 gallons

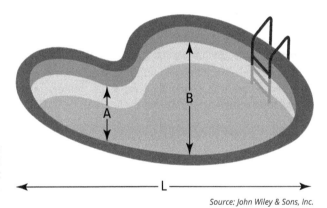

Source: John Wiley & Sons, Inc.

FIGURE 9-1:
A kidney-shaped pool's widest points, A and B.

Checking in regularly

When you have a pool in your backyard, testing it on a consistent basis is crucial to keeping up with the changing water chemistry. With an outdoor pool, all of the elements around it affect the water inside of it, and it's your responsibility to keep the chemicals in check during the season.

On average, pool owners get into the habit of testing their water once a week. That's the maximum amount of time I recommend waiting between tests — longer than that, and things can sometimes get away from you without you even noticing! Checking your pool's water weekly helps you develop a consistent schedule for both chemical and equipment maintenance. I go into more detail on what chemicals to use when in Chapter 10.

Types of home tests

Testing kits come in all different shapes, sizes, and types. All of them can give you the information that you seek, but some of them may be a little easier to interpret, and others may be a little more exact. The most common kinds of testing kits are testing strips, drop test kits, and digital test kits. Find one that fits your personal preferences, and testing your pool will be a breeze.

REMEMBER

All testing kits, whether strips or drops, have an expiration date, and they become less accurate the closer you get to that date. For test strips, they start to lose accuracy even just six months after you first open the container's cap. This is due to the oxidation of the chemicals in the pads of the test strip. So, always be sure you're using testing equipment that's less than a year old or check it against a more accurate testing system, such as the laser readers that you can find at a pool store (see the section "Testing at a store," later in this chapter), every six months.

Testing strips

Also commonly given the nickname *dipsticks,* test strips are an inexpensive, quick and easy way to check your levels in under 30 seconds. Test strips typically come in a bottle that has a chart on the back, and the bottle contains small strips that have testing pads on them. The strip will test your sanitizer, pH, and alkalinity at a minimum and some others will also test your cyanuric acid and your calcium hardness. Just follow these steps to use a test strip:

1. **Gently dip a test strip into the pool's water.**

    You can also scoop a sample of water from the pool into a cup and dip the test strip in there. Be sure to reach 18 inches down for the water sample to get the most accurate reading.

2. **Hold the test strip horizontally, pads-side up, for 15 seconds.**

3. **After the 15 seconds, match the colors of the testing pads on the strip to the chart on the back of the bottle.**

    The chart will have a range of color options for each of the corresponding pads, ranging from low to ideal to high.

Using a test strip is simple and quick, and one of the most common ways to check the levels.

There are some downsides to using the test strips, though:

>> **As simple as they are, it's a little tricky to get accurate results from them.** Most brands recommend a very controlled dip into the water — so no swishing around, and no shaking the test strip off after it's out of the water.

Too much strip jostling may cause colors to appear faded or even bleed into each other.

>> **The colors on the pad are sometimes hard for the reader to decipher.** For instance, the pH is almost always indicated by a shade of red, but not all people can easily tell the difference between one shade of red and the next.

For these reasons, I like to consider test strips a great way to tell you whether you're basically in the range. They're wonderful rough-estimate testers that can help you quickly identify whether you have an issue. If they seem off, I recommend using a more accurate or easy-to-read method of testing like a drop kit or a store's testing system before making large adjustments to your water chemistry.

Drop (or reagent) test kits

As a professional, I prefer this style of test kit as a home test kit. They may take you an extra minute or two to get the readings you want, but the colors in the charts and the accuracy of the results is what I admire. When I do weekly service on customers' pools, I personally use a drop test kit as my regular testing system. There are a lot of different brands that you can try, and a lot of different options. They range from testing only chlorine or pH levels, to being able to test all of the balancing levels in your pool like total alkalinity, calcium hardness, and cyanuric acid along with the chlorine and pH in your pool.

Drop test kids will all have the same components to them, beakers and the liquid reagents. Different brands will have slightly different instructions, but the concept with the tests are all the same. You will fill the beaker with your pool water up to the suggested fill line. There may be two different lines for two different amounts of water, so follow your test kit's instructions thoroughly. You will then add the appropriate amount of drops of the liquid reagent that is meant for testing the chemical you are looking to check. Each chemical level you are trying to check, like pH or alkalinity, will all have a separate corresponding liquid drop reagent. You will thoroughly mix the drops with your pool water and it will turn a certain color. Check that color against the color chart provided with your kit and it will indicate if the level you are testing is low, ideal, or high.

I personally don't have a preference on brand; I've used a few different brands and find them all to be accurate. The big thing in selecting your drop test kit is that you want to be able to replace the drop reagents as needed. Worst case is you could replace the whole kit, of course. But if only one bottle runs out or expires, it's much simpler to get just the drop reagent you need.

I like drop test kits that have the ability to test chlorine, pH, alkalinity, and your pool's acid demand. (I discuss the importance of those levels in later sections of this chapter.)

Drop test kits can be pricy, depending on the brand you choose. Some of the lesser-known brands can have a price ticket of around $20, but other brands can range up to $100, and they will both test for the same levels! Higher quality brands tend to be more accurate and reliable, which is where you get the price increase from. The bottles can range in size, but most of them are one or two fluid ounces each and will easily last you a whole season with weekly testing.

WARNING

Most of the reagent drop-style testing kits are made for halogen (chlorine/bromine) based pools. There aren't many that are meant for biguanide-based pools. (See Chapter 10 for more information on these pool sanitation chemicals.) So if you do have a biguanide pool, you're usually stuck with strips as your only at-home testing method.

Digital test kits

Today, it's nearly impossible to find something that doesn't have an app that you can use to control it. Well, testing your pool water is no different. And just like all things, there are a variety of brands and price points to choose from. Here are a few options:

>> **Strips that have a corresponding app that you download to a tablet or smartphone:** You dip the test strip into your pool water, then snap a photo through the app, and it reads the results for you.

But, of course, the app's accuracy is all based on how precisely you dipped the strip and the lighting in which you took the photo. The concept is great and works reasonably well, especially considering they're in the lower price range of digital options, around $15 to $20.

>> **Specialty test strips that have a separate digital reader:** With this style, you use the strips like you would any other kind of test strip, dipping them into your pool sample. And then you insert the strip into the reader. The readers are designed to work with only the strips made specifically for it, but they're quick, easy, and accurate. They're a mid-price range, usually around $75 to $90.

>> **All-in-one testing meters:** There are two styles of these meters:

● An electronic testing meter where you dip the sensor into the pool, and the results come up on the meter itself.

● A floating device that has a sensor in your pool that sends information to an app on your phone.

Both types of all-in-one testing meters are the most accurate way to test your pool at home, but they tend to fall on the more expensive side. The electronic meter is usually between $200 and $250, and the floating style is commonly priced around $500 for the good ones.

All of these readers are great ways to step up your ability to check your levels accurately at home, but none of them are perfect. It never hurts to get your pool water tested at a local pool store that you trust (see the following section), or even to check the accuracy of your main testing system with another style (which I go over in the preceding sections). Having basic test strips and a digital floating meter can only help in making you a better pool owner.

Testing at a store

Just like a digital testing meter (see the preceding section) is more accurate than a test strip (see "Test strips," earlier in this chapter), the majority of pool stores have a testing system that's even more accurate than some of the best home kits.

The system used in most pool stores has a high-tech meter that reads small plastic disks that are filled with your pool water:

>> The disk is inserted into the meter.

>> The meter spins the disk, mixing the sample water into a variety of chambers along the sides.

>> The meter uses lasers to read the colors that those chambers turn.

These meters are expensive — and, if well maintained, very accurate.

The meters are usually connected to a computer where the results are automatically entered into a program. That program creates the printout that a pool store employee reviews with you.

REMEMBER

This type of testing isn't something that you do weekly or even biweekly. Your pool's chemistry can change in that short a time period, but not enough that you need to visit the pool store. If you use a testing system like this too often, you will go slightly crazy trying to get your pool "perfect" when you have an acceptable variance within your levels. Perfect range for alkalinity is 100 ppm, and if you test it at a pool store and it says your level is 89 ppm, it can get really overwhelming to try to get it exact when 89 ppm is still considered in the acceptable variance. These testing systems are also expensive to run for the pool company, so a majority of them may limit you to only six free tests a year and begin charging for each one after that.

Testing at your pool store should be done

>> Two to three days after the pool has been opened and started running

>> One week after completing the initial balancing on your first test

>> Once a month during the season

>> Two weeks prior to the winterization of your pool

You can always test your pool water at the pool store if you're dealing with an issue in the pool that won't resolve or that you need advice on, or if you just want to be positive that your home kit is accurate.

TIP

When it's time to bring a water sample to your local pool store, be sure to follow these guidelines:

>> Take your sample from at least 18 inches below the surface of the pool to get an accurate sample and use a container that allows you to get at least 12 ounces of sample water.

The pool store may never use that full 12 ounces, but if you need to have extended tests run or have the test repeated, you want to make sure you bring enough water to cover it.

>> Use a container that has had no other liquids in it, if possible. Acidic liquids such as pickle juice, wine, or orange juice will alter your results. It doesn't matter how many times you rinse the bottle out, the traces of the acidic liquid distort the numbers, especially your pH. The only safe reusable bottle I would really recommend is an old water bottle.

>> If you just opened your pool, don't bring a sample in until the pool has been circulating for at least 24 full hours. It's amazing how much your chemicals actually sink to the bottom of the pool over the course of winter!

>> Don't bring in a water sample if you've shocked the pool with chlorine-based shock within 48 hours. (You can read about this cleaning process in Chapter 10.) Almost all testing systems are based on the color your water turns when mixed with a certain solution. Just like how chlorine bleaches your clothes, it absolutely lightens the color that the water turns when mixed with the testing solution.

This advice goes for all color-based testing systems — if your chlorine is over 8 parts per million (ppm), you probably aren't getting a very accurate reading. (I go into measuring chlorine levels in Chapter 10.)

>> If the water turns a certain color when the testing solutions are added, then water that has a distinctive color in the container in which you collect it most likely will be inaccurate when you add those test solutions. If the water in your sample bottle is green, all the colors that your test samples are supposed to turn will be mixed with green, not allowing for accurate results.

>> If your water sample has been sitting in your hot car all day at work, its chemistry changes while it's sitting in the container. If you're going to bring a water sample somewhere, always be sure to bring it as fresh as possible.

REMEMBER

>> Try not to over-test your pool water. I know that may seem crazy, but just like when you're on a diet, checking your weight daily doesn't give you an accurate representation of what's happening. If you check your pool every day — or even twice a day — you get slightly different results every time. Testing the water isn't a perfect science, and you'll make your head spin if you try to make your water's chemical balance perfect every second of every day.

Introducing the Langelier Saturation Index

The chemicals that pool professionals, such as myself, recommend adding are all part of a beautiful equation that evaluates the quality of your water. The *Langelier Saturation Index* (or LSI, for short) is a non-biased equation, and it's the deciding factor on whether your pool water is more likely to create scale or become corrosive:

>> **Scaling:** The deposit of inorganic materials onto your pool's surface

>> **Corrosion:** The long-term deterioration of surfaces or equipment

We pool people obviously want to make sure you're protecting your investment, so let me explain what makes up the LSI and what all those values and measurements mean. When you understand the LSI, you can better understand the importance of water balance, making you a better informed and more conscientious pool owner.

Breaking down the LSI equation

To begin, here are the components that make up the LSI and those components' ideal measurements (see Figure 9-2). When I say to "balance your water," the following are the factors that I am referring to:

>> **pH value (pH):** 7.2 to 7.8

>> **Temperature related factor (Tf)**

>> **Calcium hardness related factor (Cf):** 200 to 400 parts per million (ppm)

>> **Total Carbonate Alkalinity related factor (Af):** 80 to 120 ppm (see "CYA's effect on LSI" later in this chapter for a reference on how to identify your carbonate alkalinity.)

>> **Total dissolved solids related factor (TDSf):** Less than 2,000 ppm

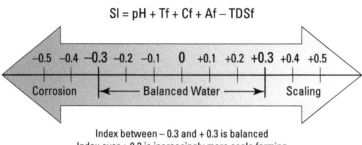

$$SI = pH + Tf + Cf + Af - TDSf$$

Index between − 0.3 and + 0.3 is balanced
Index over + 0.3 is increasingly more scale forming
Index below − 0.3 is increasingly more corrosive

FIGURE 9-2:
The LSI equation.

Source: John Wiley & Sons, Inc.

I want to point out that chlorine (which I talk about in Chapter 10), salt, and cyanuric acid (flip to the section "Chlorine Stabilizer: Your Pool's Sunscreen," later in this chapter) aren't in the preceding calculation. Although a majority of pool owners are under the impression that chlorine and salt are a part of balancing, their presence (or absence) doesn't count towards a balanced water reading at all. This is especially important for saltwater pool owners because you have to balance your pool water, even if you have one of those "maintenance free" saltwater pools.

Pool people (pros and amateurs) measure balancing chemicals in *parts per million* (ppm), a ratio of one in a million. In the pool industry, we use this measurement to define the number of chemicals that we have in a pool compared to the amount of water. The tricky part is that the measurement of chemicals in ppm needs to be converted to the correct format to be used in the LSI using a chart, as shown in Figure 9-3.

To get your pool water's LSI, follow these steps:

1. **Measure your pool water's values for pH, temperature, calcium level, total alkalinity, and TDS.**

2. **Use the chart in Figure 9-3 to find the appropriate numbers for the measurements you took.**

   Look at each factor and find where your levels lie, then the next corresponding row will give you the factor equation number that you would use to determine your LSI.

Equivalent Factors - Langelier Saturation Index (LSI)

Temperature (°F)	Temperature Factor	Calcium Hardness (PPM)	Calcium Hardness Factor	Alkalinity (PPM)	Alkalinity Factor	Cyanuric Acid (if present)	Cyanurate Correction Factor	Total Dissolved Solids	TDS Factor
32	0.0	5	0.3	5	0.7	pH	Factor	< 1000 ppm	12.10
37	0.1	25	1.0	25	1.4	7.0	0.23	1000 ppm	12.19
46	0.2	50	1.3	50	1.7	7.2	0.27	2000 ppm	12.29
53	0.3	75	1.5	75	1.9	7.4	0.31	3000 ppm	12.35
60	0.4	100	1.6	100	2.0	7.6	0.33	4000 ppm	12.41
66	0.5	150	1.8	150	2.2	7.8	0.35		
76	0.6	200	1.9	200	2.3	8.0	0.36		
84	0.7	300	2.1	300	2.5	Note: Only use if CYA is used in your pool. Only applies to >7.0pH. If so, select correction factor based on pool pH.		Note: most calculators assume 12.1 for under 1000ppm, or 12.2 for anything over 1000.	
94	0.8	400	2.2	500	2.6				
105	0.9	800	2.5	800	2.9				

FIGURE 9-3:
An LSI conversion chart.

Source: John Wiley & Sons, Inc.

3. **Enter those numbers into the LSI equation (shown in Figure 9-2) and calculate the result.**

Ideally, you want a number between –0.3 and 0.3, 0 being perfectly balanced.

REMEMBER

Anything outside that range is considered corrosive or scaling and requires adjustments to get your water perfectly balanced (or as close as you can get).

Here's an example of a pool water sample's components, where I've converted the numbers by using the chart in Figure 9-3:

>> **pH:** 7.4 (7.4)

>> **Tf:** 24 degrees Celsius/76 degrees Fahrenheit (0.6)

>> **Cf:** 250 ppm (2.0)

>> **Af:** 125 ppm (2.1)

>> **TDSf:** 2000 ppm (12.2)

So you plug those numbers into the equation to get your LSI:

$$7.4 + 0.6 + 2.0 + 2.1 - 12.2 = -0.1$$

Because –0.1 is between –0.3 and 0.3, this LSI value reflects balanced pool water.

Making sense of the numbers

When you test your pool water at a pool store, they're typically set up with an advanced testing program that enters your water's measurements, and the program automatically converts those measurements into the numbers required for the LSI equation, plugs those numbers in, and gets your answer. With that result, you also see listed anything out of range that needs to be corrected to get your water as close to 0 as possible, with instructions for how to make those corrections.

Keep in mind that even if your numbers are in the appropriate range, you may still have a scale-forming or corrosive result. If all of your results are on the very high or low end of their individual ideal ranges, that affects your LSI, even if the levels are technically in the normal range.

Here's an example of a pool sample where the chemicals are all within the acceptable range but on the higher side of those ranges:

>> **pH:** 7.7 (7.7)

>> **Tf:** 24 degrees Celsius/76 degrees Fahrenheit (0.6)

>> **Cf:** 400 ppm (2.2)

>> **Af:** 125 ppm (2.1)

>> **TDSf:** 2000 ppm (12.2)

Here's the LSI for those values:

$$7.7 + 0.6 + 2.2 + 2.1 - 12.2 = 0.4$$

Because 0.4 is outside the range of −0.3 to 0.3, this pool water needs scaling (which I talk about in Chapter 12).

TIP

The water in your pool always tries to seek a level balance or equilibrium, both physically and in chemical balance. Because the water is seeking to reach a certain level of balance, it will take minerals from things like your walls or begin depositing excess minerals on your waterline to reach its desired level. This is where you begin to see damage from poor water balance. Your water will constantly be seeking out what it needs to reach an LSI of 0, and it will take or deposit what it needs to get there.

To make a long story short, the LSI is going to be what makes or breaks your pool water. If you keep an eye on it by testing at home weekly and at a pool store monthly or as needed, while making the adjustments required to correctly balance the pool, you won't have any problems.

Understanding the Importance of pH: Don't Worry, It's Basic

Proper pH balance is the most important thing in your water. It's the part that causes the most mayhem, the most damage, and the most physical irritation to the human body. It can quietly ruin your liner, sneakily strip your heater, and in short, wreak havoc on your pool.

Defining pH

Think about pH not as a chemical, but as a condition. Just like water can be cloudy or green, it can also be acidic or basic. Without getting too technical with this definition, *pH* is the measurement of whether something is considered acidic (low pH) or basic (high pH).

Everything has its own pH: rain, leaves, pine needles, people, different drinks, foods — you get the point. So, you need to consider that everything that enters your pool will directly affect the pH of your water. And the pH of your water directly affects everything it meets.

On the pH scale (shown in Figure 9-4), the range is 0 to 14, and 7.0 is considered neutral. Anything below 7.0 is acidic, and everything above is basic. In a swimming pool, the range you shoot for is 7.2 to 7.8, with 7.4 being ideal. The reason you want to aim for 7.4, you ask? Here are a couple of them:

>> **The average pH of the human body is 7.4.** When a person enters a body of water that has a pH that's below or above that number, that person is likely to experience skin, eye, and nose irritation (depending on what the water touches). This irritation is especially prominent in young children, people who have sensitive skin, or people who have skin conditions such as eczema or psoriasis.

>> **The pH levels affect the chlorine in your water.** A high pH considerably lowers the efficiency of unstabilized chlorine, which is chlorine that is not protected by cyanuric acid (for a reference, see "Chlorine sunscreen: Your Pool's Sunscreen" later in this chapter, as well as Chapter 10). With pool water that has a pH of 8.4, for example, your chlorine efficiency is knocked down to only 9 percent. Lower pH levels increase chlorine efficiency, but acidic water has a lot of other unpleasant side effects.

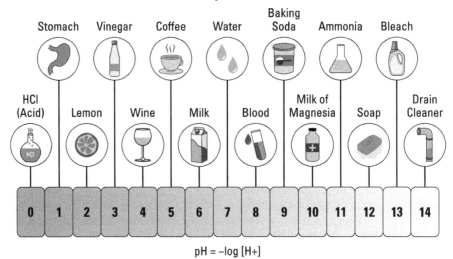

The pH Scale

$$pH = -\log [H+]$$

Source: John Wiley & Sons, Inc.

FIGURE 9-4:
The pH scale and examples of what common items line up with different pH readings.

Looking at pH cause and effect

I have gone through some of the basics about pH, but now I want to dig a little deeper. As mentioned in the preceding section, everything has its own acidity levels, thus the pH of your water can shift with every falling leaf. I want you to fully understand what the misbalance of pH is capable of.

WARNING

pH levels being off in either direction is the number one cause of skin and eye irritation in people who use swimming pools. If you think you're allergic to chlorine because your eyes burn or you have a full body rash, check your pool's pH first. It's a common misconception, and it's such an easy fix!

Basic: High pH

Let us begin with the effects of basic pH. These symptoms are typically caught more quickly than acidic ones because they create a noticeable change in the quality of your pool water. Common symptoms of a high pH include

» **Cloudy water:** Occurs for a vast number of reasons, but a common one is pH being above 7.8. Not all pools will experience cloudiness with a high pH, but it is a common occurrence.

» **Scaling:** Can be caused by pH being consistently high. Eventually, the scale buildup could cause a restriction on your water flow. (Scaling can also be caused by an LSI imbalance, which you can read about in the section "Introducing the Langelier Saturation Index," earlier in this chapter.)

- **Body irritation:** Includes rashes, burning eyes, and running nose.

- **Reduction in chlorine efficiency:** Chlorine efficiency drops by more than 50 percent every 0.5 your pH increases.

Your pool water's pH can rise for a number of reasons:

- **A solar cover:** The increased temperature and lack of gas release causes the carbon dioxide that's produced by the reaction between chemicals and contaminates in the water that have become trapped. All that carbon dioxide causes the pH to go up. Hot tubs also very commonly develop high pH for the same reason.

- **A gunite-plaster pool:** Fresh plaster has a very high pH that will constantly be leaching into the pool water, most noticeably if your pool is new or freshly resurfaced. It's definitely more noticeable with plaster less than five years old, but even old plaster can leach a high pH into your water.

- **The environment around your pool:** There are a number of different kind of trees that have a base pH in their leaves, and even the soil can have a base pH. So, if these leaves fall into your pool or you track some of the soil into the pool on your feet, it will affect your pool pH levels.

Acidic: Low pH

When it comes to acidic water, I usually have a hard time convincing a pool owner of the issues it creates because acidic water tends to have a wonderful crystal clear shine to it. When the acidity level decreases (meaning your pH drops), your pool water becomes an uninhabitable environment for most bacteria and algae (which is why the water looks so clear and rarely grows algae). The problem with acidic water is that it's incredibly bad for your equipment, pool surfaces, and bathers.

Here's a list of some common symptoms of having acidic water in your swimming pool:

- **Crystal clear water:** Of course, a low pH isn't the only reason for clear water — you can have clear water with a pH in ideal range. But acidic water is an uninhabitable environment for living things, so a very low pH (6.0 or lower) pretty much guarantees clear water.

- **Premature deterioration of your pool surface:** This damage to your pool's surface is a common and irreversible effect of poor pH balance. After a liner has been destroyed, there's no fixing it. With plaster pools, you get etching and pitting, which can be fixed by resurfacing your pool. Unfortunately, resurfacing isn't a cheap option!

- >> **Rusting and eroding of metals:** You'll see rust and erosion mostly on things that you didn't think would or should rust. When you see it, it's usually on ladders, diving board bases, and screws in faceplates. And just because you can't see it doesn't mean it isn't happening to the rods in your DE filter or the heat exchanger in your gas heater.

- >> **Overactive chlorine:** While your pH lowers, your chlorine can become overactive and burn off too quickly, rendering it inefficient. See Chapter 10 for more on chlorine.

DON'T JUDGE THE WATER BY HOW IT LOOKS

Let me tell you a short story from when I started working at my first pool store at 16 years old.

I performed a water test on an above ground swimming pool that had a pH of 3.5. (For reference, 3.5 is about the same acidity level as vinegar, the stuff you can use as DIY rust remover and weed killer!) The customer was complaining that his four-year-old pool liner was faded and very wrinkled. He also said that the stainless steel screws on his skimmer were rusting, and he had to replace the seal in his pump every year. The strangest complaint he had, though, was that the hoses that lead from the pool to his filter system kept springing tiny pinhole leaks.

What had happened? The acidity level of the water in this pool was so low for so long that it was destroying everything it touched. It faded his liner pattern and essentially stripped it of all of its elasticity, ate away at the rubber and plastic components in his hoses and seals, and started to actually rust the stainless steel in his pool. Come to find out, the walls of his pool were actually rusting, too.

You're probably saying to yourself, "How the heck does that happen?" This is what happens when you judge the quality of your water based strictly on how it looks. The customer opened the pool cover at the start of the season, and the water was crystal clear. All he thought he had to do was *shock* it (meaning you add in enough oxidizing product to eliminate all foreign contaminates; see Chapter 11 for more on shocking and oxidizing) and add some chlorine tabs all year long. I know this sounds like a dream come true, but unfortunately, it's not a reality. This customer had to spend thousands of dollars to have his liner replaced on a pool less than five years old because of unintentional neglect caused by a misunderstanding about what was needed.

Checking your pH levels should be a weekly chore, along with sanitation maintenance (which you can read about in the prior section "Testing, Testing!" and in Chapter 10). Having a pool that becomes acidic can happen for a number of reasons:

>> **The environment:** Just like with a high pH (see the preceding section), a low pH (acidic levels) in your pool can be created by the environment that surrounds the pool, such as trees or acidic soil.

>> **Chemicals:** All the chemicals that you add to your pool's water have varying pH levels. Chlorine tablets come in around a pH of 3.0, and quick-dissolving dichlor shocks come in around 6.5.

It's easy to get into a routine of adding your chlorine and nothing else — especially when the water looks so pretty.

Keeping your pH in check

First things first: Check your pH with accurate testing methods at least weekly. There are a lot of ways to check your pH (check out the section "Testing, Testing!" earlier in this chapter). If you're in a situation where you're unsure of the accuracy of your at-home testing kit, I highly recommend having your water tested at your local pool store before making any adjustments. If your testing kit is inaccurate, you don't want to accidentally adjust the pH too far in one direction.

When it comes to making adjustments to your pH, there are some easy ways to do it. Pool stores always carry pH adjusters, which can come in bottles or bags of granular material or pH decreasing chemicals can be in the form of liquid acid. They're typically labeled either pH Decrease or pH Increase:

>> **pH increasers:** Made with the active ingredient sodium carbonate, which has a pH of 11.

Adding 6 ounces of sodium carbonate to a 10,000-gallon pool will raise the pH 0.2. To prevent cloudy water, don't add more than 2 pounds of sodium carbonate per 10,000 gallons in one dose. Make sure to balance your total alkalinity levels prior to bringing your pH up. It is likely that if your pH is low, so is your total alkalinity. Reference the following section "Understanding Total Alkalinity" for more information.

TIP

TIP

>> **pH reducers:** Made of sodium bisulfate, which has a pH of around 1.

Adding sodium bisulfate to reduce your pool water's pH is a little more complex than adding sodium carbonate to increase the pH because the amount of sodium bisulfate you need to use really depends on how much water you have and what your current pH reading is. See Figure 9-5 for a chart to help you figure out the right amount of sodium bisulfate to use, given the gallon size of your pool and how far you need to bring the level down.

Decreasing pH Level in Swimming Pools Using Dry Acid
(Sodium Bisulfate)

REDUCE pH LEVEL BY:	500 GAL	5,000 GAL	10,000 GAL	20,000 GAL	50,000 GAL	100,000 GAL
–0.1	0.50 oz	5.00 oz	10.00 oz	1.25 lbs	3.13 lbs	6.26 lbs
–0.2	1.00 oz	10.00 oz	1.25 lbs	2.50 lbs	6.25 lbs	12.50 lbs
–0.3	1.50 oz	15.00 oz	1.88 lbs	3.76 lbs	9.40 lbs	18.80 lbs
–0.4	2.00 oz	1.25 lbs	2.50 lbs	5.00 lbs	12.50 lbs	25.00 lbs
–0.5	2.50 oz	1.57 lbs	3.13 lbs	6.26 lbs	15.70 lbs	31.30 lbs
–0.6	3.00 oz	1.88 lbs	3.76 lbs	7.52 lbs	18.80 lbs	37.60 lbs
–0.7	3.50 oz	2.19 lbs	4.38 lbs	8.76 lbs	21.90 lbs	43.80 lbs
–0.8	4.00 oz	2.51 lbs	5.00 lbs	10.00 lbs	25.10 lbs	50.10 lbs
–0.9	4.50 oz	2.82 lbs	5.65 lbs	11.30 lbs	26.20 lbs	56.30 lbs
–1.0	5.01 oz	3.13 lbs	6.26 lbs	12.50 lbs	31.30 lbs	62.60 lbs

FIGURE 9-5:
Decrease your pool's pH level by using this sodium bisulfate chart.

For example: Add 2.50 lbs. of dry acid to reduce the pH of a 20,000 gal. pool by .2.

Tip: An 8 oz. measuring cup of sodium bisulfate equates roughly to 3/4 of a pound.

Source: John Wiley & Sons, Inc.

WARNING

You can also use liquid acid to decrease pH, but be careful! Muriatic acid is incredibly dangerous. Handling this product should be done very carefully and according to label directions. The gas fumes are toxic to inhale and can also burn your nose and eyes. Along with the fumes, the liquid itself can blind you or burn your skin. They make "safe" versions of muriatic acid that have fewer fumes but are still very dangerous. Always handle with care.

After you have an accurate reading of your pool water's pH, you can use pH reducers or increasers (or even muriatic acid) to increase or decrease the pH into the ideal range.

Understanding Total Alkalinity

Total Alkalinity (TA) serves a few purposes, but it is most well-known for protecting your pH from rapid change. The word "alkalinity" is a very misleading term because it is not necessarily making your water alkaline. Total alkalinity is not a measurement of acidity like pH is; it is a measurement of the water's ability to prevent acidity level changes.

It is also not just the measurement of one particular thing; it is a combination (total) between four things: carbonate, bicarbonate, cyanurate ions, and hydroxyl. The main one we focus on is carbonate alkalinity, because that is the one that can cause the most corrosive damage.

If you do not add total alkalinity into your pool, anything that enters the water will add its own acidity level to the water, changing the pH of the pool little by little. By adding in alkalinity, you are adding in a buffer between the pH and the outside elements like rain, swimmers, and other chemicals. That alkalinity buffer will make the pH change minimal, if not non-existent as long as it is in the proper ppm level (80-120 ppm). Once the alkalinity begins to drop, as it will as a result of doing its job to prevent pH change, the effectiveness of the buffer diminishes, and you will eventually start to have rapid pH changes from those outside elements again.

TECHNICAL STUFF

Scientifically broken down, TA is a measure of the water's ability to neutralize acids. Water with ideal alkalinity levels of 80-120 ppm reacts to substances added to the pool that would normally cause the pH to fluctuate and absorbs them, preventing any changes to your water's pH level.

The ideal range in your pool for total alkalinity is usually 80 to 120 parts per million (ppm). That range goes for all pools, including those that use chlorine, both freshwater and saltwater.

REMEMBER

If you have a pool that uses trichlor tablets and dichlor shock (refer to Chapter 10 for more information on the different forms of chlorine), you may want to reach for the higher end of that range. Because those two chemicals have a very acidic pH to them, they bring the alkalinity of your water down faster than others. So, if you shoot for more like 100 to 120 ppm, you won't have to make adjustments nearly as often.

Why do you add alkalinity to your water?

You add total alkalinity increaser (sodium bicarbonate) to your pool water to adjust the water's alkalinity, which helps you with one of the most important parts of your water balance, the pH.

But, say you didn't do it; what would happen? For starters, you'd notice your pH levels acting like a yo-yo, jumping from one number to another, sometimes in a matter of hours, depending on what was added to the water both intentionally by you and from the environment.

When you increase the alkalinity in your pool water, just like all other things, it will affect your water's pH as well. To increase your total alkalinity, you use a chemical often referred to as a Total Alkalinity Increaser or something to that effect. The active ingredient in that chemical is sodium bicarbonate, and it has a pH of around 8.5. So, while you add this chemical, it increases your water's pH as a side effect. This pH increase isn't a major issue, especially if your pH was already low to begin with. But, if your pH was approaching the high range of normal (7.2-7.8), increasing the alkalinity would absolutely bring the pH up and out of range.

An alkalinity increaser may be one of those chemicals that you consider a less-necessary addition, but in my opinion, it's just as important as your pH. Unless you're the type of pool owner who will be testing your water and making adjustments on a daily basis, then balancing total alkalinity is absolutely necessary. Where pH is so important, due to its effects on your sanitation's ability to sanitize, is on the comfort of swimmers and the long-term protection of your surface and equipment. Keeping the consistency of that level is also very important.

Effects of poor TA balance

When it comes to any chemical in your pool, underdoing it or overdoing it both can have negative effects on your water. Total alkalinity is no exception to that rule, and the effects of poor TA balance can be pretty eventful.

High TA can affect your water in ways similar to how high pH can affect it (which you can read about in the section "Understanding the Importance of pH: Don't Worry, It's Basic," earlier in this chapter):

>> **Cloudy water:** Just like with high pH, high alkalinity can lead to scaling and cloudy water.

>> **pH lock:** When you put too much alkalinity into your pool water and your pH is already on the high end, both levels end up too high, a situation called *pH lock*. Then, the alkalinity you've added does exactly what it's supposed to do, preventing your pH from lowering — a change you actually want to happen in this circumstance. This imbalance can be very frustrating to correct.

>> **Decrease in chlorine efficiency:** When your alkalinity is high, it's very likely that your pH is also high. This would create the same effect as if just your pH was high, which means that your chlorine drops almost 50 percent in efficiency.

>> **Bather discomfort:** Any chemical levels being too high likely causes irritation to people. Alkalinity being high can cause rashes and burning eyes and noses.

All the negative effects in the preceding list are avoidable if you're testing your pool's water by using accurate and well-functioning equipment and following the instructions from your local pool professional or the chemical instructions on the container.

It's easy to just add the last 3 pounds of total alkalinity increaser from a 10-pound bag, even though your pool only really needed 7 pounds. The problem with that is, if your pool doesn't need it, those extra 3 pounds may cause your alkalinity to spike, which can have the effects discussed in the prededing list.

Low TA has some similar effects to low pH. The effects of low TA aren't quite as extreme as low pH, of course, but they're worth discussing:

>> **Rapid fluctuations in pH:** When your TA is low, there is no buffer to keep your pH from jumping up and down with every addition made to the water by you or by the environment. This will cause your pH to easily drop or spike.

>> **Premature damage to surfaces and equipment:** Having low alkalinity inevitably leads to low pH, which will cause all of the same damage I talk about in the section "Acidic: Low pH," earlier in this chapter.

>> **Bather discomfort:** Having the acidity levels fluctuate is more likely to cause bather discomfort, and fluctuations occur when you have low alkalinity levels.

Bringing your alkalinity up and down

The different ways to adjust your alkalinity based on your current readings:

>> **Alkalinity and pH are both too high.** The only way to bring them down is with the addition of an acid, such as sodium bisulfate or liquid acid. Lowering your alkalinity and pH can take some time, and you'll need to test between chemical additions to be sure you don't bring the levels down too far.

Alkalinity is high, but pH is low. Essentially treat your alkalinity and pH levels as two separate issues, but at the same time. Use sodium bisulfate (which decreases pH) to bring down the alkalinity, then follow it with sodium carbonate (which increases pH). Repeat these additions, testing in between, until both your alkalinity and pH are in the desired ranges.

Don't worry, this particular imbalance doesn't happen often!

>> **Both alkalinity and pH are low.** You may be able to use just sodium bicarbonate (which increases TA) to bring them both up. This approach works if your pH is only a little low because alkalinity will raise your pH, but not drastically.

TIP

This is also the route you'd take if your pH is in range. The only difference would be to check your levels after 24 hours to be sure your pH didn't rise out of range. If it did, you need to use sodium bisulfate to decrease the pH, adjusting that level back into ideal.

>> **Alkalinity is low and pH is high.** Raise your alkalinity level first. This will prevent erratic pH change, and then you can bring your pH down afterwards using sodium bisulfate. You may need to add sodium bisulfate a few times to get your numbers correct. Check the pH every 24 hours and make adjustments if needed. Once both levels are in range, you can go to your regular weekly testing.

WARNING

One thing I've seen numerous times is a pool rejecting the effects of a total alkalinity increasing chemical if it's added too quickly. If your pool's current alkalinity is 0, and you need 25 pounds of a sodium bicarbonate to get your pool's alkalinity to the ideal level, add that chemical in increments of 10 pounds for every 10,000 gallons of water, with six to eight hours between doses.

Here's the best way I can explain why a pool rejects the effects of an alkalinizing chemical: It's like a person who's severely dehydrated. If they're given water and chug a gallon of it, their body is likely to reject the water and cause stomach pain — or even possibly cause the water to "vacate the premises," if you know what I mean.

Just like adding water to a dehydrated body, if you need to increase your pool's alkalinity or pH drastically and you add the chemicals to the pool too quickly, it can cause a reaction. It could be minor, such as cloudy water (stomach pain), or it could just not dissolve all together (rejection).

If the chemical is rejected and will not dissolve into the water, you'd have to vacuum out the chemicals that settle to the floor to waste (see Chapter 7 for more details on vacuuming to waste), have the water retested after 24 hours, and treat your pool as if you hadn't added anything yet.

TIP

Here are the general rules for adding chemicals to adjust alkalinity:

>> **To increase alkalinity:** 1 pound of sodium bicarbonate per 10,000 gallons of water raises alkalinity by 10 ppm.

>> **To lower alkalinity:** Similar to lowering your pH by using sodium bisulfate (see the section "Keeping your pH in check," earlier in this chapter), lowering your alkalinity depends on where your levels are and how much they need to come down. See Figure 9-6 for a chart on dosing.

Lower Alkalinity w/ Sodium Bisulphate

Reduce By	Pool Volume			
PPM	5000 GAL	10000 GAL	15000 GAL	20000 GAL
10	12.8oz	1lb 9oz	2lb 6oz	3lb 3oz
20	1lb 9oz	3lbs 3oz	4lbs 13oz	6lb 7oz
30	2lb 7oz	4lb 13oz	7lb 3oz	9lb 10oz
40	3lb 3oz	6lb 6oz	9lb 10oz	12lb 15oz
50	4.0lb	8.0lb	12.0lb	16.0lb
60	4lb 13oz	9lb 10oz	14lb 6oz	19lb 4oz
70	5lb 10oz	11lb 4oz	16lb 13oz	22lb 6oz
80	6lb 6oz	12lb 13oz	19lb 3oz	25lb 8oz
90	7lb 4oz	14lb 8oz	21lb 10oz	28.00lb
100	8.00lb	16.00lb	24.00lb	32.00lb

Raise Alkalinity w/ Sodium Bicarbonate

Increase By	Pool Volume			
PPM	5000 GAL	10000 GAL	15000 GAL	20000 GAL
10	0.75lbs	1.5lbs	2.25lbs	3.0lbs
20	1.5lbs	3.0lbs	4.5lbs	6.00lbs
30	2.25lbs	4.5lbs	6.75lbs	9.00lbs
40	3.00lbs	6.00lbs	9.00lbs	12.00lbs
50	3.75lbs	7.50lbs	11.25lbs	15.00lbs
60	4.50lbs	9.00lbs	13.00lbs	18.00lbs
70	5.25lbs	10.5lbs	15.75lbs	21.00lbs
80	6.00lbs	12.00lbs	18.00lbs	24.00lbs
90	6.75lbs	13.5lbs	20.25lbs	27.00lbs
100	7.50lbs	15.00lbs	22.50lbs	30.00lb

FIGURE 9-6: Decrease water alkalinity by using this sodium bisulfate chart.

pixinoo/Shutterstock

Hardness Isn't the Hardest

Minerals make a difference! In pool chemistry, water can be "hard" or "soft" based on the amount of minerals in your pool water. Hard water has a high presence of minerals and soft water a low level. One of the main minerals to cause hardness or softness is calcium. In this section, I discuss calcium hardness (as used in the Langelier Saturation Index [LSI] equation, which you can meet in the section "Introducing the Langelier Saturation Index," earlier in this chapter) and how it affects the balance of your water.

Why balance your calcium?

Ever cut your toes on the floor of a pool? That's what happens when a plaster pool surface becomes damaged from poor calcium balance — it etches or scales, causing a sharp and irregular surface.

Calcium hardness plays a very important role in all pools — it's part of the LSI for a reason. But it does play a particularly important role in plaster pools and salt-to-chlorine pools (which I discuss in depth in Chapter 10). When water needs something to reach a 0.0 saturation balance, it takes it from anything it touches. On a plaster pool, all of its surfaces contain these minerals, and your pool will pull them right out, causing pitting and etching in your pool wall. After your pool has begun to etch, there's no repairing it easily or inexpensively.

When you have a salt-to-chlorine pool, the platelets inside of the generator itself go through a process called *electrolysis*, which involves splitting the sodium chloride (salt) molecule added to the water to create chlorine by using electricity. And in that process, a chemical reaction within the water occurs and creates a high pH and high temperature, which is the perfect breeding ground for severe scaling if the water's calcium is off-balance.

Effects of low calcium

The ideal range to shoot for with calcium hardness is between 200 and 400 ppm. If you have a liner pool, you'd be safe around 200 ppm, but with plaster pools, you want to aim for more of the 350 to 400 ppm range. Calcium levels decrease with dilution, so this happens any time you add water or it rains. This takes quite a while to lower your levels into a position where more calcium is needed to be added, so balancing it once in the beginning of the spring, checking and adjusting mid-way through the summer, and then a week before closing is enough to keep this level in its ideal range.

In a liner pool, if your calcium is too low (meaning the water is too soft), you're likely to experience foaming as a side effect, as well as corrosion of metals or plastic pieces. Low calcium for long periods of time will also affect the vinyl in your liner, and it might even fade the pattern.

I've actually had a customer who had a relatively new, six-year-old liner, and that customer never added calcium to their pool — the corrosion was so bad that the liner pattern would just wipe off with your hand.

In a plaster-surface pool, when you have low calcium, the surface of your pool will begin to etch and pit. This deterioration will inevitably lead to chunks of the surface falling off. If your pool's surface is starting to deteriorate at a rapid rate, it's almost always from lack of chemical balance. This situation, unfortunately, is commonly seen in public pools, where water chemistry is being handled by multiple people and balancing becomes secondary.

REMEMBER

Also, keep in mind that the water from in your pool will end up on the deck as well. It's absolutely possible for pool water that has low calcium levels to cause damage to your deck the same way it would your plaster surface.

Effects of high calcium

When you end up with high calcium levels in your pool water, that's when you start developing a high LSI and can start to see scaling. *Scaling* is the deposit of excess calcium in the water. In pools, you'll see it along the waterline or pool surface mostly, but it can also build up in your pipes, filters, and even your heater if you have one. It's also very likely to form a much quicker and more aggressive calcification buildup on your salt chlorinator platelets. If that happens, you'll ruin the effectiveness of your salt cell, or even destroy it beyond repair.

I was once taught to think of calcium buildup on a pool like plaque on your teeth or in your arteries. (Gross, I know!) After it starts to build up on the surface, you'll start to see it the most on the waterline. If you have tile up at the top of the wall, it'll begin to form there. An acid, such as muriatic or hydrochloric acid or even a scale remover, which is acid based, along with brushing where it's needed, is the best way to remove calcium buildup.

WARNING

Handling acid to clean anything on your pool can be very dangerous, so always be careful and follow all instructions that come with the acid you buy.

Just like most other chemicals, high calcium can also cause cloudiness in the pool. The water stops being able to properly dissolve the chemicals that you add, so they'll either stay suspended in the water or settle to the bottom.

If you do find that you have calcium buildup on your plaster pool surface, you can use a stainless steel wire bristled brush to brush the surface daily to try to break it down. In addition to this daily brushing, bring the calcium levels down into their ideal range by partially draining and refilling the pool. This approach isn't an option for vinyl, fiberglass, or pebble surfaces (reference Chapter 2 for more information on pebble-texture inground pools). For surfaces other than plaster, you can use a regular nylon brush, along with short-term pH drops (adding muriatic acid or sodium bisulfate into the water to lower the pH to as low as possible) to try to brush it off. Bringing the pH to a low range isn't a long-term fix — drop the pH quickly, and then correct it quickly.

You can raise calcium levels in your pool water only by the addition of calcium. So adding calcium chloride to your pool is the way to increase your water's calcium levels purposefully. Adding calcium-based products can raise the numbers indirectly. The main calcium-based product added to pools is calcium hypochlorite (which is a type of powdered chlorine). You can find more on the different forms of chlorine, calcium hypochlorite specifically, in Chapter 11.

How to change your calcium numbers

After your calcium hardness levels go out of range, adjusting them is either super easy (if it's too low) or very complicated (if it's too high)!

Adjusting low calcium content

If the calcium content in your pool is too low, the fix is as simple as adding the correct amount of calcium to your water. The chemical used to do this is called calcium chloride, and the additions are 1 pound of calcium chloride per 10,000 gallons of water to bring the calcium up 10 ppm. Add the calcium chloride directly to the pool by either pre-dissolving it (mixing it in a bucket of pool water prior to pouring it into the pool) or brushing the calcium off of the floor with your pool brush immediately after adding it until it dissolves completely.

WARNING

Never add calcium chloride into your skimmer because it doesn't dissolve quickly enough just from the flow of water. Calcium chloride can cause severe clogs in your skimmer or even your pump by solidifying into a concrete-like substance and this will create havoc in your filter system.

WARNING

Calcium chloride gets extremely hot when mixed with water. When adding this product to your pool by pre-dissolving it first, always add small doses into larger quantities of water. In my experience, it's capable of warping a hefty plastic bucket, so it's absolutely capable of burning you. Adding it to the pool and brushing immediately instead of pre-dissolving is a much safer option. The calcium chloride will dissolve much faster in your 10,000-gallon pool than it will in a 5-gallon bucket.

Modifying high calcium content

Bringing your calcium hardness level down isn't as easy as raising it (see the preceding section). There are two main ways you can bring it down:

>> **Add water:** Lowers the levels because most source water has a very low calcium content. If you have high calcium in your source water, try the next option.

>> **Add calcium reducing chemicals:** The options available to do this are often marked as either stain and scale inhibitor/removers, waterline control, or calcium reducer. They all work the same way, which is to prevent scaling by lowering the calcium. The main ingredients in them are primarily acids, mostly phosphoric acid.

Adding water is usually the easiest and most effective way to lower your water's hardness. Your calcium level doesn't like to change easily just from chemical additives like calcium reducers or scale inhibit products, so dilution is the quickest option. Here are a couple of things to keep in mind:

>> Partially draining and refilling your pool will lower your calcium levels, but also effects the other chemicals in your pool, so after diluting the water you will want to test your pool water and re-balance your other levels like alkalinity and pH.

>> If the water you're going to fill the pool back up with has a high metal content, that will lead to other chemicals needing to be added to correct it (see Chapter 12 for more information on hard water and staining).

Over time, your calcium levels will drop naturally while you add water to the pool that you lost from evaporation or while you gain water from rain. If you discontinue the use of calcium-based products, the calcium level will lower on its own.

In severe cases, you can manually bring your calcium level down one other way — *floc,* which is when you add a flocculating product to the water that drops all suspended particles to the floor. This should really only be done in cases where the calcium levels are causing cloudy water, which means that the water simply can't handle any more and you need to remove it. Using an aluminum sulfate–based flocculant will drop all of the suspended particles to the floor, allowing you to vacuum to waste (see Chapter 7) and get the numbers down quickly. Using floc has some steps that go along with it to make sure it works properly, so refer to Chapter 12 for step-by-step guidelines.

Getting the Details on Total Dissolved Solids

When you add sugar to your hot tea, the sugar may disappear, but you can still taste it and you know it's in there. Picture your pool as a cup of tea and the chemicals you add to it as the sugar to understand the definition of TDS (total dissolved solids). Defining *total dissolved solids* is simple as pie — it's the measure of dissolved organic and inorganic substances in your pool water. Any time anything has dissolved in your water, it contributes to your TDS level.

Your TDS is measured using a specific TDS meter that is at all pool stores that do water testing. Your TDS level does not need to be tested weekly at home, which is why they don't really make at home testers. The best way to check your TDS levels is at a pool store when you go in for your monthly visit. This level is not something I would stress too much about, the range is very vast and the only time it gets out of hand and needs adjusting is mostly on indoor pools. This is because they do not have the elements of weather and rain the same way outdoor pools do, to the water does not get diluted naturally, leading to a TDS that never lowers.

The ideal range for TDS is anywhere from 0 to 2,000 ppm. There are some exceptions to that rule, such as pools that have salt added to them. In salt-to-chlorine pools, you add hundreds of pounds of salt into the water, which will greatly increase your TDS levels.

In pools that aren't saltwater, average TDS is far below 2,000 ppm — closer to 500 to 800 ppm. In comparison, salt pools have an average TDS over 3,500 ppm, all the way up to 5,000 ppm.

When it comes to having a high TDS, it's controversial whether this high level is a problem. In some pools, you may not even notice any side effects. If you do have side effects, it can cause these symptoms:

>> **Cloudy water:** Even with perfect sanitation and filtration.

>> **Ineffective chlorine:** If your TDS is high, there are too many suspended particles in the water, which makes chlorine, your sanitizer, less likely to efficiently get from point A to point B.

It's like seeing an attractive person on the other side of a very crowded bar. You may get so worn out shoving through all of the people that you give up entirely halfway there or are too exhausted to talk by the time you get there!

TIP

If you need to lower the TDS level, the only good way is dilution. Because the majority of source waters (whether from a tap or a water truck) will have such a low TDS, you can partially drain your pool and then top it back off. This dilution will cause changes in your other chemical levels as well, so be sure to test your water after 24 hours of circulation.

Partially draining and refilling your pool isn't a thing pool professionals commonly like to have you do because your pool and liner rely on the weight and pressure of the water to keep everything in place and structurally sound. It's usually a very last resort because this is such an uncommon occurrence in outdoor pools and due to rain and regular water additions it is not likely the levels will stay high long enough to cause physical effects as previously mentioned.

If your TDS is low, there are no real side effects, as long as the other participating levels are in their ideal Langelier Saturation Index (LSI) levels. (See the section "Introducing the Langelier Saturation Index," earlier in this chapter, for what levels comprise the LSI.) Freshly filled pools or pools that contain a lot of new water will typically have a low TDS because most source water contains very little dissolved solids.

Temperature Is More than a Preference

If you're anything like me, you prefer your pool water temperature to be well above 70 degrees Fahrenheit (82 degrees Fahrenheit for me, to be exact!). There are, of course, those crazy kids who will swim until their lips are purple and they have to speak through chattering teeth.

But aside from personal comfort, what you need to know is that the temperature of a pool will determine how certain chemicals react at a molecular level.

How heat makes a difference

I know having your pool at 85 degrees Fahrenheit during the summer sounds like a dream, but let me explain how it can also be a big pain in the you-know-what. If you have a chlorinated pool, your water will go through chlorine much faster at a higher temperature because chlorine burns off quicker in warm water. Although many people believe it's the UV (which, don't get me wrong, definitely does play a part — flip to the section "Chlorine Stabilizer: Your Pool's Sunscreen," later in this chapter, for details), it's actually the physical temperature that will lower your levels.

Bacteria and organic material thrive in warm water. (Hence getting more algae growth in the middle of July and August.) Your pool is likely to be at its highest temperature of the year in those months, along with being in the sun for longer periods of time during the day. If your algae spawns faster, it'll use up your free chlorine reserve faster, too (see Chapter 10 for more on chlorine).

With higher water temperatures, the water is also less aggressive (meaning the LSI is lower, which creates a more corrosive environment). If you live in a warmer climate, where your water temperature doesn't drop below 32 degrees Fahrenheit, your winterization and balancing routine is different than those of us who live where the water freezes solid.

The difference in freezing water

Water that freezes is more aggressive because the LSI is lower, creating a corrosive environment. That means that even when your chemicals are all in their ideal ranges, your overall LSI will be more on the corrosive side of the scale. (You can find out how to calculate LSI in the section "Introducing the Langelier Saturation Index," earlier in this chapter.)

Let me show you a couple of examples.

Pool A, a beautiful plaster pool in sunny Florida in May, has the following LSI values:

>> **pH:** 7.5 (7.5 in the LSI)

>> **Water temperature:** 84 degrees Fahrenheit (Temperature factor of 0.7)

>> **Calcium hardness:** 250 ppm (Calcium factor of 2)

>> **Total alkalinity:** 100 ppm (Alkalinity factor of 2)

>> **Total dissolved solids:** 800 ppm (TDS factor of 12.1)

To calculate the LSI, you plug these numbers into the LSI equation:

$$LSI = pH + Tf + Cf + Af - TDSf$$

$$7.5 + 0.7 + 2 + 2 - 12.1 = 0.1$$

An LSI value of 0.1 means the pool water is balanced.

Pool B is another beautiful plaster pool, but in New Hampshire in December:

>> **pH:** 7.5 (7.5)

>> **Water temperature:** 37 degrees Fahrenheit (0.1)

>> **Calcium hardness:** 250 ppm (2)

>> **Total alkalinity:** 100 ppm (2)

>> **Total dissolved solids:** 800 ppm (12.1)

Here's the calculation for Pool B's LSI:

$$7.5 + 0.1 + 2 + 2 - 12.1 = 0.5$$

Pool water with an LSI of 0.5 is corrosive and likely to cause your equipment, liner, or plaster surface to deteriorate prematurely.

As you can see, the water temperature made a massive difference, and if the plaster pool in New Hampshire wasn't balanced properly for winterization, then that unsuspecting pool owner could be finding a pitting surface when they open their pool in the spring.

Making sure you properly prepare your pool for winterization in a climate where pools freeze is a necessity to keep your pool's surfaces protected. In most cold states, the pool is closed longer than it's open, so winterizing it (read all about winterizing in Chapter 8) is crucial.

Always make sure that, when you're testing your water before closing your pool, you take the temperature into consideration. And always inform the pool store associate who may be testing your water at a store the temperature of the water in your pool. There's a setting on all testing programs (at least, all the ones I'm familiar with) that direct the results to proper winterization levels.

Chlorine Stabilizer: Your Pool's Sunscreen

With chlorine stabilizer — specifically, cyanuric acid (CYA) — new discoveries on its benefits and side effects have recently been discovered and are being studied still. Like most things in this world, as scientists study a subject for years upon years, they figure out new aspects of that subject and change recommendations based on those new discoveries. Chlorine stabilizer plays a large part in your pool water's LSI, even though, technically speaking, it isn't included in the calculation's factors.

Introducing chlorine stabilizer

CYA is like a sunscreen for the chlorine in your pool water. UV directly affects your chlorine levels by breaking the chlorine molecules apart and causing them to dissipate.

TECHNICAL STUFF

A more advanced explanation on how that happens is this: UV is a form of electromagnetic radiation. This radiation is very powerful and capable of breaking chemical bonds. Chlorine forms hypochlorite ions, which are used to sanitize by destroying bacteria and other organic or inorganic contaminants. If the UV breaks apart the hypochlorite ions, those split ions will dissipate into a gas and no longer kill bacteria. The amount of hypochlorite ions in pool water is measured as free chlorine. You can read more on free chlorine and total chlorine in Chapter 11.

When you add chlorine stabilizer to the water, it gives the chlorine something to bond to so that the chlorine can't be broken down by UV. If you picture it like safe zone in a game of tag, the chlorine bonds with the stabilizer (its safe zone) and waits for a contaminant to come by that it wants to oxidize (the chlorine version of tagging).

As soon as the chlorine lets go of the CYA, that chlorine is free to go burn off the bacteria. And now that the CYA has no chlorine bonded to it, another chlorine molecule will jump on over and make contact with the CYA safe zone. While chlorine is in the safe zone, the sunlight can't get to it; but as soon as it disconnects from the CYA, it's susceptible to UV rays.

Make sure that your chlorine is working at its fullest capabilities by keeping a steady chlorine stabilizer level, or it may never reach the bacteria that it's leaving its safe zone to tag.

Your role with CYA

Maintaining the CYA level in your pool is an important step in keeping a good balance of chemicals overall. It prevents the quick dissipation of your pool's chlorine from UV rays when it's in range, but it can adversely affect your chlorine and render it ineffective when it is too high. It is your job to keep your chlorine stabilizer levels in the ideal range of 30-50 ppm to keep your pool's chlorine sanitation at optimal efficiency.

In the start of your season, or right now if you are a new pool owner, you want to get a handle on what your current CYA readings are. You can check those numbers by using an at-home testing kit or you can bring a sample of your water to a local pool store. I recommend going to a pool store to start so you get a more accurate and exact number for your CYA. If your levels are lower than the ideal range of 30-50 ppm, you will want to add CYA, which is the chemical used to increase chlorine stabilizer, at a rate of 13 ounces per 10,000 gallons of pool water to raise your level 10 ppm.

REMEMBER

Adding CYA to your pool is slightly more complicated than other powdered chemicals. The reason for this is because it dissolves at a painfully slow rate, so you can't just dump it directly into the water or it will settle to the bottom and stay there for a long time. The best (and kind of only) way to add CYA to the pool is to mix it in a bucket of pool water at no more than a pound per five gallons of water and dump it directly into the skimmer of your pool while the pump is running. You want to pour it in slowly so that it doesn't fill tight spots or the pump or skimmer basket too quickly and solidify.

Your CYA will make its way into your filter where it will dissolve unseen. It can sometimes take two days for the CYA to dissolve completely while inside your filter, so if you have a backwashing feature (see Chapter 3 for more details on backwashing), you want to avoid using it for at least that two-day period, or you may end up backwashing out some CYA before it dissolves completely.

Once your CYA is in the ideal range, you want to test it weekly. You are not going to need to adjust it that often, maybe only once a month or even once a season if you're lucky, but its good to keep an eye on it just like all of your other chemical levels. Your CYA level will only change if more CYA is added through chlorine products that contain CYA (such as dichlor and trichlor, explore Chapter 10 for more information on different chlorines) or if the water is diluted from heavy rain fall or addition of outside tap water.

Effects of poor CYA-to-chlorine balance

It's been discovered that when chlorine is attached to CYA, it becomes slightly sluggish. It's bonded to something in the water, so when it wants to reach out and sanitize bacteria, it first has to disconnect from CYA.

On average, your chlorine should be at least 7.5 percent of your CYA level to stay effective. The ideal CYA range for all chlorine pools is 30 to 50 ppm, and not to exceed 70 ppm. After you get into higher concentrations, you'll require a very high chlorine level to still have proper sanitation.

Here's the ideal free chlorine level calculation:

CYA (in ppm) x 0.075

If your pool has a cyanuric acid level of 40 ppm, your free chlorine level should be maintained at 3 ppm (40 x 0.075 = 3).

If your pool has a cyanuric acid level of 100, your free chlorine level should be maintained at 7.5 ppm (100 x 0.075 = 7.5).

WARNING

For most people, a free chlorine level that high could cause skin and eye irritation.

REMEMBER

Here's the kicker: If you don't have any CYA in your pool, chlorine exposed to direct UV light could break down by between 75 to 90 percent in just two hours. So if you start your day with a 3 ppm chlorine level, you certainly won't end that way. There's a very happy balance to be found here, and when it's properly maintained it's exceptional.

CHLORINE LOCK

CYA is capable of creating a chlorine lock in your water. *Chlorine lock* is when both your CYA and chlorine levels are extremely high, and your chlorine level isn't coming down. Because stabilizer is added to the pool to prevent chlorine dissipation, it can become overbearing and prevent the chlorine from dissipating at all. If this happens, you can use a sodium thiosulfate (chlorine neutralizer) to try and bring the chlorine numbers down manually.

Dealing with high CYA levels

Cyanuric acid is obviously one of those chemicals that you'll have a love/hate relationship with. When it works, it's a huge money and time saver. When it's not in range and not working the way you want, it can be a nightmare.

How did the CYA levels get too high?

There are two ways that CYA gets too high:

>> Improper dosing and addition of cyanuric acid

>> The constant introduction of chlorines that contain stabilizer

I explain how to use chlorine further in Chapter 12, but if you use chlorine tablets made of trichlor or powdered chlorine made of dichlor, these chemicals actually contain cyanuric acid within them. If you use them all season, as some pool owners do, you'll rapidly increase the CYA. If you are not testing weekly to watch your CYA levels and switching to an alternative chlorine that does not contain CYA, you could end up having CYA levels that are much too high.

For every 10 ppm of chlorine that you add to your pool using trichlor, you'll add 6 ppm of CYA, too. If your pool goes through 2 ppm of chlorine to keep bacteria at bay, that's a 1.2-ppm increase in CYA a day. Over 10 days, you're looking at a 12-ppm increase in CYA. If your levels started at the ideal range of 50 ppm in the beginning, you're looking at 62 ppm by the end of the 10 days. It's not uncommon for trichlor users to get over 100 ppm of CYA by mid-summer if the numbers were balanced in the beginning.

To prevent this overabundance of CYA, you can use unstabilized chlorine options, such as liquid chlorine or calcium hypochlorite–based products and balance your CYA in the start of the season by testing the level at a local pool store and adding in CYA to bring your curreny level to the idea range. Or you can just adjust the CYA levels throughout the season while you go.

How to bring the CYA levels down

Similar to your total dissolved solids (TDS; flip back to the section "Getting the Details on Total Dissolved Solids," earlier in this chapter), cyanuric acid doesn't dissipate on its own or chemically. It builds up and up until you start to become a victim of the side effects. After you're in that boat, there's really only one way to bring it down — draining and refilling your pool (at least partially).

If your CYA is over 120 ppm, your best bet really is to just dilute the existing water and get your numbers back in check.

For pools that are partially drained in the winter, your levels will lower by spring because of the pool being filled back up either by hose, melted snow, or rain. Sometimes, in situations where the CYA is extremely high (over 130 ppm), I recommend an owner drain the pool lower than usual for winterization (see Chapter 8 for more information on winterizing), and then fill the pool back up to the ideal level for winterizing, which is 18 inches from the top of the pool's edge. It's the easiest way to lower your numbers without having to drain your pool completely in the middle of summer!

CYA's effects on LSI

High CYA levels influence your chlorine's efficiency and while this does cause you some complications when sanitizing your pool, it does not directly affect your LSI. Another implication high CYA can have is the effect on your total alkalinity. In the section "Understanding Total Alkalinity," I mention how the "total" in total alkalinity is a measurement of 4 different levels together, bicarbonate, cyanuric ions, carbonate, and hydroxyl. For your pool's safety, to prevent corrosion I mainly focus on your carbonate alkalinity, that is the one that when it is low can cause corrosion to your surface and metals in and around the pool.

What your cyanuric acid contributes to in the four elements of your total alkalinity is cyanuric ions. This factor when high or low, does not have any corrosive side effects at all. So, if you are taking a measurement of the four elements contributing to your total alkalinity but your cyanuric ions are incredibly high due to a very high cyanuric acid level, that factor is removed from the equation. Removing the cyanuric acid addition is known as a stabilizer correction, and it makes it so you're getting a true reading on your carbonate factor. If you left the cyanuric ion addition, your alkalinity level may read in the ideal range of 80-120 ppm, but the reality is that the carbonate alkalinity is much lower if there is a high cyanuric ion reading in the equation.

On the LSI chart in Figure 9-3, you can see a LSI factor conversion for the cyanuric acid correction (stabilizer correction). It's the factor number that you would subtract from your alkalinity factor to get your true carbonate alkalinity. You take your current CYA level and multiply it by the "Cyanurate Correction Factor" on the chart, based on your current pH reading.

For example:

> If your pH is 7.4 and your stabilizer is 60 ppm, you would multiply your CYA reading of 60 ppm by the correction factor next to the pH 7.4 which would be 0.31. Your result would be 18.6, and that is the amount of ppm you would decrease your current total alkalinity reading to give you your carbonate alkalinity reading that is used on the LSI chart.

> If your current total alkalinity reading (which you can get on any type of home testing kit such as strips or a drop test kit) is 100 ppm, you would minus the CYA correction of 18.6 and get a true carbonate alkalinity reading of 81.4 ppm. You then use the Alkalinity Factor associated with 81.4 ppm (or the closest number rounding up or down), which is 75, and use the factor 1.9 in the LSI equation.

Chapter **10**

Step 1 to a Clean Pool: Sanitation

O ne of the most important things you can do for your pool is to keep it properly sanitized. A pool — or spa or hot tub, for that matter — that's not properly sanitized will not only leave you with stinky, unappealing water, it can also make people very sick. But sanitation is more than just preventing sickness. It also prevents algae growth and keeps the pool clean, even if outside contaminants enter the water.

Safety First

WARNING

Chemicals can be dangerous. Regardless of whether they're in your basic kitchen cleaner or what you use to clean your pool, all chemicals need to be used with caution.

Approach chemicals as if you're in a science lab and you need to carry around a beaker containing dangerous liquid. Not all pool chemicals are hazardous, but it's safest to treat them all as if they were hazardous. If you use proper safety precautions with any and all chemicals, you'll decrease the chance of any problems. Coming from someone who has been in the industry far too long and has made some close-call mistakes, believe me. Check out the sidebar "Avoiding my mistakes," in this chapter, for a couple of examples of when things went wrong for me.

WARNING

Never let children handle pool chemicals! Children can easily spill chemicals or get it on their hands and clothes without realizing it and end up with chemical burns or worse!

Here are two important tips for safely using chemicals:

>> Pick a specific brand and store to purchase your pool chemicals from.

>> Always carefully read the instructions that come with the chemicals you use.

The following sections talk about these tips in detail.

Picking a store and brand for your pool chemicals

I've said this tip so many times in my career: When it comes to buying chemicals, stick with one store and one brand. Different brands may have different names for the same chemicals. Or they may have the same name for different chemicals! Super Shock is a great example because I've seen that name used to describe liquid chlorine, cal hypo powdered chlorine, and a trichlor powdered chlorine — all three of which are incompatible with each other. (You can read more about the wonderous variety of chlorines in the section "Considering Chlorine," later in this chapter.)

REMEMBER

Purchasing your brand of chemicals from the same store every time is so important because, when it comes to advice, not all answers are the same. For example, if you have a cloudy pool, one company may suggest one route, but another pool store may give a completely different suggestion. That doesn't mean one is necessarily right or wrong, but it does mean you're likely to get different answers to the same question. I've always felt that if you can find one or two people at one pool store that you trust, it's best to just use them for all your pool-related questions: That way, your information and recommendations are consistent, along with the brand of chemicals being offered.

AVOIDING MY MISTAKES

The first time I had a bad encounter with a chemical was with hydrogen peroxide shock, often used as the oxidizer for biguanide-based systems. (Flip to Chapter 11 for the details on shocks and oxidizers. I go into more detail on biguanide in the section "Biguanide — Fun to Say, More Fun to Use!" in this chapter.) A customer had brought in three empty bottles for this hydrogen peroxide product and asked us to dispose of them for him. Being a newbie, I was sent off to throw them into the recycling bin out back.

My dad always taught me to crush my bottles before tossing them, so that's exactly what I did. I removed the cap, placed the bottle on the table in front of me, and crushed it with both hands. In doing this, the gasses and leftover liquid inside the bottle shot up into my face. Now, this was just the remnants of what used to be in the empty bottle. It got into my eyes, my nose, and my mouth, causing severe stinging in my sinuses and eyes. The gasses caused my chest to tighten up, and I had a hard time breathing. The kind of hydrogen peroxide used in pools isn't like your everyday medical hydrogen peroxide, and I took it for granted. With some fresh air and level breathing, I was okay, but it really scared me.

The second time I can recall is when I was helping a father and his little girl gather some chemicals for the summer from the store where I worked. The customer needed two gallons of liquid chlorine and a few other heavier things. I carried the heavier products while the customer carried the chlorine.

About halfway up to the register, I heard the dad ask his daughter if she wanted to help him carry something. The dad, who also was unaware of the move he was making, handed the daughter one of the gallons of chlorine.

She was only about 5 or 6, and she made it about three steps before dropping the bottle on the floor. When it fell, the bottom cracked open, and the chlorine splashed up all over her clothes. The chlorine was rapidly pouring out on the floor, which could have led to a whole other world of problems. So I acted quickly and called for a manager.

I directed the customer to take his daughter into the bathroom to rinse her and her clothes off right away. Luckily, the girl's shirt was the only thing damaged in the process, but the chlorine had burnt holes in her shirt by the time they left the store. How easily a small gesture like that could've become tragic.

These are mistakes I've only ever made once, but once is all it takes. Chemicals are chemicals — treat them with respect and always handle them with care.

Following directions

Follow instructions! Follow all safety protocols on label directions and advice from pool professionals, and never add chemicals without knowing what can safely go together. Always make sure you familiarize yourself with them before opening the container. If you're trying to decide when or how to use a chemical for your pool and you aren't sure you're making the right choice, don't guess. You could cause more harm than good, and you could possibly make a costly (or harmful) mistake.

When it comes to following directions on chemicals, it's especially important to follow the dosing instructions and the directions about how to apply these chemicals to your pool. If you add chemicals to the skimmer that shouldn't go in there, you could clog a line, or even blow something up! If you have a salt generator, always take into account every chemical that's being added to the pool. Some algaecides don't work well in saltwater pools, and some chemicals can ruin your salt generator if there's too much or not enough.

Getting Familiar with Sanitation

When it comes to keeping your pool clean, clear, and safe, follow three very important steps:

>> Sanitize.

>> Oxidize.

>> Prevent algae growth.

Not one of these three steps alone would keep your pool consistently clean and safe — but do all three together, and you have the perfect recipe!

A lot of times, people assume that chlorine alone is enough to keep your pool clean (the sanitize step), and in some ways, that's correct. But, not all pools use chlorine. And a lot of times, chlorine at regular sanitation levels is too low to prevent algae growth.

When sticking with a consistent 1, 2, 3 program, you can control the clarity and look of the water, even during the hottest times of the year.

For this chapter, I'm sticking to discussing sanitation. Turn to Chapter 11 for details on oxidizing and algae prevention.

In reference to sanitation in swimming pools, there are only three Environmental Protection Agency (EPA)–approved ways to do it:

>> **Chlorine (or salt-to-chlorine):** The most common sanitation method. You can read all about chlorine in the section "Considering Chlorine," later in this chapter.

>> **Bromine:** A slightly less common pool sanitizer than chlorine; often used for indoor pools or hot tubs because of its endurance against high water temperatures. Check out the section "Deciding on Bromine," later in this chapter, for all the details.

>> **Biguanide:** A completely chlorine- and bromine-free option. Definitely a lesser-used option because of its expense and common difficulties you can run into when using it (which I go into in the section "Biguanide — Fun to Say, More Fun to Use!" later in this chapter).

When you add sanitizers to your pool water, it's to keep the water clean between one person and another using the pool. I'm sure you're grateful for properly sanitized water when swimming with young children — in case of, shall we say, bladder issues. Sanitizers also help keep algae growth and bacteria at bay.

Sanitizers should be in their ideal range at all times — this consistency is so important! Having low sanitizer levels in your pool can lead to all sorts of complications, from something as simple as a haze to the water, all the way to someone getting sick after swimming in your pool (see Chapter 5).

If you never use a regular sanitizer and only add your oxidizers (also called *shocks*, which I talk about in Chapter 11) you probably have a yo-yo effect with your water quality. This up-and-down water quality is especially prominent in chlorine pools but can also happen in biguanide- or bromine-treated pools.

Getting Clear on Your Sanitation Options

As I discuss in the preceding section, there are three Environmental Protection Agency (EPA)–approved chemicals that you can use to sanitize your pool: chlorine, bromine, or biguanide. Whether you choose one over another is really based on personal preference. In the following sections, I give you a brief introduction to each sanitation option.

Getting acquainted with chlorine

Coming in strong, we have the sanitation option of chlorine. Most people are pretty familiar with what chlorine is. In common pool use, chlorine comes in tablets, powder, or liquid, and is used as either your regular daily sanitizer by adding in powder once a day or letting chlorine tablets float around in a little duck.

TECHNICAL STUFF

Of course, I can't help myself — I have to go into more detail about how this chemical works. Chlorine is a powerful disinfectant that breaks down the chemical bond in bacteria and other organic compounds in the water. Chlorine, when it attacks contaminants, steals part of the contaminants' molecules to break them down through *oxidation,* meaning burning off of the elimination of bacteria, combined chlorine (chloramines) and other foreign contaminates. This process leaves behind a byproduct called chloramines that can lead to cloudy water, a strong chlorine odor, and irritation to the eyes and skin of swimmers.

WARNING

Don't ever mix two kinds of chlorine together. The reaction between them could be incredibly dangerous, and even deadly!

What's so great about chlorine is that, if done correctly, it can be easy to maintain, incredibly effective, and inexpensive to keep up. When you start running into issues, it's usually because of outside elements that weren't properly dealt with at the start and have gotten out of control. Figuring out how your chlorine is affected by your environment and use of the pool takes time and experience, which you get with consistent water testing. But, after you understand the idea that your chemicals will change after large parties or with rainstorms, it all just becomes a habit!

IT'S A GAS!

When you use a chlorine sanitizer in your pool water, you're not using it in its elemental state. Chlorine by itself is actually a gas, and that gas is released when you use products that contain chlorine and mix it with water. When your salt cell (the device added to your pool that creates chlorine from salt) splits the salt molecule through electrolysis and creates that free chlorine, it is in its elemental state of gas. Chlorine gas itself being pumped into the water through a specialized feeder can be very dangerous because chlorine gas alone is unstable. When the chlorine gas is introduced into the water using a salt-to-chlorine generator, it is the only safe way to get pure chlorine gas to sanitize your pool.

Opting for bromine

Bromine is a much less commonly used sanitation option than chlorine, unless you have an indoor pool or a hot tub. Bromine, although highly effective and a very aggressive sanitizer on bacteria, can't be stabilized against the sun (see Chapter 9). So if you have a pool in a beautiful sunny area, bromine can't keep up with the sun, and there's no way to fix that problem. Unlike chlorine bromine is not affected by hot water temperatures, which is why it's so well-suited for warm indoor pools and hot tubs.

Bromine is much more stable and dissipates more slowly in environments that have no UV exposure, as compared to chlorine, which is much faster acting but will fluctuate quickly and has more of a yo-yo effect when it comes to outdoor exposure and sunlight. Bromine also works in a similar fashion to chlorine when it comes to bacteria, but it's slightly different. With bromine, it more or less forces the bacteria molecule apart, separating its key functions until the bacteria fails. In doing this pull-apart, the bromine mostly remains working and active but leaves behind a byproduct called bromamines. This byproduct is not as unpleasant as the byproducts of chlorine which is chloramines.

Bromine also has a much gentler effect on your skin and eyes than chlorine, which is a huge benefit if you have very sensitive skin or eyes. It's also gentler on your respiratory system, a concern if you have severe asthma.

WARNING

Although bromine is known for being less aggressive to the skin, it is still very common for those users who have eczema or psoriasis or just sensitive skin issues to still be just as affected by bromine as they would chlorine. Hives, itchy skin, and burning eyes are all possible if you use bromine.

Introducing biguanide

The bromine- and chlorine-free EPA-approved sanitizer is called polyhexamethylene biguanide — also known as PHMB or biguanide, for short. Originally created to be an antimicrobial preoperative scrub, it was found that biguanide is an effective pool sanitizer. With its gentle nature on skin and eyes, this sanitizer is best known for making the water feel soft when you're swimming in it.

REMEMBER

Biguanide is highly effective as a sanitizer and has algae preventative qualities as well. When you use this type of sanitizer, you don't want to mix it with any other types of sanitation chemicals, such as chlorine or bromine. They're very incompatible with biguanide, and they'll cause a chemical reaction that resembles uncooked scrambled eggs (yuck!).

While biguanide is a very effective sanitizer, it has its cons such as being much more expensive than chlorine, along with being more prone to water molds that are difficult to remedy.

Considering Chlorine

The most common chemical people use to sanitize their pool is chlorine. Chlorine is a very highly effective sanitizer that has a lot of great, and not so great, qualities. If regulated properly, chlorine can be just as comfortable in a pool as any other alternative out there. As long as you test weekly and keep your chlorine levels in the ideal range of between 2 to 4 ppm, chlorine is not going to affect people negatively (smell, rashes, dry skin, burning eyes). Chlorine just happens to be more complicated to keep "perfect" since it will dissipate with use and from outside elements, such as sun or rain. It is the most common option due to the fact that it is inexpensive, effective, easily accessible, and easy to maintain once you get the hang of it by testing the levels regularly.

REMEMBER

Most of the time, when chlorine is blamed for a problem such as fading liners, burning eyes, or dry skin, it's typically caused by something being off balance. It could be that the chlorine levels were far too high, or maybe your pH was actually off the whole time. Of course, this isn't always the case — but remember that a well-balanced pool, even with chlorine as your sanitizer, shouldn't have a harsh feeling at all.

In the following sections, I give you information on the ingredients that make up different chlorines, and I offer a rundown on what form of chlorine may work best for your pool.

Checking on pool chlorine ingredients

To choose a chlorine form that works best for you, it's helpful to know the five main ingredients that make up different types of pool chlorine: trichlor, dichlor, sodium hypochlorite, calcium hypo, and lithium hypochlorite. I go over these five chlorine types in the following sections.

Trichlor

Trichloro-s-triazinetrione, or trichlor, is the most commonly used as the main ingredient in chlorine tablets (or sticks). It contains cyanuric acid (CYA, a chlorine stabilizer to protect chlorine from the effects of UV rays) and dissolves slowly, which is best when it comes to tabs.

Dichlor

Dichloro-s-triazinetrione, or dichlor, is what is commonly found in powdered chlorine and can be used as an oxidizer (see Chapter 11 for more information on what oxidizing is) or as a daily sanitizer. It dissolves quickly and contains CYA as well. This product is also a more expensive type of chlorine.

Cal hypo

Calcium hypochlorite, or cal hypo, is almost always found in a granular form and can also be used as a daily sanitizer or an oxidizer. It does not dissolve very quickly and does not contain CYA, so it is not stabilized against the sun.

Sodium hypochlorite

Sodium hypochlorite is the main ingredient in liquid chlorine. It only comes in a liquid form and is most commonly used as an oxidizer only (see Chapter 11) but in some cases, it can be used as a daily sanitizer. It is not stabilized with CYA.

Lithium hypochlorite

Lithium hypochlorite is a very outdated type of chlorine due to its extreme price increase as lithium becomes more desirable for other things like batteries. If you find it in a pool store, it is a quick dissolving powder that is not stabilized with cyanuric acid and was mainly used as an oxidizer.

Finding the best method to add chlorine

When it comes to chlorine, companies have made it easier and easier to keep your pool consistently stabilized and sanitary. In years past, you had to go out with your big ol' bucket of chlorine granules and throw a few scoops in every day. Now, we have easier slow-feeding methods, such chlorine tablets or salt-to-chlorine generators. The three main methods are tabs, powder, and liquid, which you can read about in the following sections.

Chlorine tabs

Chlorine tablets are one of the most common ways to add chlorine into your swimming pool because they're easy to maintain and regulate. They are most commonly made with trichlor because trichlor does not dissolve too quickly and it compacts well into a shape. When I say tabs, I really mean any solid form of the chlorine; it can be in 3-inch tabs (fondly known as hockey pucks), 1-inch tabs, cylinders, or sticks (kind of like a bar of soap!). It is possible to find chlorine tablets made with different types of chlorine such as dichlor or cal hypo, but those two kinds of chlorine do not compact well, and dissolve very quickly.

Trichlor tablets are easy to find and easy to use. The best way to use them is in a floating chlorinator, which is a small plastic device that chlorine tablets can fit into. It floats around the pool and the chlorine tablets dissolve and release chlorine into the pool through holes in the floater. I recommend using one 3-inch tab or 1 stick for every 5,000 gallons of water. On average, the chlorine tables will dissolve enough to be replaced every 4 to 5 days.

Another option would be to put the chlorine tablets into an in-line or off-line chlorinator. More information for chlorinators is available in Chapter 2, but they are cylindrical canisters that are plumbed in near your pool filter. The chlorine tablets fit into the canister and as the water passes through the chlorinator, it slowly erodes the tablet and feeds the chlorine into the water through the pipes. This is going to be the most effective way to use chlorine tablets because you can fit significantly more tablets in a chlorinator than you can a floater, and you won't have a floater in the pool that is tempting kids to play with. It is also easier to regulate the chlorine output because chlorinators will have a dial that allows you to change the amount of chlorine that is going into the pool.

WARNING

The one place you should not be putting chlorine tablets is in any of your baskets, such as your skimmer basket or your pump basket. While this is a common practice for pool owners because it is quick, simple, and out of sight, the chlorine dissolves and goes directly into your plumbing and filter system. That means you have a high concentration of chlorine flowing through all of the metal and rubber components in your pump and filter, along with going through a heater if you have one and causing internal damage.

Safety precautions when using chlorine tabs

Chlorine tablets are a chemical that most homeowners have to handle on a regular basis, and there are some things you want to be careful about when using them.

One of the first tips is to never open chlorine tablets in an enclosed area, and keep your face back when you take the lid off. Gasses can build up inside the bucket and can be very overwhelming, so do your best to prevent breathing that in. That goes for chlorinators and floaters as well; wet chlorine releases a lot more gas than dry chlorine does, so be very careful when opening up anything that contains chlorine inside.

In the preceding section, I mention that chlorine tablets are normally made with trichlor, but in some cases you can buy them made with dichlor or cal hypo. Never mix any chlorine tablets together if they are made with different ingredients. They are not compatible with each other and will cause a chemical reaction that creates incredibly strong and dangerous gasses, and, in some cases, those gasses can build up inside of a chlorinator and cause an explosion. I have seen the damages of this firsthand, and if anyone had been around that chlorinator when it exploded, it could've been deadly.

Another note about dichlor and cal hypo tablets: Never use them in a chlorinator to begin with. Dichlor and cal hypo tablets dissolve at a much more rapid rate than a trichlor tablet does and the gasses will build up inside the chlorinator and will also cause an explosion. Trichlor tablets are the only type of tablet you can use inside of a chlorinator unless it is specially designed to be used with something else.

Powdered chlorine

Powdered chlorine is available in many different kinds, so trying to figure out which to use and why can be a little overwhelming. Powdered, or granular, chlorine is most commonly made with cal hypo or dichlor, but it can also be made with trichlor. Trichlor is not as commonly used as a powder because it works more efficiently as a tablet, but it dissolves quickly and could be used as a shock.

Using powdered chlorine is really not as common of a way to sanitize your pool as it used to be. If you use powder as a sanitizer, it typically has to be added daily. Having to go out to your pool every day to sanitize is a lot more work than just having chlorine tablets dissolve on their own. The benefits to using powder is that it is easy to regulate, because you are the one regulating it on a daily basis, and if you use cal hypo it tends to be the least expensive way to sanitize this way.

You have a few choices when it comes to powders. The two most common are dichlor and cal hypo. The two of them are very different in a few ways and knowing those differences will make it easier for you to choose between them.

POWDER CHLORINE WITH DICHLOR

This option is the more user-friendly option for sanitizing purposes. It is a fine powder, so when it is added into the water it dissolves very quickly and you will have little to no settling of chlorine on the floor. Dichlor is also a stabilized chlorine, meaning it contains CYA and will last longer in the pool during the summer, especially on hot days. It does still need to be tested and adjusted almost every day, but in some cases, it may hold up and may be able to be added every other day. The biggest downside is that this chemical is fairly expensive per pound, especially in comparison to cal hypo.

POWDER CHLORINE WITH CAL HYPO

Cal hypo is more of a granular chlorine, meaning the texture is closer to coarse salt than it is to a powder. That thicker texture makes it so it does not dissolve quickly in water. The best way to add it is to either take a clean bucket and fill it with your pool water, then add in 1 lb of cal hypo at a time into the water and mix it until it is dissolved as much as possible. Then you add it right to the pool, ideally in the deepest part so that it has time to dissolve the remaining granules before settling on the floor. The other option is to carefully toss the cal hypo into the pool and to use your pool brush to sweep the chlorine off of the floor until all of the granules have dissolved.

WARNING

Undissolved cal hypo on the floor can bleach out any colored surface and could also possibly cause the liner (if you have one) to become brittle in that spot and be more likely to tear in the future.

Cal hypo is not stabilized, so it must be added daily to maintain proper chlorine levels between 2 to 4 ppm. The biggest plus is that cal hypo tends to be the least expensive chlorine available.

Safety precautions when using powdered or granular chlorine

Powdered chlorine is an easy-to-use product as long as you use it safely.

Cal hypo is best used when it is pre-dissolved, but you want to make absolutely sure you are using a bucket that has no remnants of any other chemical, especially any other chlorine. The mixing of cal hypo with any other chlorine could be deadly, so always be sure to use a clean bucket when pre-dissolving. Cal hypo is also highly reactive to many liquid chemicals, especially algaecides. If those two mix, you will create a very dangerous chemical fire! Keep your powdered chemicals separate from your liquids, and especially keep your chlorine away from any other liquid chemicals.

You also want to be very careful when adding the chlorine to the pool. If you are gently broad casting the chemicals in, which I don't recommend, be sure you are at least down wind. If you toss chlorine into the air and it comes back at you, you could get it in your eyes or mouth and be in a serious situation.

Lastly, never add chlorine, or any chemical for that matter, into your skimmer unless the directions on the chemical specifically indicate to do so. There are so many ways adding chemicals into your skimmer can go wrong, so never use that method unless you are told to directly by a chemicals label or a professional in the pool industry.

Liquid chlorine

I'm sure all you chlorine users out there have heard of liquid chlorine, commonly called *pool bleach.* Among pool owners, liquid chlorine is strong, fast-acting, and safe on all pool surfaces.

TECHNICAL
STUFF

Liquid chlorine isn't like your typical store-bought bleach, although the active ingredient is the same. Just like hydrogen peroxide in pools, the concentration of sodium hypochlorite in liquid pool chlorine, as compared to store-bought bleach, is between twice and four times as potent. Name-brand cleaning bleach may reach a concentration of 7 percent sodium hypochlorite, and generic brands can have as low as 3 percent. They also can contain other ingredients that are added to keep the pH in the bleach maintained along with whiteners and a few other things. Pool liquid chlorine is usually 12.5 percent, which means you have fewer additives like any byproducts being added to the water, using a more concentrated version.

Liquid chlorine can be used as a maintenance sanitizer if you have a liquid chlorine feeder or if you add it twice a day. It is not a common way of sanitizing due to the bulkiness of liquid chlorine and the fact that it is unstabilized against the sun, so adding it frequently is a necessity to maintain your ideal chlorine level of 2 to 4 ppm. Most commonly, though, it's used as a shock. (I go into the nitty gritty of shocking your pool in Chapter 11.)

WARNING

Handle liquid chlorine very carefully. It is the easiest one to get on your hands or clothes and it will destroy clothing and dry out the skin it touches.

How chlorine works with saltwater

Oh yes, one of the most controversial topics in the pool world between customers and pool techs — saltwater pools. Over the last 10 years, saltwater pools have taken over the pool world. Everyone and their dog wants salt, and most of the time, it's not for the right reasons. Now, I'm not a salt hater in any way, but I'm not sure I understand the hype (see the next section, "What's with All the Saltwater Hype?"). Salt pools still use chlorine-based sanitation. The reason I'm not a huge advocate for this sanitation style is because of the lies that people are told to convince them to buy it.

TECHNICAL
STUFF

Salt is the common name for the chemical sodium chloride. A salt-to-chlorine generator uses electrolysis to split the sodium chloride molecule. In the process of splitting the sodium from the chloride, the salt cell (which is the unit plumbed in with your filter system that does the chlorine creating) creates chlorine in the form of sodium hypochlorite and hypochlorous acid. Hypochlorous acid, which is the main disinfectant, is the same gas that powder or tablet chlorine releases as it dissolves in water. It's not the salt that sanitizes; it's the chlorine created from putting the salt through a chemical reaction that sanitizes your pool.

What's with All the Saltwater Hype?

You may be wondering if a saltwater pool is for you. After having customers come up to me say that they want to switch to saltwater a hundred times a week, my first question is always, "Why?"

The number one answer I get is, "I want to stay away from chlorine." And they want to avoid chlorine for a number of reasons:

>> "It smells."

>> "It makes my eyes burn."

>> "It bleaches my bathing suits."

>> "I'm allergic."

All of these reasons are things that have almost nothing to do with the chlorine itself, but more with a misuse of chlorine. Switching to salt will solve none of these problems. To clarify, when you switch to a saltwater pool, you are adding in a device to your filter system called a salt-to-chlorine generator (or salt cell). You dump salt into your pool water, and the salt cell will take the sodium chloride (NaCl — a.k.a. table salt) and split the molecule. The sodium stays sodium (Na), but the chloride becomes free chlorine (Cl). That free chlorine is the same chemical you get from all other kinds of chlorine (tabs, powder, and liquid). The following sections go over some things to consider in choosing a saltwater pool.

The effects of saltwater on your pool and equipment

Salt is not a one-and-done kind of product. Switching to a saltwater pool actually makes it so you need slightly more products, not fewer. Your only change is going from using chlorine tablets or powder to using the salt to create chlorine. Balancing your water (see Chapter 9) is even more important now that you are creating a very harsh environment for all metal components in or around your pool water. If you have big box store furniture on your pool deck, prepare for premature rusting! If you have tile at the waterline of your plaster pool, get ready to use an acid cleaner to remove the scale forming. Oh, and anything you may have in your pool that's not made of surgical steel is going to rust or corrode over time. It's not an if, it's a when. The salt cell is also susceptible to scaling and corrosion damage from improper water balance, which is another reason balancing the pool is so important.

There are ways to prolong the inevitable breakdown of the things surrounding your pool, such as using chemical softeners or something called a zinc anode. Both of these things will help keep the effects of salt at bay, but neither will prevent saltwater corrosion completely.

TIP

A *zinc anode,* also known as a *sacrificial anode,* is a small tee that contains a bar of zinc. You can plumb it into your filter system after the pump, before any other pieces of equipment. Zinc is a very soft metal and will corrode much faster than any other metal in the pool, preventing rusting or corrosion of equipment by corroding first. This isn't a guarantee, and it may not prevent all other metals (ladders, bolts, and so on) from corroding at all. But it will drastically minimize the possibility.

Lastly, salt-to-chlorine generators are susceptible to calcium buildup (scaling) inside the generator itself on the titanium plates when the levels of your pool water balance is off. In Chapter 9, I go over the effects of poor water balance in much more detail but, your balancing chemicals, especially total alkalinity and calcium hardness levels, play a big role in the protection and quality of your salt cell.

The feel of saltwater

A saltwater pool is definitely softer on the skin than regular pool water. Salt is a natural exfoliant and is used to help people who have skin conditions such as psoriasis or eczema.

However, the chlorine that salt produces can be just as harsh as chlorine from tablets or liquid if it reaches a high level. Chlorine in the water at 8 ppm will be harsh to some bathers, and it may leave your skin feeling itchy or dry. That discomfort will still happen in saltwater pools that have high chlorine levels.

Another reason a saltwater pool can still feel not-so-great on your skin is because your pH balance is off. Even in a pool that uses the softest chemical system, you can still have skin and eye irritation because of poor pH balance (see Chapter 9). With a salt-to-chlorine generator, during the process of electrolysis, the reaction causes a pH of around 13 — which is crazy high! If you never checked your other chemical readings, the pH would end up out of range and could become very uncomfortable for bathers.

So, yes: Salt feels better because it's salt. But, if you are not diligent in testing the water and balancing it as needed (see Chapter 9), then a saltwater pool can be just as irritating and skin drying as any other chlorine pool.

The use of chemicals in saltwater

When you think saltwater, you tend to think chlorine- and chemical-free because that is how the industry likes to portray it. Unfortunately, if we could find an efficient and safe chemical-free alternative for taking care of your pool, no other option would ever be purchased. The reality is that saltwater pools are only an alternative kind of chlorine pool. They are still chlorine pools, they still require chemicals, and they still need to be tested regularly (weekly at home and monthly professionally).

Another common misconception is the belief that saltwater pools don't need to be *shocked* (meaning oxidizing extra contaminates and chloramines in the water; see Chapter 11 on oxidation and shocking). The fact of the matter is that chlorine, regardless of the way it enters the water, will create dirty chlorine (chloramines) and need to be shocked to break it up.

The thing with using a saltwater system is that you want to keep the addition of outside chlorine to a minimum. You can use non-chlorine-based oxidizers, such as potassium monopersulfate (see Chapter 11), to break down non-organic matter (such as *chloramines,* which are combined and dirty chlorine) without raising the actual chlorine level. Note that even though the assumption is that the saltwater pool will take care of itself without your intervention, you will end up with a pool that is very corrosive or scaling in nature (see Chapter 9 for more information on proper water balancing).

The costs of the salt system

In this section, I run down the approximate cost to upkeep a chlorine pool compared to a saltwater pool. I don't account for the balancing chemicals because both types of pool use approximately the same types and amounts of those chemicals.

Say that we have two 25,000-gallon pools, one chlorine and one saltwater. Both pools are open for six months, on average.

Here's what you need to keep a chlorine pool in good shape:

>> **Chlorine tablets:** You'd go through about 25 to 35 pounds of chlorine tablets. For this scenario, I'm going to round up to 50 pounds. At the time of writing, the running price for a 50-pound bucket of chlorine tabs is around $250.

>> **Shock:** Say that you use the more expensive kind of shock (which is the oxidizing product you use for chlorine pools; see Chapter 11), such as dichlor powdered shock. The average cost of a 24-count case of that shock is around $150. Because a pool of that size would need two bags a week for 24 weeks, you would need two cases, coming to $300.

GIVE YOUR SALT SYSTEM A BOOST

You have the ability on most salt-to-chlorine systems to boost your chlorine output using the button labeled "boost" or "super chlorinate." The reason would be to shock your pool using the salt cell itself. Your salt system, which includes your salt cell and its computer, is programmed to work on 100-minute cycles. On your control panel for your system, you usually set a percentage between 20 and 100 percent. That percentage is the number of minutes out of 100 that the cell will actually work to produce chlorine gas. So, selecting 40 percent means that your system produces chlorine for 40 minutes out of 100 minutes. When you boost your system, you're essentially producing chlorine 100 percent of the time for 24 hours.

There are two problems with this technique:

- If you run your pump for only five hours after hitting "boost," you won't produce enough chlorine in that time period to properly oxidize the contaminants in your water.

- Your salt cell's life is based on how many hours it produces chlorine. Therefore, if you use the boost every week for the full 24 hours, the salt cell will deplete its 10,000-hour lifespan much more quickly.

Combining the cost of chlorine ($250) and shock ($300) brings this chlorine pool's total to $550 in upkeep for a six-month season.

For the saltwater version of this pool, you need to include the cost of starting up on salt. So, a 25,000-gallon pool would need the salt system and salt:

>> **Salt system:** Assume that you went with a name-brand salt system so that you get the best quality. In that case, the salt system, which includes the salt cell and its control panel, costs $1,800.

>> **Salt:** Comes in 40-pound bags, costing around $10 per bag. Because you are starting from no salt at the start up, you need 17 bags of salt, making that total $170.

Those totals, with a $1,800 salt system and $170 in salt, is $1,970. And that doesn't even include the cost of the pool tech and electrician needed to install the salt system.

Now, a saltwater pool comes with some additional potential expenses over the years:

>> **Salt cell:** The average lifespan of a salt cell is between three and five years, and the cell needs to be acid-washed every 500 hours (or approximately three months). If you don't acid-wash it, you'll decrease its lifespan. For the sake of this scenario, assume your salt cell lasts for five years. After the cell dies, the average cost of a name-brand quality cell to replace it is $800.

>> **Fresh salt:** If you're in an environment where you need to winterize your pool and you get snow, on average, you'll need 340 pounds of salt every spring, which is another $85 a year.

So, over a five-year period, here are the costs for upkeep for the two types of pool:

>> **A traditional chlorine pool:** $550/year x 5 years = $2,750

>> **A saltwater pool:** $1,970 for the first year + ($85/year x 4 years) + $800 = $3,110.

These estimates assume balancing is done the same way, as it should be (see Chapter 9 for proper balancing), and that you need to replace your salt cell within five years, as most people do.

The pool types that work and don't work with saltwater

Some pool types are better than others at accommodating saltwater. Here are a few:

>> **Resin-framed above ground pools with aluminum walls:** The resin frame and aluminum wall is really the only combination I would recommend if you want an above ground pool with saltwater. Anything else and you are setting yourself up for damages to the pool from corrosion.

>> **Gunite-plaster pools:** There is little metal in gunite-plaster pools, leaving very little opportunity for salt corrosion.

>> **Concrete wall liner pools:** The concrete wall is protected by the liner and is a much better alternative than steel walls for corrosion reasons.

This may seem obvious, but saltwater systems aren't compatible with steel-frame or steel-wall above ground pools. In most cases, using saltwater in those pools will actually completely void the pool manufacturer's warranty. If you're getting a new above ground pool or you have one now, make sure you're aware of the damage switching to salt will cause, and weigh out whether it's worth it. All pools, inground or above ground, steel or aluminum, are susceptible to the corrosive damages of salt.

Deciding on Bromine

Although bromine isn't as commonly used in the swimming pool industry as it is in hot tubs, it's still an option that you have access to. Bromine does have some features you may like; but all ups have downs, and bromine is no exception. I go over the good and the bad of bromine in the following sections.

Looking at the bromine pros

Because bromine and chlorine are so closely related, it's easy to think they're pretty much the same. Well, in some ways, I guess they are. But as a whole, they're still two distinct sanitizers.

Here are a few pros about bromine when compared to chlorine:

>> **Gentle on skin:** Bromine can be less harsh on the skin than chlorine, so if you have sensitive skin, bromine can be a little less irritating.

>> **Best for warm water:** Bromine is much easier to regulate in heated bodies of water, such as indoor pools or hot tubs. Chlorine burns off very quickly in hot water, but bromine will withstand the high temperatures and stay consistent longer.

>> **Less smelly:** Bromine is known to have a less aggressive scent. (Chlorine typically has a pretty intense smell.)

Here's one kind-of pro about bromine: It doesn't burn off the same way that chlorine does, so it's possible to use a non-chlorine oxidizer to rejuvenate the existing bromine. (You can read about oxidizers in Chapter 11.) The fact that bromine doesn't burn off is also a con, which I get into the following section.

Checking on the cons of bromine

Of course, bromine has a few downsides:

>> **Hefty price tag:** The big negative that I think really matters is the drastic price difference. Bromine is currently almost double the price per pound of chlorine. Fifty pounds of chlorine tablets costs around $250 at the time of writing, and 50 pounds of bromine costs upwards of $450. This price difference has progressively gotten worse over the years (but, of course, it's subject to changes).

>> **Doesn't play well with UV rays:** Bromine can't be stabilized against UV rays. So, in a pool that's outdoors, this is a major issue. You'll use a lot more bromine than chlorine over a season in an outdoor pool, and there's really no way around it (so that hefty price comes back into play here). For a description on how stabilization of chlorine is done and how it helps, check out Chapter 9.

>> **Certain side effects:** If the levels of bromine in your pool are too high, it can have the same negative side effects as chlorine, such as rashes, skin and eye irritation, strong chemical odor, and bleaching of bathing suits or colored surfaces.

SWITCHING FROM BROMINE

Needing to change sanitizer isn't a common occurrence, but if you're currently using bromine in your pool or hot tub, there's only one way to switch to a different sanitizer, and that's to drain it completely. Bromine leaves behind bromine ions in the water when it's added, so even if your test is showing a bromine level of zero, if you add chlorine, the bromine ions will convert it to bromine. This isn't so complicated in hot tubs — a 400-gallon spa is easy enough to drain, clean out, and then refill. But if you're currently using bromine in a pool, completely draining your pool could potentially be dangerous for your pool or liner, if done incorrectly. Your liner uses the pool water to keep it in place and stretched against the surface. If you drain the pool, the liner can pull away from the wall and actually begin to shrink. Then if you go to refill the pool, the liner won't set back against the wall as it was before and you could end up with wrinkles or even gaps between the liner and the wall.

If you're considering switching from bromine in your spa, hot tub, or pool, for whatever reason, when draining the water that contains bromine, make sure you remove all water from the pool and the pipes. Even small amounts of bromine ions in the water will prevent you from completing your conversion because when the bromine ions come in contact with the hypochlorous acid produced by chlorine, it converts it to bromine version called *hypobromous acid*. Essentially making your chlorine into bromine!

Biguanide — Fun to Say, More Fun to Use!

Using biguanide as your pool sanitizer isn't for everyone, and that's based on a lot factors. In the following sections, I dive into what biguanide is and why this may be a great or not so great option for your pool. Factors affecting whether biguanide is for you include the environment, the usage, and maybe even your availability to maintain it the way it needs.

If you're diligent with this chemical option — and you do it as you're supposed to and watch it as needed — it's a fantastic sanitation option. It's safe, easy, and gentle on everything it touches, including you and your pool.

Sorting out the biguanide positives

I'm sure you can think of a reason or two why being chlorine- and bromine-free can be beneficial. Here, I'll hit the obvious points:

>> **A soft touch:** Chlorine- and bromine-free pools are much softer on a person's skin. Using a biguanide-based system allows you to effectively kill bacteria while keeping the water nice and soft.

In the section "Introducing biguanide," earlier in this chapter, I mention that biguanide was invented to be a gentle but effective antibacterial scrub for surgeons. If you were to clean your hands as vigorously and often as surgeons do with chlorine-based scrub, your hands would begin to crack and dry out very quickly. But biguanide as a scrub was much gentler on surgeons' hands. In the same way, it's much gentler on you in the pool.

>> **No smell:** Biguanide pools have very little to no smell, which is a huge plus for a lot of people. The smell of chlorine, for some people, can be nauseating.

>> **Doesn't cause fading:** Biguanide won't bleach out anything it touches. No more faded bathing suits or liners! One of my pools that uses biguanide as the sanitizer has a 14-year-old liner that looks like it was installed this year.

>> **More resilient against things that affect chlorine:** It's stabilized in the sun, effective even with a poor pH balance, and easily regulated and maintained.

Following up with the negatives of biguanide

Of course, biguanide has some faults:

>> **Less aggressive sanitizer:** Biguanide, although it's soft, is a less aggressive sanitizer against bio-slimes. *Bio-slimes* are not like algae — they're actually made of a water mold that can be very stubborn when you try to get rid of it. In the process of fixing a large algae or water mold bloom, you'll go through a lot of the chemicals used in a biguanide system.

>> **Expensive:** A pool that size, using chlorine, would need approximately 10 pounds of chlorine tablets for four months. That 10-pound bucket would run you around $90 at the time of writing. In comparison, biguanide would use 2 gallons, and that would run closer to $199.

>> **Poor tolerance to surrounding trees.** Due to its gentle nature and its susceptibility to water molds forming, using biguanide in a pool surrounded by a lot of trees would not be a good fit. Trees and the leaves, acorns, bird poo, and pollens that fall from them are the main source of water molds, so if you have a lot of trees, it can be almost impossible to prevent a bloom from forming on a biguanide-sanitized pool.

>> **Can't handle a lot of swimmers:** Biguanide is so gentle that a lot of people in the pool regularly could create such an increase in contaminants that the biguanide couldn't keep up.

>> **Requires a strict schedule:** Something that can lead to a biguanide pool owner getting frustrated is that this system works best on a strict weekly schedule, with regular testing. If you're in a situation where you can't run the filter at its recommended time every day, or add chemicals weekly without skipping, then this system won't work for you. The start of a water mold can become a large bloom very quickly and it's a costly and time-consuming process to bring it back.

CONVERTING TO CHLORINE

The only way this conversion is easy is if you drain the pool and start over. It's not impossible to switch without draining, but it can be a time-consuming process. Basically, the biguanide sticks to a water molecule with every ounce of its strength. It's very hard to separate it from the water molecule, so you really have to try to break it down using chemicals or partially dilute your biguanide-sanitized water with fresh water. If you try adding chlorine or bromine into a biguanide pool while your levels are in their normal 30 ppm range, you will end up with a very messy and ugly chemical reaction that resembles scrambled eggs. Chlorine/bromine is very incompatible with biguanide.

If you live in an environment where you partially drain your pool to winterize it, that's when you want to start the switch:

- Stop adding biguanide about a month before you plan to close your pool. If you winterize in October, stop using your biguanide in early September. Let it run out as much as you can.

- When you go to drain the pool a little for closing, drain it a foot or two lower than usual, and then fill it back up to normal closing level with plain water. Diluting the biguanide will make your life much easier.

Come spring, you should have very low levels of biguanide in the water. You'll want to get it tested at a local pool store to make sure it's at or below 10 ppm. If it's higher than that, you have to manually detach the biguanide from the water molecules by either diluting it further and removing biguanide-treated water and replacing it with biguanide-free water or adding potassium monopersulfate to the pool. The potassium monopersulfate will attack the biguanide and peroxide (the oxidizer in biguanide pools; see Chapter 11) like it is an organic and will force bond to the water apart. Either of these options will lower the biguanide levels down to 10 ppm or lower over time.

After your biguanide levels are low enough, you have to start the conversion by adding liquid chlorine to the pool at 1 gallon of chlorine per 15,000 gallons of water once a day until the water stops reacting. This reaction usually starts off with the water getting cloudy and yellow for a few hours. After a while, you stop seeing that reaction, and it's at that point that you want to start working on the next step. Make sure that the pool holds chlorine after 24 hours and that you don't have a combined chlorine. A combined chlorine is a sign that the chlorine you're adding is still working to separate the leftover biguanide from the water. The easiest way to get an accurate test on your combined chlorine is by using a testing system at a pool store — those testers can read race amounts of combined chlorine. The other option is to use an at-home testing system like test strips, as long as it tests for free and total chlorine. You would get a reading on both of those numbers and see if there is any combined chlorine. See Chapter 9 for more information on testing your pool.

You'll hit a point where the chlorine will hold over 24 hours with no visual reaction and no combined chlorine — you're officially converted (yay!). This process can take anywhere from one to eight weeks, so you want to make sure you give yourself plenty of time to do it; don't start mid-summer.

The pool isn't usable during this process because you're creating a chemical reaction. If you were to swim in your pool during this conversion from biguanide to chlorine, you'd have severe skin and eye irritation because of the nasty chemical reaction happening between two very incompatible chemical systems.

Supplements to the Common Sanitizers

If you didn't like the sound of any of the regular sanitizing options I discuss earlier in this chapter, then this section is for you. These alternatives may not mean that you never have to use chlorine, bromine, or biguanide ever again, but they will certainly lessen your need for them.

Ozone

Ozone is by far the best add-on for any pool. A small device called an ozonator produces ozone gas. This gas is designed to kill bacteria and impurities in water. Ozonators are more commonly used on hot tubs, but they're started to become more popular in the swimming pool world because everyone is always trying to get away from chlorine one way or another.

An ozonator can be used with any chemical system to help kill bacteria, so you don't need as much of your main sanitizer. If you're using biguanide, there's a brand or ozonator called Oxygen that takes the ozone purification and makes it a whole program. This program uses a copper sulfate mixture as its weekly *shock* (to oxidize unwanted or left over contaminates), along with peroxide-based oxidizers for trickier scenarios. (Flip to Chapter 11 for the details on shocks and oxidizers.) Because peroxide is the main ingredient in biguanide systems' oxidizers, this system is an easy alternative if you're looking to get away from biguanide but don't want chlorine. You could just add the Oxygen ozonator and begin to use their brand of chemicals with very few issues.

Ozone is also compatible with chlorine and bromine, and it works well with them.

WARNING

Ozone is an excellent gas that kills bacteria, but it's not safe to breathe in. If you have an indoor pool or spa that has poor ventilation, the gasses can become toxic. Ozone should only be used in a body of water than can expel the gasses safely.

Ultraviolet (UV)

A very common add-on for hot tubs, UV sanitizers are another way that you can help kill bacteria in a more natural way. And it's compatible with all pool shapes, sizes, and chemical sanitizers. UV is exactly what it sounds like: It's a unit that gets plumbed into your pool's water that contains a UV bulb. While the water passes around the bulb, the UV light will stop bacteria growth in its tracks, preventing any reproduction.

The UV bulb is like any other bulb and needs to be changed from time to time. Some bulbs are easy to change; others can be more complicated. Be sure that you know how to do this part of the maintenance before investing in this system. And just like ozone, it's not a standalone sanitizer. It needs to be used in conjunction with one of the three Environmental Protection Agency (EPA)–approved sanitizers. But using a UV bulb helps limit the amount of sanitizer that you need to keep your pool sparkling clean and sanitized.

Copper ion/silver ion/zinc systems

You can use copper, silver, and zinc in as an added natural sanitizer and algaecide to a chlorine or bromine pool. These metals aren't compatible with biguanide systems because the metal actually works so well that it sees the biguanide as a contaminant and lowers that level. And because biguanide is so pricey, you want to make sure you get full use from it.

Mineral systems are typically sold as a combination set with a chlorinator, but you can buy just a mineral feeder on its own. With pools, it is usually an inline chlorinator of the same brand that is added in conjunction with the mineral feeder. The mineral feeder will accept a cartridge that contains a mix of minerals that will slowly feed into the water, aiding with keeping algae at bay and killing bacteria. The usage differs for hot tubs and pools:

>> **Hot tubs:** Silver, copper and zinc can come in small tubes that float inside the filter area or in a cartridge that floats with the bromine or chlorine. In some cases, the mineral cartridge will snap together with the chlorine or bromine back, and, in other cases, they are two separate cartridges that connect into one floating device and submerge in the water and float together.

>> **Pools:** The minerals, which can consist of silver, zinc, or copper, come in a canister that goes into an erosion canister, from which the mineral feeder releases these minerals for six months (or one season, whichever is shorter).

Copper, silver, and zinc are all natural metals that have antibacterial and *algistatic* (algae-inhibiting) qualities to them. When they're introduced into the water, they'll work to kill bacteria, prevent algae growth, and keep the water nice and clean.

IN THIS CHAPTER

» Shocking your pool by using oxidizers

» Weighing your chlorine shock options

» Considering hydrogen peroxide for your pool shock

» Finding the right algaecide for your pool

Chapter **11**

Steps 2 and 3 to a Clean Pool: Oxidation and Algae Prevention

Treating your pool water is a multi-step process. It's more than just throwing chlorine tabs into the skimmer and running the filter. There's a reason for the procedures and practices that professionals like me tell you. Keeping your pool clean, clear, and safe is not as simple as one step, but the process is simple after you know the basics.

In this chapter, I cover the basics of oxidizing and preventing algae. (The first step to a clean pool is sanitation, which I discuss in Chapter 10.) In this chapter, I also explain what shocking your pool means.

Shocking Information on Oxidizers

Oxidizing your pool water is done for many reasons, and if you don't think you need to do it, then you're in for a shock (see what I did there?). Not everyone is familiar with the word *oxidizers* but almost everyone knows the term *shock*. Well,

I'm here to tell you that in the pool care world, they're the same thing. *Oxidizing* (or *shocking*) your pool is a way of cleaning up byproducts left behind from your regular sanitation.

The main reasons to shock your pool — and to do so regularly — are

>> To kill bacteria

>> To break up *chloramines* (which are what is treated when your chlorine attaches to a contaminate but does not burn through it; it just clings to it)

>> To eliminate foreign contaminants

Shocking your pool is done for both maintenance reasons and treatment purposes. The maintenance part is really a treatment as well, but it's more preventative. Your pool needs to be oxidized routinely, typically once a week.

How shock works

This may be hard to believe, but *shock* is actually a verb and not a noun. When you *shock* a pool, you're performing the action of burning off organic and inorganic impurities in the pool water. Of course, I'm sure your first thought is, "Well, isn't that what your sanitizer does?" And you're not wrong!

Your sanitizer does work to clean up bacteria and keep the water consistently clear and safe. However, if you ever have a situation where a large amount of contaminants enters the pool at one time — say a heavy rain fall or a pool party — regular sanitation can't keep up with an overdose of pollutants. Oxidizing (shocking) is meant to be a much larger dose than your regular sanitizer to pack a bigger punch and kill all pollutants. But, if you've been shocking your pool on a regular basis, your oxidizer will compensate for the extra contaminants.

REMEMBER

Every time your chlorine burns through a contaminant in the water, it leaves behind a byproduct. That byproduct will keep building up every time your sanitizer does what it's supposed to do. And at a certain point, the byproduct begins to create problems, such as smelly or cloudy water. When you shock, meaning oxidize, the pool water, that process eliminates all the buildup and cleans your pool-water slate.

Shocking can be done a number of ways, as long as you're adding enough product to the pool water at one time to break up the amount of contaminants in the water. That means you can use a liquid or powder, or the boost button on your salt system.

How shock fights combined chlorine

Picture this: You and your family decide that for your February vacation, you're going to stay at a hotel that has a big indoor heated pool. You walk into the hotel lobby, and you can just smell that rich chlorine scent already.

My mom always said, "I love the smell of chlorine. It makes me feel better that the pool is so clean." Well, I have some unfortunate news for her (and you). That smell isn't, in fact, free chlorine. That's the smell of combined chlorine, also known as chloramines.

Chloramines form when the chlorine that's in the pool water has already attached itself to a foreign body in the water. It's no longer active and available, so it can't kill bacteria and keep you safe. It already has a soulmate to cling to, and it's not letting go.

Chlorine that's combined with an organic contaminant gives off a very strong chlorine smell and is a main cause for skin and eye irritation for swimmers. Unfortunately, because of the amount of organic material that's introduced into public swimming pools because of their heavy bather load, it's nearly impossible to have a public pool that has 0 parts per million (ppm) of combined chlorine. The stronger it smells, the dirtier it is!

Common shock products

When you can find pool shocks available to you just about anywhere, such as grocery stores, big box stores, and local pool stores, it's good to familiarize yourself with the common ones you might use. Not all shock products are built the same, and what's even more important is how incompatible they can be with each other. Always be sure that you're getting the pool shock that's best for you and your pool — or you may end up making an expensive mistake.

Shocks can be made up of chlorine, hydrogen peroxide, or a non-chlorine oxidizing agent (most commonly potassium monopersulfate, or MPS). All of these options work, but not all of them work on every sanitation system. Although chlorine shocks are the most common type of shock to find, it's not impossible to find non-chlorine options hanging around in the same section of the store.

WARNING

If you're the type of pool owner to pick up chemicals at your local hardware store because it's on your way home, that's fine — but know what you're getting. Products can have similar names but have totally different chemicals in the container, or vice versa. If you're not going to stick to a brand, find out the active ingredients of the products you're buying to stay consistent and safe.

Chlorine-based shock products

A chlorine-based shock is the most common kind of oxidizer you'll find out in stores other than dedicated pool stores. Chlorine is the chemical used to sanitize the majority of pools, so finding compatible shock products in stores will be fairly simple. But not all chlorine products you can get in big box stores are the same quality as what you can buy in pool stores. Typically, the products found in pool stores have no additives, have a stronger percentage of active ingredients, and end up being cheaper in the long run because you don't have to use as much product.

Chlorine-based options are used for chlorine-based pools but can also be used in bromine-based pools. If you have a bromine pool, you can use either chlorine or non-chlorine oxidizers and get a very similar result. There are four common forms of chlorine-based oxidizers:

>> **Powdered dichlor:** This is a much finer powder chlorine that does contain CYA and doesn't need to be pre-dissolved or brushed after adding. It will usually dissolve completely before touching the floor of the pool.

>> **Powdered trichlor:** This is a fine powder that contains CYA and dissolves quickly. Mostly seen in big box stores.

>> **Powdered cal hypo:** This is a granular chlorine that does not contain chlorine stabilizer (CYA) and needs to be brushed or pre-dissolved when adding.

>> **Liquid sodium hypochlorite:** This is the only active ingredient in liquid chlorine; it comes in array of different gallon sizes and is much stronger than traditional household bleach.

All of these forms of chlorine-based oxidizers will produce the same end result, as long as they're used in the correct dosage and in the correct manner. You can use any of them at any time, even switching from liquid to powder week to week.

I go into further detail on how to use these products in the section "Choosing and Using Chlorine Shock Products," later in this chapter.

Hydrogen peroxide

Hydrogen peroxide is the oxidizer you'd use in biguanide-based sanitation systems, and it's really only compatible with that type of system. (You can read about biguanide systems in Chapter 10.)

Hydrogen peroxide is a very aggressive oxidizer when it comes to doing its job of cleaning, but it's not aggressive on your skin after it's in water. If the normal dose for peroxide shock is 1 gallon used for every 10,000 gallons of pool water, and you added 4 gallons into a pool that size, it still wouldn't raise the peroxide levels high enough to cause physical irritation to skin. If you put in four times the recommended amount of chlorine, your skin and eyes would know it right away! Hydrogen peroxide's relative gentleness makes this type of oxidizer so beneficial because you could shock the pool and go swimming 15 minutes later.

WARNING

In its concentrated form in the bottle, pool hydrogen peroxide is nine times stronger than the average household hydrogen peroxide (3% versus 27.5%). It is dangerous to handle because if it gets on your skin or in your eyes in its concentrated form, it will burn you and turn your skin white. It feels like bee stings and can be very uncomfortable. These side effects are not permanent, but you want to handle with care.

TIP

Hydrogen peroxide does have some chlorine neutralizing qualities to it, so if you find yourself in a situation of dire need, it could be used to shock a chlorine pool. You'd need to consult with and follow the directions of a pool professional.

The other guy — potassium monopersulfate

The non-chlorine oxidizer potassium monopersulfate (MPS or KMPS) can be used with all types of sanitizers, but it's most commonly used with bromine and chlorine pools. MPS, also known as potassium peroxymonopersulfate, works great to break down organic waste, such as sweat, urine, sunscreen, oils, and other impurities in the water. In doing this, it frees up your sanitizer to focus on more important matters at hand, such as bacteria and algae.

REMEMBER

However, MPS shouldn't be used as a standalone oxidizer because it doesn't kill algae or bacteria that can make you sick. Always use chlorine- or peroxide-based oxidizers when you're dealing with a large organic problem like algae growth. But if the water is clean and clear and you're looking for sanitation of byproducts like chloramines or non-organic material, such as sunscreens, this is a great option.

Choosing and Using Chlorine Shock Products

Why is one chlorine shock better than another? Which one would be better for my pool and why? With all of these questions in the air, I'm here to help. (Head to Chapter 10 for information on chlorine sanitation systems.)

When you go to a store to buy shock for your pool, you may come across four bags of powdered chlorine shock, and all four are made by using a different type of chlorine. None of them are really compatible, and none of them are added in the same way in the same doses.

In the following sections, I cover dichlor, trichlor, and cal hypo shock, as well as liquid chlorine. All of these chlorine shocks have unique features, and you can do a process of elimination to decide which may work best for you.

Dichlor and trichlor

Coming in strong, we have dichloro-s-triazinetrione (dichlor, for short) and trichlor-s-triazinetrione (abbreviated trichlor). Either type of chlorine shock is versatile and easy to use. Dichlor is far more common as a shock than trichlor is because trichlor is much more commonly used as the main ingredient in tablets. But I've worked with both, and they share very similar qualities.

The positives of dichlor and trichlor

Here are a few pros to consider in regards to dichlor and trichlor:

>> **Made with a fine grit:** Because of the finer grit, they dissolve quickly with no settling on your pool floor. That means if you sprinkle it in, you shouldn't have to pre-mix it or brush it afterwards.

>> **Uses a CYA stabilizer:** These chlorine shocks are stabilized with cyanuric acid (CYA), which is the chemical used to prevent the UV rays from dissipating chlorine levels from the water.

However, the CYA can be a con, as well — see the following section.

>> **Allows swimming soon after adding:** Some dichlor shocks can also be purchased as a *shock-and-swim,* which means it's a lower percentage of the chlorine and is mixed with other oxidizing and sanitizing products. Therefore, the chlorine levels aren't raised too high, and you can swim 30 minutes after adding.

The negatives of dichlor and trichlor

There are a couple of downsides to these products:

>> **Expensive:** They're pricey in comparison to cal hypo or liquid. They typically cost about $7 to $10 a pound at the time of writing, which makes it a much less economical choice, compared to cal hypo (which you can read about in the section "Cal hypo," later in this chapter).

>> **Contain CYA:** CYA levels will rise when you use dichlor and trichlor shocks, and that level change can cause the stabilizer reading to become too high. Once that begins to happen, your chlorine stops working as affectively and reversing these effects is not always easy. I cover more on high CYA in Chapter 9.

Cal hypo

Calcium hypochlorite, more commonly called cal hypo, is a type of chlorine widely used all over the pool world. The main reason for that is that it is less expensive than most. It is usually in a granular form, sold in buckets or 1-pound bags, and is a very reactive chlorine. It should always be kept away from all other chemicals just to be safe, as there is a good chance it doesn't play nice with what's next to it.

TIP

When you add this product to your pool, either pre-dissolve it in a bucket or brush it in the water until it dissolves completely. You can add some of the cal hypo to a bucket of pool water and mix it with a stick until it is mostly dissolved. This will allow you to pour the mixture into the pool and prevent a lot of settling. You still want to brush any settling granules as they can bleach the surface if they lie there for too long.

The positives of cal hypo

Some of the pros to this chemical are

>> **Contains no CYA:** This product won't raise the CYA (chlorine stabilizer) number in your pool at all, which means you won't have to worry about that going out of range and causing you problems like you would with drichlor or trichlor (high CYA level issues are explained in Chapter 9).

>> **Inexpensive:** Costing around $4 to $6 a pound, cal hypo is a less expensive shock product than dichlor or trichlor (which I talk about in the section "Dichlor and trichlor, earlier in this chapter).

The negatives of cal hypo

A few cons to cal hypo are

>> **Can raise your pool water's calcium hardness levels:** Because it's made of a calcium base, over time, using cal hypo shocks will raise your calcium levels, which can lead to scaling or cloudy water. In Chapter 9, I cover all of the side effects of high calcium hardness levels.

WARNING

>> **Hazardous to use:** This chemical is incompatible with pretty much all other chemicals in its concentrated. If cal hypos mixes with another chlorine or a bottle of algaecide, it can cause a very dangerous chemical fire or create gasses that can be deadly to inhale.

>> **Difficult-to-follow directions:** Cal hypo is very commonly used incorrectly because it is either not pre-dissolved and bleaches the surface of the pool

after it settles or it is poured down the skimmer (which is a big no-no) and causes an explosion in the system. It can also rust out metal components in the filter.

The last thing you want to do is add cal hypo to your pool through the skimmer. In some instances, putting cal hypo through your skimmer could unintentionally cause an explosion or ruin internal parts of your filter or pump.

Liquid shock

Liquid chlorine (or liquid shock) is known as *bleach* to a lot of people, and although it contains the same main ingredient as household bleach, it's not exactly the same. Liquid chlorine that's used for pools will have a much higher percentage of sodium hypochlorite in it than household bleach and contains no additional additives.

TIP

I personally think liquid shock is the best option because it doesn't have any other chemicals added to it, such as calcium or cyanuric acid. It does have a high pH to it, so over time, it can raise your pool water's pH level. But if you're using trichlor tablets for maintenance sanitation (which you can read about in Chapter 10), the low pH of those tablets tends to somewhat balance out.

The positives of liquid shock

Here are a couple of good things about liquid shock to keep in mind:

>> **Inexpensive:** Compared to dichlor and trichlor (see the section "Dichlor and trichlor," earlier in this chapter), liquid shock is inexpensive, typically running at $6.00 a gallon, which will treat 15,000 gallons of water at 12.5%.

>> **Easy to use:** Because it's liquid, there's no pre-dissolving or brushing needed, which you may need with powdered chlorine, whether it's dichlor, trichlor, or cal hypo.

The negatives of liquid shock

A couple of downsides to this product are

>> **May cause damage to clothing:** Liquid chlorine can ruin your clothes because if it splashes on you, it will bleach the color out of wherever it touches and possibly even lead to holes in those spots.

>> **Can be an irritant:** Be cautious not to get it into your eyes; rinse your eyes with water for 15 minutes and seek medical attention immediately.

>> **Bulky to store:** Most of the time, liquid chlorine is sold in 1-gallon or 5-gallon bottles, and they tend to be heavy and not very user friendly.

Hydrogen Peroxide — Not Just for Cuts!

Hydrogen peroxide is an excellent oxidizer for biguanide-based systems (flip to Chapter 10 for information about the different sanitation systems), which comes in only liquid form. And really, hydrogen peroxide is the only way to properly oxidize your water if you have a biguanide-based system. You can't use anything chlorine based because chlorine and biguanide are not compatible chemical systems, and non-chlorine shocks, such as MPS (see "The other guy — potassium monopersulfate," earlier in this chapter), can end up causing more problems than they solve.

Some bonuses to working with hydrogen peroxide in your biguanide pool are

>> It works incredibly well on bacteria, algae, and organic waste, such as sweat and lotions.

>> It's fast acting, and you can safely swim in your pool within one hour of adding it.

>> Because it is a liquid, it is nice and easy to use! It can be poured directly into the pool while the pool is running, and depending on what brand of biguanide-based chemicals you are using, the program will either recommend weekly additions or monthly.

The big thing you want to remember with hydrogen peroxide for pools is that it's nine times more potent than medical grade peroxide. The stuff we use on our cuts is only 3 percent, but the pool shock is 27.5 percent. Because of this higher percentage, you will need less product to get the same job done.

WARNING

If you get this product on your skin, you'll experience a whitening of the skin that it comes into contact with, along with a burning, stinging sensation. This discoloration can last up to an hour, and it feels like you're being stung by an insect the whole time. If you get pool hydrogen peroxide on your skin, be sure to rinse it thoroughly with water to prevent this unpleasant outcome. If you get this hydrogen peroxide in your eyes, rinse your eyes in fresh water for 20 minutes. Seek professional medical care if symptoms persist after you thoroughly rinse the area.

Don't use hydrogen peroxide in chlorine pools because it works like a chlorine neutralizer (meaning manually bringing chlorine levels down at a fast rate) and can also cause some cloudy water side effects. If you're intentionally trying to bring your chlorine levels down, you can accomplish that by adding hydrogen peroxide. Just remember that it's possible you'll have to deal with physical chemical reactions such as cloudy or even smelly water.

Arming against Algae

If you're in a climate where your pool season is six months or shorter, having a pool that you can't use because of algae is one of the worst things that can happen. Algae is not only unsightly, but it can also make bathers sick. It's possible to get inner ear infections, bacterial eye infections, rashes on your skin, and even symptoms that are similar to a stomach virus (nausea, fever, diarrhea, and so on). Never swim in a pool that has an algae bloom, even a mild one. An algae bloom is typically a sign of low sanitation, and that can cause its own illnesses.

Preventing algae is one of the best money savers you can do for yourself. I know it seems counterintuitive because it's another chemical to buy and add routinely. But, just like oxidizing your pool regularly prevents a nasty buildup of byproducts and foreign contaminants, adding an algaecide regularly prevents the buildup of algae. Preventing an algae bloom is always much less hassle and money than treating it after it has taken over your pool.

In the following sections, I explain the different types of products to use to prevent algae (for a deeper look on the kinds of algae that can disrupt your pool and what to do if that happens, see Chapter 12).

Types of algae products

There are a lot of algae control products out there for you to use, and picking the right one for your pool can sometimes be tricky. All of them are in liquid form for easy application. When it comes to algae-related products, you are using them for two reasons, maintenance or treatment.

The common kinds of algae products are

>> Copper-based algaecides

>> Quatalgistats

>> Poly, also known as polyquat algaecides

Here's the difference between an algaecide and an algistat:

>> An *algaecide* kills algae.

>> An *algistat* helps kill algae and prevents algae growth.

All of these products can be used as preventatives, but not all are good for treatment.

Copper algaecides

Copper algaecides are one of the best and worst algaecides available:

>> **The best:** They're incredibly effective algaecides and actually have some bacteria-killing qualities. They can be used weekly, or you can add them every three months. And they have no foaming side effects.

>> **The worst:** This type of algaecide isn't all that great because the copper can have some unfortunate, and unsightly, side effects. The side effects include staining on pool surfaces, causing green hair, and turning the water green.

WARNING

Copper algaecide isn't ideal for biguanide or salt-based pools. The copper level in the product will react with the biguanide, effectively neutralizing the biguanide. And with salt-to-chlorine generators, the copper can actually cause damage to the plates on the inside of the generator, which can lead to the salt generator needing to be replaced.

Copper can be in an algaecide in one of two forms, chelated and non-chelated. That really means the copper is either bonded or unbonded with something in the water. Chelated copper won't cause negative side effects such as staining on the pool surface or steps, or light-colored hair being tinted green, but of course, the chelated version is always a little more expensive.

Using copper-based algaecides is highly effective. If you don't use them for maintenance, you can always use them for treatment. This algaecide treats all kinds of green, yellow, and black algae more effectively than any other algaecide. If you're willing to pay the extra money to buy chelated copper products and use this chemical regularly, you'd have to really try to get an algae bloom.

Quat algistats

Next, we have quaternary ammonium (quat)-based algistats. I don't call it an algaecide because unless you use a lot of the product, it doesn't have algaecide qualities to it. So it's great at keeping the problems away, but it's not great at shutting them down after they start.

This product is completely metal free, so you don't have any issues with staining or green hair like you would with some copper algaecides. But it does have the bad side effect of foaming. The foaming can range from a few bubbles on the surface when you splash all the way to a frothy bubble bath in severe cases. Because of this side effect, this product isn't recommended for a pool that has any type of water feature. Anything that will agitate the surface consistently and excessively is really not a good mix with a quat algistat.

If you use a quat algistat as your maintenance algae control product in a regular pool that has no water features, you won't really notice any foaming. The only time you may notice it is if you have to put a large dose of this chemical in at one time. Usually, you add a large amount of a quat algistat in the beginning as your initial dose or to treat algae in the case of an algae bloom.

On the plus side, quat algistats are safe for all pool and chemical types. It takes a lot of the guess work out of finding the right algae treatment. It's also the least expensive option that you can use, so it can't hurt to try it.

Poly algaecide

The actual name for this algaecide is incredibly long — poly-oxyethylene-dimethyliminio-ethylene-dimethyliminio-ethylene dichloride. (I told you!) So it's commonly referred to as poly or polyquat algaecide. This type of algaecide has a lot of really great features. It's completely metal free (unlike copper algaecides, discussed in the section "Copper algaecides," earlier in this chapter) and has no foaming side effects (unlike quat algistats, which you can read about in the preceding section), so poly algaecide is the best of both worlds. It can be used as a preventative and for treatment, and it's safe for all types of pools. This, in my opinion, is the best and most well-rounded option if you're not going for a hybrid option (which I talk about in the following section).

These are the only real downsides to this product:

>> **Limited efficacy:** It's not super great on black algae and yellow mustard algae.

It's highly effective on green algae, though, which is much more common. Poly algaecide is also great on bio-slimes such as white water mold and pink slime.

>> **Expensive:** Tends to be the most expensive option ($40 for a quart) for algaecides, especially if you're getting a 60 percent active ingredient option. That's the strongest it gets, and I think it is totally worth it.

IN THIS CHAPTER

» Figuring out why your pool water is cloudy and the best way to clear it

» Dealing with unwanted visitors in the form of algae and bacteria

» Making sure your pool looks and smells great

» Avoiding swimmer discomfort

» Identifying the cause when your pool water can't keep chlorine

Chapter **12**

Solving the Problems in Your Pool Water

As much as you want a swimming pool to be a perfectly clear oasis with no problems or hard work, that's unfortunately not possible. Now, that's not to say your pool can't be without problems for a whole year — that's definitely possible! But the likelihood of your pool needing some elbow grease from time to time has a high probability. The thing with pools is that, most of the time, there's an underlying reason for any issues that arise: It could be a lack of sanitation because you just had a big rainstorm or your gardener recently fertilized the plants around your pool deck. Knowing the root of the problem is just as important as treating it because, most of the time, it's easier to treat a disease after you have a diagnosis.

If your pool is cloudy and you just start throwing clarifiers at it without trying to figure out how or why it started, you could be throwing money into a cure that won't ever work. In some cases, trial and error with different treatment options can end up solving your problem: You'll hit the right combo and your water issue will correct itself. But that particular combo may not be the right combo every time, so if you use that same regiment every time you have a similar-looking problem, the results may vary.

Basically, in this chapter I do my best to explain to you how it happened (whatever the problem might be), as much as I show you how to fix it. Both of those things are equally important in keeping your pool in tip-top shape with the smallest amounts of chemicals and labor as possible! From cloudy water to slime to staining, I get down and dirty to cover these issues and more, and I offer up fix-it tips to get you in the clear.

Identifying How Your Pool Got Cloudy

Cloudy water is one of the most complex obstacles to navigate. There are a multitude of causes, and sometimes it's more than one cause at a time. What also makes correcting cloudy water more difficult is that with each filter type, your treatment course may be different.

I've figured out over my years of pool care that there are four main reasons for having cloudy water in your pool. You might have a problem with

>> Sanitation

>> Filtration and/or circulation

>> A chemical imbalance

>> Past or present contaminants getting into the pool

All of these possibilities are common causes. And although some of them can be fixed the same way, not all of them can be and not every time. In the following sections, I go over how each suspect may be the cause for your cloudy water.

A sanitation situation

Sanitizing your pool is what keeps the water clear, clean, and safe. (I go into all the details about sanitation in Chapter 10.) So, if your water isn't looking pristine, sanitation is a great place to start.

A lack of sanitation in the water will lead to a buildup of bacteria, and outside contaminants will also lead to cloudiness in your pool. If your pool is chlorine based and you haven't shocked it in over seven days, there's a strong possibility that your water will start to grow enough bacteria to lead to cloudy water. *Shocking* is the act of adding in specific oxidizing chemicals like chlorine-based products to break down organic and inorganic material left behind by regular sanitation. I go into detail about shocking in Chapter 11.

It is also very possible that even if your pool does get shocked every seven days and you have a stable feed of chlorine being contributed to the water, those measures aren't enough to prevent bacteria growth. If your chlorine level was 1.5 parts per million (ppm) on Friday morning, then you had four people use the pool for four hours in the sun that afternoon, your 1.5 ppm could be less than 0.5 ppm by the evening. At that number, bacteria basically have free reign of the pool — and voila, cloudiness!

A filtration and circulation issue

Proper filtration and circulation play a huge part in proper sanitation and cleaning up debris, and these processes are also responsible for removing things from the water that aren't supposed to be in there. That can range from dead algae floating around, to pollen, to sunscreen oil slicks.

If your pool begins to get cloudy and your sanitation levels are where they need to be (see the preceding section), it may be because your filter is either not filtering properly, or your filter is not filtering for long enough at a time.

In the following sections, I cover good ways to keep up with proper filtration and circulation. These tips are good to know for when you need to make adjustments.

Keeping proper filtration

REMEMBER

The simple rule for proper filtration time is between 8 and 12 hours of filtration time every day. The exact amount of time a day your pool should filter is really based on the size, the pump size, and the hydraulics of the system (for more on filters, see Chapter 3). But to make it easy, run your pool pump as often as you can — a minimum of 8 hours and during the day. If you forget to turn the pump on, or if you're running it only 5 hours a day at night in the middle of the summer, you may end up with some cloudy water.

TIP

In my professional opinion, the best time to run your pump and filter is during the times the sun is the hottest because stagnant water is a much better environment for algae growth, and during the hot times of the day that is especially perfect for a bloom. The hottest time of day changes while the seasons change, so your filter time can change with it. But you want your pump on during the day. If you only run your pump at night, your pool water is stagnant in the heat, day after day, and your pool is more likely to develop cloudy water or algae growth.

Maintaining proper circulation

In Chapter 3, I go over the proper techniques for getting your pool's circulation as perfect as you can get it. Although filtration is a key player, it's nothing without proper circulation. If you have your pump running 24 hours a day but your water flow is moving only 25 percent of the pool, you're not doing a whole lot of good.

Here's a quick summary (you can get the details in Chapter 3):

>> **Return jet angle:** You want your return jets facing down and away from your skimmer at a 45-degree angle.

>> **Jet angle variation:** If you have more than two returns, you can have one angled up towards the surface for better skimming action (making sure all the other returns are facing at a 45-degree angle down).

   If you faced all of the return jets towards the surface, then you'd only ever move the top 18 inches of water.

>> **With or without suctions:** Circulation does improve if you have suctions at the bottom of the pool. But not all pools have those suctions. And if your pool does have these suctions, you don't want to rely on them to give you all of the circulation you need because the flow of the water is most efficient the more times you can turn it over. The more suctions you can pull from the better.

A chemical imbalance

The balance of your pH, alkalinity, and calcium hardness will directly affect the visual quality of your water (see Chapter 9). Balancing the chemicals in your pool water isn't optional if you want a safe and long-lasting pool.

If you have water that looks hazy or severely cloudy, take a moment to check your water's chemical balance. Here are tips about what to check for and how to solve imbalances you may find. If any of these values are too high, they can cause cloudy pool water:

>> **pH:** If your water's pH level is at 8.3.

>> **Alkalinity:** If your alkalinity level is over 160 ppm.

>> **Calcium or cyanuric acid:** Both of those things can cause cloudy water as well in severe enough cases, although they are less commonly the cause.

REMEMBER

If either your pH level or your alkalinity level is elevated, your chlorine levels may now be ineffective.

If you're dealing with cloudy water, always check your sanitation levels first. But you might as well check the balance of the other variables that can be problematic at the same time.

A sudden change

A good idea, if you aren't sure where to start, is to think back to two days before your pool water got cloudy. Events such as these might affect your water clarity:

>> A big rainstorm

>> Multiple days with temperatures over 90 degrees Fahrenheit and a lot of sunshine

>> A summer party for your kid's soccer team

>> When friends came over for drinks and tanning

Your cloudy-water cause could be as simple as forgetting to turn the filter on for a day or forgetting to put in your weekly dose of shock.

Here are some more obvious causes of cloudiness:

>> The gardeners recently landscaped around your pool deck and filled the pool with debris.

>> You accidentally added 10 pounds of a chemical when you should have added 2 pounds.

>> You just added a product to your pool that you've never added before, which created an instant cloudy-water reaction.

Cloudy water means contaminants

The first thing a doctor asks when you show up with a broken bone is, "How did this happen?" They make you think about what led you up to your situation. With a pool, the cloudy water may not have as obvious an explanation as a broken bone would, but it does have an explanation. Your pool doesn't change for no reason; it changes because of outside variables. And those variables caused the change — either their presence or absence.

REMEMBER

If the water condition changed in a matter of days — or sometimes even hours — there's always a main trigger that started it. The majority of the time, it happens from excessive contaminants entering the water at one time.

If your water isn't clear, that means there are particles floating around in the pool water. Chemicals alone won't make those particles just disappear; they either fall to the bottom or get caught in your filter. So filtration is a huge key factor in clearing a cloudy pool:

>> **Tackling green algae:** If your pool was a green swamp and you added a bunch of shock and algaecide products into the water to kill the algae, the algae will die and turn white. That dead white algae will still be in the water, so filtering it out is really the next step to get your water clear.

>> **Dealing with water mold:** If you had any kind of water mold in your pool, that can cause cloudiness in your water, which is treated the same way that you treat green algae. You add in your shock and algaecide products and let it filter to remove the actual particles from the pool water.

TIP

If your pool had any kind of previous issue, such as algae or white water mold, that's likely your cause for cloudy water. Start by treating the living bacteria and algae first, and then proceed to treat the cloudiness by following the steps in the following section.

Noting the level of cloudiness

To help you identify how cloudy your water is, I break down the severity of the water's condition into three stages:

>> **Stage 1:** Light cloudiness. On an inground pool, you can see the bottom of the deep end. I consider that to just be hazy. For above grounds, you can see the bottom of the pool and recognize a leaf shape versus a frog clearly.

>> **Stage 2:** Medium cloudiness. In this stage, you can see that there is debris on the floor but maybe not exactly what it is when looking in the shallow end of an inground pool or at the bottom of an above ground pool. For inground pools, you cannot see the bottom of the deep end at this stage.

>> **Stage 3:** Heavy cloudiness. If you can't see more than one or two steps down into any pool, that's a severe problem.

Clearing Up a Cloudy Situation

All of the different causes of cloudy water have different solutions. I go over each possible cause and offer up some ways to correct each situation in the following sections, based on your pool water's stage of cloudiness (see the preceding section).

Sanitation

Check your sanitizer levels first by using a home testing kit. If the pool is cloudy and the sanitation seems low (see preceding section "A sanitation situation" to know what proper levels to look for), add shock products to the water. Add enough shock to compensate for the severity of the cloudiness. Be sure that if your pool is salt or chlorine based that you use shock that is chlorine based. Follow these tips, depending on your pool water's stage of cloudiness:

>> **Stage 1:** A normal dose of your regular shock products will almost always fix your problem.

>> **Stage 2:** Double the amount of shock you'd normally add. This amount of shock will most likely be enough to fix your problem. Also, let your pump and filter run for at least one 24-hour cycle. If the pool water's clarity doesn't improve at all and the chlorine is still low or even zero after that 24 hours, repeat the process (it means you're dealing with high contaminate levels and your chlorine was used up). If the pool looks no better but the chlorine is way above 5 parts per million (ppm), move on to the following section, "Filters and circulation."

>> **Stage 3:** Have your pool water tested at a local pool store and get some help from the professionals. If you don't want to do that, you can either follow the instructions in the following section for your filter type or move onto the section "Floccing your pool," later in this chapter.

Treating cloudy water becomes easier the more experience you have with your pool throughout the seasons. You'll figure out that if your pool gets used heavily or if there's a lot of rain or outside contaminants, you'll need to overcompensate for that contamination. By overcompensate, I mean add extra sanitizer to kill the extra germs. Rain, parties, windstorms, dogs swimming — all these things make a pool thirsty for sanitation.

TIP

If you're not sure what may qualify as heavy use or enough rain, just use your at-home testing system to check your levels. If you do that every time you think there's a possibility that your pool needs extra attention, you become familiar with what does and doesn't affect your pool's sanitation levels; it becomes second nature, and you'll know what's okay and what's too much without even testing.

Filters and circulation

With different filters come different problems and corrections. And remember that circulation ties in with filtration because the water will only filter as well as it is being moved around.

Filter aids may be used for different filter systems. They are:

>> **Liquid water clarifiers:** Group the small microscopic particles together so that they become a larger particle that the filter can catch more easily. This type of product is mainly used in sand filters, but it can also be used in cartridge filters.

>> **Powdered filter aids:** Work in sand filters by making your sand a little *dirty*, which will fill the large gaps in the sand. The small gaps that are left will catch small particles.

>> **Flocculants:** A chemical that attracts particles in the water using positive and negative forces. (See the section "Floccing your pool," later in this chapter.)

In the following sections, I go over some solutions based on the type of filter you have.

With a sand filter

A sand filter, unlike other filter types, will usually need some form of a clarifier or filter aid to get your water back to its ideal quality. But start with identifying the cause of your problem.

DUE TO POLLUTION

If you had a large amount of contaminants, which you can get with a big party or a rainstorm, start by shocking your pool with your usual shock products. Follow these tips based on the water's stage of cloudiness:

>> **Stage 1:** A normal amount of shock will usually cure your problem.

>> **Stage 2:** Double your maintenance dose. After that treatment is added, allow your filter 24 hours of continuous filtration for maximum results.

>> **Stage 3:** Add a double dose along with a form of clarifier, filter aid, or floc.

DUE TO A FILTER AND CIRCULATION ISSUE

If the cause of your cloudy water wasn't a rapid increase in pollution, do a water test, even if it's just a home test. Make sure that the water is in prime condition and make any adjustments that you may need at the start.

If your water's balance seems to be in decent condition and your sanitation levels are at an ideal level (you want 2 to 3 ppm, at a minimum — flip to Chapter 10 for all the down and dirty about sanitation), then consider whether the issue is coming from filtration and circulation problems. To start treating a filtration and circulation issue, first determine the severity of the water condition. If you're able to see the bottom of the pool, start with just filtering the pool for 48 hours continuously. If the water doesn't improve after those 24 hours, move on to using filter aids.

TIP

A sand filter, unlike other filters, will work better when it gets slightly dirty from particles in the water. Let your filter build at least 5 pounds per square inch (psi) on the gauge before backwashing. (You can read all about filter pressure gauges and identifying the need for backwashing in Chapter 3.)

WARNING

Backwashing isn't good for your filter and doing it too often won't help you clear the water. Only backwash when needed.

If your water isn't super cloudy, start the clean-up process by using a liquid clarifier or a powdered filter aid — or you can go straight into using them together. If the water is severely cloudy, where you can't see more than 12 inches down, consider floccing your pool (which I talk about in the section "Floccing your pool," later in this chapter).

TIP

I personally think it's just easier to start by using both a liquid clarifier and powdered filter aid together to clear up the problem faster. To give your cloudy water this one-two punch, follow these steps:

1. **Add liquid clarifier directly to the pool's water.**

2. **Add the powdered filter aid into the skimmer.**

   From the skimmer, it will be sucked into the filter, where it will coat the sand.

3. **Allow the pool filter to run with both products for at least 48 hours before reassessing your water quality.**

   If you see an improvement, even a small one, it's working!

WARNING

   Always follow the instructions that you find on the chemical's bottle. Some liquid clarifiers will cause the water to become more cloudy, and you can clog your filter too quickly by overusing a filter aid.

4. **Keep using the clarifier and filter aid together.**

   Continue filtering and backwashing as needed until the pool is clear. And, as long as the other balancing chemicals (like pH, alkalinity, calcium, CYA, and chlorine) are kept in check, the pool is safe and swimmable.

TIP

If your filter is functioning properly, the preceding steps will get your water clear over a course of a few days to a week. If it's not improving, consider reading Chapter 4 to see whether there are some underlying issues that need to be addressed.

With a cartridge filter

With this kind of filter, your options are very similar to sand filters (see the section "With sand filters," earlier in this chapter), but you don't need powdered filter aids. Try these suggestions:

>> Add shock based on the severity of your cloudy water and let the pump and filter run for 24 continuous hours. If you see an improvement, continue with round-the-clock filtration until the pool is clear.

>> If the shock isn't working, get a water test done to determine whether there are any chemical issues that may be leading to a cloudy pool.

If you try both of the preceding suggestions with no success in three days, follow these steps:

1. **Make sure your filter is in good condition and spray it down thoroughly to clean it.**

   A cartridge filter works at its best if it's clean. Even if your pressure gauge isn't indicating a large pressure increase, keeping your filter extra clean is key to getting the water clear.

2. **Run the filter 24 hours a day.**

   With a clean and functional filter, there are very few particles that won't get caught by your filter, so 24-hour-a-day filtration should clear most issues if they're not from a lack of sanitation or a balance issue. (Those issues are discussed in Chapter 9.)

3. **(Optional) Add a liquid clarifier to speed up the clearing process.**

   Adding a liquid clarifier to your pool water will allow the filter to catch those really small particles faster, which will clear the pool water faster.

TIP

If you're running your filter continuously for days on end and keeping up with cleaning the filter, and there's little to no improvement on the water's quality, you may have an alternate issue. Turn to Chapter 4, where I discuss reasons why your filter may not be functioning the way that it should, which can mean your water will never get clear.

With a DE filter

If there's one thing that I like to stress anytime I talk about diatomaceous earth (DE) filters, it's that when they are working properly, it's almost impossible to have cloudy water. If you have a DE filter and cloudy water, start simple by following these steps:

1. **Test your chemicals.**

   Whether it's a lack of sanitation and the pool just needs to be shocked, or the balance of some of the core chemical levels is off and needs to be adjusted, chemical issues are commonly the cause for a DE filter pool having cloudy water.

WARNING

   I don't ever recommend using any kind of clarifier if you have a DE filter. If you use one, it will most likely cause the filter to become clogged faster than needed and make it so that you need to backwash too often. A clarifier should never be necessary if you have a DE filter because this type of filter can catch any particle in your pool.

2. **Shock the pool.**

   If you shock your pool and it has good balance on your other levels such as pH, alkalinity, calcium, and CYA, and then you run it for 24 hours, it will almost always cure your cloudy water.

REMEMBER

If the severity of the cloud is really bad because you're dealing with the dead algae from an algae bloom, run the filter for 24 hours a day until the water is clear — and backwash when it needs it. (See Chapter 3 for details on knowing when to backwash.)

In the case of a really severe cloud to your pool water, even with a DE filter, I sometimes recommend floccing the pool if you have the ability. Because the DE filter is so efficient, if you're trying to clear a severe cloud, the filter may get clogged too quickly and be more work than you have time for. If you have the time and ability to backwash the filter as needed — which could be hourly — then you can certainly do that. Unless something obvious, such as an algae or water mold bloom happened and caused the water to be cloudy, there's a high probability that the pool is cloudy because of a problem with the filter itself.

TIP

In Chapter 4, I cover a few key things that could lead to a DE filter allowing the diatomaceous earth back into the pool. That would cause the water to become severely cloudy, and it wouldn't improve if you kept the filter running. If anything, it may get worse! So, if you shock your pool, check your chemical balance, filter continuously, and backwash when needed, it should fix your cloudiness. If it doesn't, check out Chapter 4.

Chemical correction

Keeping your pool's chemicals in balance is an important component of clear water. To keep the balance, check your pool water's chemistry as frequently as you can, but a minimum of once a week. (See Chapter 9 for the details on keeping your pool water's chemicals in balance.)

If you find your water is cloudy, test your pool to see which levels are off:

>> **Low sanitizer levels (chlorine, bromine, or biguanide):** A lack of sanitation, which is fixed by shocking the pool.

>> **High pH or total alkalinity:** Add in sodium bisulfate to decrease both.

>> **High CYA:** Can prevent your sanitation levels from functioning at all, which is adjusted by partially draining and refilling your pool with fresh hose water to dilute the level.

All of these are common chemical causes for cloudy water and should be adjusted before any other steps.

TIP

If you're ever unsure about what steps to take or how much of which chemicals to add, check with your local pool professional. Your at-home testing system isn't as accurate as the tests you can have run in stores, and you don't want to over- or under-adjust your numbers. If you don't have a local pool store, just make adjustments in small doses, giving four to six hours between each dose, so that you don't overdo anything. Sometimes, coming back from an overcorrection is complicated and takes time. For more information, flip to Chapter 9, which can help you better understand what to look for in balanced versus unbalanced chemical levels and how to properly look for them.

Floccing your pool

Floccing your pool is the process by which you add flocculant chemicals to your pool water. *Flocculants* are substances that promote clumping of materials. So while the flocculants sink to the bottom of the pool, they clump with and carry everything suspended in the water with them.

Most flocculants work within 24 hours, but some can take up to 72 hours. I personally use a liquid floc when I need to because they tend to work more quickly than the powdered floc. Here are the differences between the two:

>> **Powdered floc:** The active ingredient is usually aluminum sulfate.

>> **Liquid floc:** One of a few different combinations of chemicals.

TECHNICAL
STUFF

The chemicals in liquid floc are *cationic,* meaning they're positively charged ions. Their positive charge allows them to attract the negatively charged suspended particles in the water.

Here are a few key things to remember before floccing your pool:

- **Your pool water level has to be higher than normal.** After the particles and floc settle to the bottom of the pool, they create a very fluffy thin layer that must be vacuumed out of the pool with your filter on the Waste setting. In this process of removing the flocced materials from the pool, you'll lose between 4 and 8 inches of water, depending on how quickly you move and how big your pool is.

- **Your filter needs to be able to vacuum to waste.** In Chapter 7, I cover how to vacuum to waste and how to determine whether you even can. Basically, all sand filters can vacuum to waste, most inground DE filters can, and the majority of cartridge filter systems can't unless they've been specially plumbed to do so.

WARNING

It's possible that floccing simply won't work, that the flocculant product doesn't sink. This can happen for a few reasons, such as adding too much floc or adding too much algaecide prior to floccing. The floc can take up to 72 hours to sink and must remain completely undisturbed and unmoving until then. This can be a really inconvenient process to follow in the middle of July when everyone is itching to swim.

Floccing a pool is usually my last choice in clearing a cloudy pool because the process takes a while, and the pool is unusable during that process. If your pool is severely cloudy, floc only if you can't seem to make progress with the methods I talk about in the preceding sections.

From Algae to Mold: Taking Care of Unwanted Growth

Even with the most diligent regiment of pool care, it's possible that, once in a while, your pool will start to grow a little something-something. It can be as minor as some algae on the steps to a full-blown swamp with frogs swimming around after you take a week away on vacation. Either way, the treatment is basically the same. You need to determine the severity of the situation and then attack it accordingly. Your goal is to terminate all living things in the water and then remove the remains so that you can get back to having a beautiful, clean, and clear pool.

Identifying algae

Here are some identifying features to determine which kind of algae you may have:

>> **Green algae:** Can have a yellowish coloring to it, but it looks slimy and sticks to surfaces.

>> **Yellow mustard algae:** Kind of looks like what green algae looks like after it dies and falls to the floor. Yellow mustard algae has a yellow-beige color to it and settles to the floor like sand. It's fluffy, and if you brush it, it just settles right back down.

Yellow mustard algae can also sometimes be confused with sand or DE on the floor, so check to make sure it isn't that first. Mustard algae is much finer of a settlement. DE looks more like mud and is heavier and gathers in patches. Sand has a very obvious consistency that you can feel if you scoop some up. Mustard algae is like a cloud, very fluffy and easily disturbed.

>> **Black algae:** Looks more like black spots or stains. Picture the mold that can grow under your sink — small black patches. It can start off pretty minor and look non-threatening, but if you don't get on top of it right away, it can take over your pool.

On liner pools, black algae tends to be a little easier to wipe off, but on plaster pools, it won't budge when you brush it. That's how you know what you're dealing with has roots and many layers of protection.

TIP

There are excellent reference photos of these all over the internet. But if you need to confirm with anyone, I recommend asking your local pool professional. It's easy to post a photo of what's growing in your pool on a local pool-help Facebook page and get a million wrong answers. Ask a professional to be sure you're treating it properly based on what exactly it is.

Going from green to clean

Green algae growth is the number one problem you'll deal with when it comes to something living in your pool. I'm sure that, if you have a pool or are even considering having a pool, you've heard of the dreaded algae. In fact, there are over 20,000 different varieties of this pesky green slime, but they're all treated in a similar way.

REMEMBER

Even though you may treat them all the same way, that doesn't mean they'll react the same way. You may treat an algae bloom with a certain regiment one time, and the next time it doesn't work.

An *algae bloom* is an excessive growth of algae in a body of water. It can be caused by contaminants in the water, warm temperatures, and an abundance of sunlight.

Make sure that all of the other elements that go into keeping your pool clean are where they need to be before you begin treating for algae. If you start treating it without proper chemical balance or circulation (which are covered in the preceding sections), you won't get the proper results from your work:

>> Your pool balance levels are in their proper ranges.

>> Your filter is in functional condition with good circulation.

If you just start shocking your pool to try to kill the algae but your filter is barely running because it's so dirty, or the pH is so high that the chlorine you're adding is basically useless, then you're wasting your time and money.

The following sections guide you through getting your water clear and free of green algae.

Testing the water

In a chlorine-based pool (or a salt-to-chlorine pool), your path to a clean pool starts with prep work. The prep begins with a water test, at home or in a store. Check the water is to make sure that whatever treatment chemicals you're planning to add to get rid of the algae are going to be effective. All of your balancing numbers work together, and if one is off, the system can collapse. These are your major chemical-balance priorities for algae treatment:

>> pH at 7.2 to 7.6

>> CYA at 30 to 50 parts per million (ppm)

The pH and CYA are the two values that will cause you the most problems if they're off.

For non-chlorine-based pools like biguanide, your job is the same. Ensure all of your balancing chemicals like pH, alkalinity, and calcium hardness are in their ideal ranges and adjust them if they are not.

Vacuuming up the algae

After you make sure your water chemical levels are where you need them (see the preceding section), spend some time brushing and/or vacuuming the bulk of the algae:

>> **Vacuum to waste.** If you have a bad algae bloom — bad enough that you can't see the bottom of the pool — you're best off vacuuming the majority to waste if you have that option. (Check out Chapter 7 for the details on vacuuming to waste.)

>> **Brush, shock, and run the pump and filter:** If you can't vacuum to waste, you're basically stuck brushing the pool to get all of the algae suspended in the water, and then shocking the pool heavily, along with a strong dose of algaecide. If you have a specific kind of algaecide that you are used to, you can use the treatment dose of that product for algae blooms. Then continue filtering your pool as normal until all dead algae has been removed.

Shocking the pool

If you're treating algae in a chlorine- or bromine-based pool, do a minimum of a double dose of your regular chlorine-based shock product.

TIP

If you don't have a regular shock product yet, I personally find liquid shock to be my favorite because it is inexpensive and works quickly.

If you're using liquid shock, you add 2 gallons of 12.5 percent sodium hypochlorite per 15,000 gallons of water. Your main objective here is to make sure you add enough chlorine to the pool to break through the entirety of your algae problem. Typically, you're looking to reach a chlorine level of 10 ppm at a minimum — slightly higher is okay, but not lower because then you will be opening the door for the algae to bloom due to lowering chlorine levels. In some cases, algae can regenerate in as little as three hours if the environment allows it, so you want to make sure you kill it all the first time.

Adding algaecide

During the time of an algae bloom, you will want a strong algaecide on your side to give your shock the extra hand it needs to kill the plant. The best algaecides for killing algae are poly or copper-based algaecides because they are the stronger more effective options. In Chapter 11, I cover in depth the benefits and cons of the two options.

TIP

After choosing your algaecide, you want to add in the algae treatment dose that is listed on the bottle of the algaecide you are using. It is to be added at the same time as your shock treatment and can be added directly to the pool water.

Running the filter

Run the filter overnight. The next day, you're looking for a few things in your pool water:

>> A clear (or clearer) pool

>> A chlorine level in the ideal range (2 to 4 ppm)

>> Very little to no combined chlorine

When you test the pool the next day, if the chlorine level is lower than 2 ppm and the water is still green or cloudy, repeat the process from the preceding sections until the pool is clear. Run and clean your filter as often as you need to. If your pool is cloudy the next day but your chlorine residual is still holding high, your worries now are strictly about clearing up the cloudy water. When the algae dies and you still hold a high chlorine residual, that means you killed all of the algae and had sanitation to spare. That's perfect!

You know you've successfully treated an algae bloom when:

>> Your pool is clear.

>> Your chlorine stays in a normal range after 12 hours.

>> Your combined chlorine is less than 0.5 ppm.

Troubleshooting for algae

If you follow the steps in the preceding sections but the pool doesn't improve at all — and you check your chlorine, and it's very low or even zero — that means you didn't add nearly enough chlorine in one dose. Try repeating the process with twice as much chlorine-based shock and filtering for another day.

Look for physical improvements in the water daily, and if you're not seeing that improvement, you're not adding enough chemicals to kill the algae. The key is to get the chlorine over 10 ppm and maintain it there until the pool clears up. You need to prevent the water from going back to green.

If the pool water isn't green anymore, only cloudy, the next day, but your combined chlorine is over 1 ppm, repeat the process in the preceding sections again. A combined chlorine of over 1 ppm indicates that your chlorine got to only partially do its job, and now it's locked in with the contaminants. Add another double dose of chlorine shock to break up the combined chlorine itself and break up whatever it's trying to combine with.

More truths on algae troubles

With algae treatment, there can sometimes be causes and solutions that are out-side of the normal recommendations. Not to say that my methods above have not proven themselves time and time again, but there are always ways that people are looking for that are faster, easier, and cheaper.

In this next section, I cover some algae related topics that touch on ways algae can be worsened, cured, or even misdiagnosed.

Is it algae, or is it metals?

A lot of times, people will find themselves with a green pool that's not green from algae. Metals in your water can become oxidized after being introduced to chlo-rine, and that can cause your water to turn a really pretty shade of green. (I go into problems with metals in your pool in the section "Staining and Discoloration from Metals," later in this chapter.) Green water caused by metals will usually be crys-tal clear, and the water itself has a green tint. In comparison, algae grows on the pool surface and usually starts to make the water cloudy.

There are three questions that you can ask yourself to figure out whether you have metal in your water:

>> **What's the water source?** Metals almost always come from your source water, typically a well. If you're filling the pool with city water, you're less likely to have a strong metal content, but it's not impossible. So, if you recently added water or you just filled the pool with water that you know has a high metal content, the chlorine you introduce after that will likely oxidize the metals and make them turn green (or an array of other colors).

>> **Does the situation improve with the addition of chlorine?** If you think your green-pool culprit is algae and add your chlorine shock, then the next day it looks exactly the same and your chlorine level stays high, it's likely metals causing the color. Algae is an organic contaminant, and removing it will use up your chlorine levels, but metals won't affect your chlorine levels at all.

>> **How does the water feel?** Not all people will touch the water to find this out! But algae will be slimy, and metals won't.

Check those phosphates

Over the last 10 years, phosphates in pool water have become another factor that can disrupt our easy-going pool care life. *Phosphates* are chemical compounds that contain phosphorus, which is essential for all living things. They're in everything and transfer through almost everything. The reason we pool people can't stand them is because they're an excellent source of nutrients for algae in pools. Due to their abundance and dramatic effect on the increase in algae growth, treating for them has become necessary for many pool owners. It can be taken care of in one big sweep, or it can be routinely kept up through weekly additions of phosphate removers.

The issue is that phosphates will always be introduced into the water, and so you end up with this cycle of treatment and removal. Phosphates are in your lawn fertilizers (or your neighbor's lawn fertilizers) and it is being added into drinking water because it does a great job at protecting the pipes underground from corrosion. Any time you walk through your grass to get to the pool, add water from your hose, or any time it rains, phosphates can enter your pool water and begin its job as an excellent source of nutrients for algae.

In pools, it's ideal to keep your phosphate levels below 150 parts per million (ppm). If you have phosphate levels higher than that, you begin to see algae growth. And the algae that feeds on phosphates are more difficult to kill than algae in a pool with phosphate levels lower than 150 ppm because now they have a great food source to keep regenerating. The phosphates themselves aren't harmful to you or your pool. They just have a habit of making you work harder to keep your pool green free. Look into treating them when they get over 500 ppm because that's when I most often notice that issues begin. Every pool is different, and how and when to treat phosphates is the choice of the pool owner.

Here's the way I look at it: If it isn't causing a problem, then there's no reason to fix it. But having an elevated phosphate level does come with some risks:

>> **Aiding algae:** Your pool is more prone to algae growth when the water contains phosphates, and that algae may be more complicated to get rid of.

>> **Hampering chlorine:** You may have issues with excessive chlorine usage. The phosphates are probably helping living organisms thrive in the water, so the chlorine is constantly in battle against those organisms. This back and forth will cause your chlorine levels to be harder to keep in their ideal ranges.

WARNING

>> **Calcifying:** There's the possibility that, with really high phosphate levels in a saltwater pool, you could create calcification on the salt generator platelets. The phosphates combine with the calcium hardness and cause a buildup on the generator, which can render it useless.

If you think the preceding list are problems you'd like to avoid, it's time to treat your phosphates. You want to start by getting a water test to determine your exact phosphate level and to ensure that your other balancing levels are in range so that you can start proper treatment.

If you're dealing with phosphate levels under 500 ppm, you can usually use a more mild treatment that can also be added into your weekly regiment. If your levels are over 500 ppm, or even into the thousands, you'll want to take a more aggressive approach and attack it with stronger forms of phosphate removers. See your local pool professional for help.

WARNING

Here's the catch about treating high phosphate levels — there's a high probability that you'll end up with a cloudy pool, if not worse. When you add a phosphate remover, it does exactly what the name says: It pulls the phosphates out of the solution of the water and drops them to the floor of the pool, often in a fluffy cloud-like layer. So then they have to be removed from the pool, ideally by *vacuuming to waste* (see Chapter 7). It's way too fine a consistency to be vacuumed, especially with a sand or cartridge filter. The fluff will either go right through the filter or clog it within a few swipes. This vacuuming to waste can be quite an annoying process because that fluffy cloud will poof up into the water if you make even the slightest movement close to it.

So, if you're treating a high level of phosphates in your pool water, I recommend breaking up that large initial dose of phosphate remover into small daily doses until you reach the full amount. This process will get the same job done when it comes to removing the phosphates from the water without the really annoying side effect of it settling all over the floor. After this big phosphate removal, you can begin using a more mild phosphate remover weekly to keep the levels from getting too high again.

The SLAM method and PoolRx

I think it's only appropriate that I cover two common pool fads that I read about on the internet. The SLAM method is a series of steps to take, not a product. In the section "Going from green to clean," earlier in this chapter, I go over how to clear an algae bloom in a chlorine-based pool. Basically, you get your pH and CYA into range, and then shock the pool to hit the breaking point for long enough to eliminate your problem. Well, the SLAM method is exactly that.

The SLAM method stands for shock, level, and maintain. The concept behind it is to not just shock your pool like you normally would by adding in a dose of shock and waiting to see what happens next (does the pool clear or look worse).

The first step in the process is to check your pH and CYA levels. Your pH should be around 7.2, which is on the low scale for regular balancing — normally 7.4 to 7.6. Your CYA will need to be between 30 and 50 ppm.

Next you shock your pool, but not like normal. It involves maintaining a high chlorine level of 12 ppm for a few days, and sometimes up to a week. To do that, you test the pool with your at-home kit and read the chlorine level. Your job is to maintain the chlorine level over 12 ppm continuously until the water is clear, free of any combined chlorine, and holds a consistent chlorine level overnight.

My only qualm with this particular method is that it should be used as a last resort for very stubborn algae problems, and not used just any time there is algae in the pool. You still want to learn the more basic techniques that I cover in this chapter because most of the time, a basic treatment will do the trick!

PoolRx, on the other hand, is something I'm pretty sure just resurfaced as a great pool cleaning technique because people want to find safe and chemical-free ways to sanitize their pools. PoolRx was actually founded in 1994 and has been pretty great since day one. It's a mixture of natural minerals, such as copper and silver. This mixture is highly effective at killing bacteria and preventing algae growth.

In Chapter 11, I dive into the different kinds of algaecides, one of which is copper based. Copper is a fantastic algaecide. Silver is another excellent algaecide, and it's also able to kill bacteria. Using PoolRX or any type of mineral system with chlorine together is smart, effective, and easy. I recommend all chlorine-based pools use a mineral add on to help kill bacteria and prevent algae growth. It will save you money on chlorine and algaecide because you won't have as much algae to kill!

WARNING

NOT SO MAGICAL MAGIC ERASERS

Magic Erasers are a viral fad that flooded the internet in the last few years. They were shown absorbing algae while in a pool skimmer, and everyone went wild. Here are the issues I have with Magic Erasers:

- **Toxic chemical reaction:** The component in Magic Erasers is melamine, which is not toxic. What is toxic, though, is the chemical reaction it has with the cyanuric acid (CYA) in your pool. It's really not safe to have in a chlorine pool under any circumstances.

- **Better options available:** The absorbing algae attribute is not something to write home about. There are far better and more effective ways to clean algae in a pool than to use your kitchen counter cleaner.

- **Liner pattern destroyer:** Warning to anyone who tries to use it on a liner — it's absolutely capable of removing the pattern from your vinyl.

Treating algae with biguanide or an Oxygen system

Green algae in a biguanide pool is less common than in a chlorine pool, and that's because the biguanide contains an algaestat and is a great sanitizer. If you're getting algae in a biguanide pool, follow these steps:

1. **Test and make sure other balancing chemicals (pH, alkalinity, calcium hardness) are in range.**

   They play less of a roll in a biguanide pool, but they do matter.

2. **Brush or vacuum your pool.**

   Brush or vacuum to waste if you need to. At a minimum, brush and get the stuff stuck to the bottom of the pool up into the solution of the water.

3. **Top off your biguanide.**

   The biguanide is your sanitizer, after all.

4. **Add hydrogen peroxide.**

   Add your hydrogen peroxide shock at 2 gallons of shock per 10,000 gallons of pool water.

5. **Do a treatment dose of your weekly algaecide (if you have one).**

   This step is especially important if the bloom is severe.

   If you don't use an algaecide and instead have an alternate weekly step, do your treatment or initial dose of that product.

6. **Run your filter 24 hours a day until your pool clears.**

7. **Repeat Steps 1 through 5 if your water doesn't clear up the first time.**

With an Oxygen pool (which I cover in Chapter 10), you can attack an algae bloom in one of two ways:

>> **Follow the preceding steps.** If you want to maintain a completely chlorine-free pool, you can follow the steps in the preceding list for biguanide systems, except you'd skip adding the actual biguanide (Step 3). An Oxygen pool should clear a little more quickly than a regular biguanide pool because when you run the filter, you're also having your Oxygen Ozone systems produce your sanitizer at the same time. You'll likely see a clear and clean pool by the end of the second day (depending on the severity).

>> **Use chlorine-based shock:** If you're dealing with a really bad algae bloom and want to use something a little more potent than hydrogen peroxide, use chlorine-based shock. Follow the steps for chlorine pools in the section "Going

from green to clean," earlier in this chapter. Oxygen is compatible with all chemical types, so you have a choice on how you want to handle treatment of water problems.

I personally would choose chlorine because it's inexpensive, quick, and easy. And the chlorine level will dissipate so quickly that you'll be chlorine free again in no time!

Breaking down black algae and yellow mustard algae

Some algae are just built different, and these two — black algae and yellow mustard algae — prove it:

>> **Black algae:** To start, I should clarify that black algae isn't, in fact, an algae at all. It's actually a type of bacteria called *cyanobacteria*. Black algae has roots that will imbed themselves into the surface of their choosing, making it incredibly hard to get rid of.

>> **Yellow mustard algae:** Unlike black algae, yellow mustard algae actually is an algae. And it's an incredibly stubborn one. Yellow mustard algae has a defense mechanism against the compounds of chlorine, even at high levels.

So, here's where each organism comes from:

>> **Yellow mustard algae:** Can get into your pool in from the rain, pollen, or trees around the pool

>> **Black algae:** Likely comes from a natural water source and was introduced to your pool through an unwashed bathing suit or pool float

All those potential sources are constantly introduced into your water, so it should be no surprise when they turn up in your pool. But these organisms can grow into a problem because of insufficient pool water care. It could be a bad balance of chemicals, a lack of proper sanitation, or poor circulation. The best way to prevent a black algae or yellow mustard algae bloom is by doing your weekly maintenance and keeping the pool properly filtering and sanitized.

Treating for yellow mustard algae

Yellow mustard algae is fairly resistant to chlorine, but you know what it's not resistant to? Sodium bromide, also known as bromine.

I've heard that you can use chlorine at extremely high levels to treat yellow mustard algae, such as adding a triple dose of shock, and it will work. But, in my experience, I've found bromine to be far more effective because it combines with chlorine creating hypobromous acid, which is much more aggressive on this kind of algae.

To treat yellow mustard algae in your pool, follow these steps:

1. **Make sure your water balance is perfect.**

   See Chapter 9 for all you need to know on balancing your pool chemicals.

2. **Remove as much of the yellow algae from the pool as possible.**

   The more algae you can remove by vacuuming (to waste, if possible) the more effective your treatment will be because there will be less algae remaining for the chlorine or bromine to have to kill.

3. **Add shock to your pool.**

   Depending on whether you want to use chlorine or bromine, follow these instructions:

   - *Chlorine:* Add a minimum of a triple dose of your preferred shock product. You don't have to use a certain product; any chlorine shock will do.

   - *Bromine:* You can sometimes find it in a small bottle that's labeled specifically as a yellow algae treatment. Add this powder along with a strong chlorine-based shock. You may not need to do a triple dose of chlorine shock, but you do want at least a double dose.

   If you have a biguanide-based pool, don't use chlorine or the bromine; add hydrogen peroxide at a rate of 2 gallons per 10,000 gallons of pool water.

4. **Add in a strong copper-based algaecide to your pool.**

   Minerals like copper or silver are excellent at killing algae.

   TIP

   If you can find a silver-based algaecide, it may be worth spending the extra money because silver works really well against yellow mustard algae if you are having a hard time getting rid of it.

5. **Run the filter 24 hours a day until you have no visual remnants of the algae.**

6. **Vacuum and brush your pool at least once a day until the algae seems gone.**

7. **Check your chlorine levels daily and add shock, as needed.**

Treating for black algae

Getting rid of black algae is a pain in the you-know-what. It's especially difficult in pools that have porous surfaces, such as plaster, which is where you tend to see black algae the most. To get rid of black algae, follow these steps:

1. **Check your water balance and make sure that it's perfect.**

   Get the pH and stabilizer where it needs to be so that you're not wasting any time or money. I go into the details of getting balanced pool water in Chapter 9.

2. **Shock the pool very heavily, ideally with a powdered chlorine.**

   If you use a powder, do a triple dose of chlorine (usually around 3 pounds of chlorine for every 10,000 gallons of pool water).

TIP

   If you have a white plaster pool, feel free to add calcium hypochlorite directly on top of the spots and let it sit. The surface can handle it, and the more direct chlorine you get on that black algae, the better.

3. **Add a strong copper-based algaecide (over 3% of copper).**

   Copper-based algaecide is the most effective algaecide on black algae.

4. **Brush your pool until your arms fall off.**

   Brush at least once a day and be thorough. It's so important that you get rid of the black algae's roots to prevent it from ever coming back.

TIP

   If you have a plaster surface, be sure to use a stainless-steel bristled brush for optimal results. The steel bristles can really break into the defensive layers of the bacteria and expose the part that you can kill.

REMEMBER

Clean your filter at the end of this treatment, especially if you did any vacuuming, to ensure that you get all of the bacteria out of the pool. This is a long process, and although the black algae itself isn't dangerous to swim in, it's not something that will easily go away and should be treated immediately.

Finding the origins of pink slime

Pink slime, also known as pink or red algae, has a pinkish-brown-red color to it, and it's slimy. You'll typically first see it inside your skimmer or on your steps. Pink slime isn't an algae. Similar to black algae (flip back to "Breaking down black algae and yellow mustard algae," earlier in this chapter), it's actually a bacteria. In severe cases, you'll start to see pink slime in low-flow areas in the pool, but its ideal environment is warm, dark places. Another place you may have seen pink slime is in your shower, maybe on your shower curtain or in the corners of the tub, because it likes the warm and moist environment.

It's hard to determine exactly where the bacteria may have come from in your pool, but it's usually airborne and naturally occurring, so it's hard to prevent it. You can only treat it before it gets bad. With a pool, you'll likely have the pink slime start in areas where you can't see it. It will start inside your filter, and then work its way through the pipes. And by the time you see it in your skimmer or on your return, it's already quite established. That's why it's so important to watch for the signs and to act quickly.

Pink slime is more commonly seen in a biguanide pool, but it can occur in chlorine pools, as well. So I cover how to know you have a pink slime invasion in your pool, as well as treatment options for both types of pool sanitation systems, in the following sections.

Signs of pink slime

If your pool has a DE or cartridge filter, with a pink-slime problem, you'll notice a spike in pressure, but the water still looks clear. If that happens, either

>> Backwash to see if you notice any red or pink, a sure sign of pink slime.

>> Add a quart of hydrogen peroxide in front of your skimmer slowly while the filter is running. If you notice bubbles coming from your return, that's a sign of bacteria in your filter.

Clean the inside of the filter thoroughly with a water-and-bleach solution, and then follow the treatment plans in the following sections (depending on what type of pool you have).

Another thing to look for is a sudden drop in your shock levels, which is especially important in biguanide-based pools because your hydrogen peroxide levels typically keep pretty consistent. In some systems, such as Baquacil CDX, the oxidizer level is kept high, in the 100-to-200 parts per million (ppm) range consistently, and a sudden drop will indicate the growth of a contaminant. If that happens, clean your filter then start treatment right away.

Treating pink slime in chlorine

Luckily for you, if you're using chlorine in your pool, there's a very slim chance you'll ever have this bacteria even start to grow. Chlorine is highly effective in killing this bacteria, and if your chlorine levels are properly maintained, then you'll never really see any pink slime in your pool.

The main reason you may get pink slime, or any water bio-slime, is because you have little to no chlorine in the pool while it's hot and the pool isn't circulating. It sort of has to be a perfect storm of neglect for pink slime to grow in a chlorine-based pool.

When it does happen, follow these steps:

1. **Test your water and be sure your balancing chemicals (pH, total alkalinity, calcium hardness, and CYA) and your chlorine levels are all in their ideal ranges.**

2. **Clean all removable items with a water-and-bleach solution.**

   This list includes floats, ladders, DE or cartridge filters, cleaning accessories, and things like that.

   TIP

   If you have a sand filter, you can add in an acidic filter cleaner to remove excessive pink slime remnants if you feel the issue is severe enough. This would be if you find the filter unable to backwash due to the amount of pink slime in the sand.

3. **Wash any bathing suits that may have been used within the last week or so.**

   You want to launder anything that may have been in the water since the pink slime started.

4. **Shock the pool.**

   You can usually do just a regular dose of your maintenance chlorine shock, but if you feel it needs something a little heavier, you can double it.

5. **Brush any surfaces the pink slime may be attached to.**

   Don't forget your pool walls and floor because you may not be able to see the pink slime, but it is likely already creating a layer on the floor and walls and you don't want to miss it.

   TIP

   You can use the rough side of a sponge to wipe down the inside of skimmers or returns.

6. **Run the filter for 24 hours.**

7. **After the pool is clear, clean, and holding chlorine levels resume your normal running settings.**

   If you are battling cloudiness or lack of chlorine, repeat Steps 4 through 7.

The problem should be rectified fairly quickly and won't return as long as you maintain proper water sanitation, balance, and filtration times.

Preventing pink slime in biguanide

Most biguanide pools will get pink slime as often as chlorine pools get green algae. There are ways to prevent it, and it's good to remember that prevention is cheaper than rectifying.

Pink slime will mostly happen during the hottest times of the year, so for most of the U.S., that's June, July, and August. During those times, to prevent bio-slimes, increase your filtration time and at least double the amount of 27.5 percent hydrogen peroxide oxidizer you add to your pool for maintenance. There are two ways your hydrogen peroxide gets added for maintenance:

>> Once a month in the dose of 1 gallon of hydrogen peroxide per 10,000 gallons of water

>> Weekly at 1 quart of hydrogen peroxide per 10,000 gallons of water

The dose is the same; one is just more spread out. I personally prefer adding your peroxide weekly, and in the hot months, I'd do a half-gallon of hydrogen peroxide per 10,000 gallons of water. Keeping those numbers higher has no negative effects on equipment or bathers, but it'll work really well to keep bio-slimes at bay.

TIP

When adding your maintenance dose of hydrogen peroxide, add it slowly about 6 inches from the front of your skimmer, which will allow your main defense against pink slime to attack the most common starting point, in the filter. If you start to get a lot of agitated bubbles coming from your returns, slow down even further or stop adding it there all together for safety's sake.

WARNING

Never add hydrogen peroxide into the skimmer! If you have pink slime or any other bacteria, the peroxide will foam when it comes in contact with bacteria. And this reaction can actually cause enough pressure to build in the filter that things can break or even explode.

Keep your sanitizer level on the higher end and keep your pH and calcium hardness in range. All of these factors together should be enough to prevent your pool from becoming overtaken by a water mold or bio-slime, but it isn't always enough. In some cases — especially in pools that get a lot of direct sunlight or ones that are surrounded by a lot of trees — it's more likely that pink slime will start anyway because the sunlight or tree droppings will give the pink slime a better environment for growth.

Treating pink slime in biguanide pools

The first symptom of pink slime in your biguanide-based pool will be that

>> Your filter clogs quickly, even if the water is clear.

>> The pool has started to become cloudy.

If you've noticed those two things, it's time to start treatment. Just follow these steps:

1. **Test your water to check all balancing chemical levels and sanitation levels.**

   For better accuracy, I always recommend having your water tested at a pool store.

2. **Clean all removable pool accessories with a water-and-bleach solution.**

   This includes ladders, floats, DE or cartridge filters, pool cleaning accessories, and so on.

3. **Brush the pool's floor and walls and any surface around the pool that has visible pink slime (such as in the skimmer, around the return, in or on steps/ladders in the pool).**

4. **Add hydrogen peroxide to your pool.**

   If the water isn't cloudy yet, you can usually fix the problem with a double initial dose of your hydrogen peroxide. That would be 2 gallons of hydrogen peroxide for every 10,000 gallons of water, and I recommend adding half of that slowly in front of the skimmer.

   This step of shocking will kill all bacteria in the skimmer, filter, and pipes, and the high peroxide levels in the water will help kill the bacteria in the pool.

   If the water is cloudy, it is best to do a minimum of a triple dose to ensure you are adding enough hydrogen peroxide to kill your algae problem. If the water is cloudy, that means the algae has been affecting the filter and eating up your sanitation for longer than what you thought.

   If you use Baquacil CDX, add in your maintenance dose of CDX (one pint per 10,000 gallons) into the skimmer right after you add your hydrogen peroxide in.

5. **(Optional) Use your weekly algaecide in a treatment dose.**

6. **Let your filter run for 24 hours, and then resume normal filtration.**

7. **After three days, check to be sure that your pool water still has a hydrogen peroxide level over 50 ppm.**

   If it's lower than that, you may not have killed all of the pink slime, and it will come back in a few days if you don't do anything.

8. **Repeat Steps 4 through 7 if your hydrogen peroxide level is under 20 ppm.**

   If it is, it means you are still dealing with a residual pink slime problem that is depleting your peroxide levels.

TIP

In severe cases — say the water is very cloudy and the pink slime is visible beyond just your skimmer — it's time to go a little more intense on the treatment. Follow the preceding steps, but in Step 4, add a minimum of 3 gallons of hydrogen peroxide for every 10,000 gallons of water. I know this may seem excessive, and biguanide-based systems are good at sanitizing, but they're not highly aggressive. They won't have the same effect on bacteria that chlorine would, so you have to dose higher. Run the filter 24 hours a day until it's clear, adding more hydrogen peroxide any time the hydrogen peroxide level in your water reaches 50 ppm or lower.

If you want to have even more of an effect, you can do one of two additional actions:

>> **Add 1 pound of potassium monopersulfate oxidizer per 10,000 gallons of water into the skimmer.** This oxidizer will help break down the pink slime in the pipes and filter, but it does have the negative side effect of lowering your biguanide levels.

>> **Add a single chlorine tablet into each of your skimmer baskets.** Even though chlorine and biguanide are incompatible, the chlorine feeding into the lines will be enough to kill pink slime without causing a severe chemical reaction with the biguanide in your pool. You must run the filter continuously until the tablet (or tablets, if you have more than one skimmer basket) either dissolves completely or is removed to prevent a buildup of high chlorine in the skimmer basket.

REMEMBER

Pink slime isn't too complicated to remove, but it is pesky and may return days or weeks later, depending on the pool water environment. So, keep up with your sanitizer and oxidizer, run the pool extra-long during the hot months, and keep an eye out for signs it's starting so that you can get on top of it quickly.

Introducing white water mold

If you've never seen what this fungus looks like in person, I'm very jealous. To be honest, I think this is one of the more unsightly water molds you can get. Luckily, it's not dangerous to humans — but it sure is ugly.

White water mold will appear in two different ways:

>> As a white-ish gooey mucus-looking substance (eww!)

>> Like you shredded tissue paper and threw it in the water

Just like any organic material that grows in a pool, it starts because the water's environment allows it to. There isn't enough circulation or sanitation to prevent it from growing, so it does what nature intended it to do and grows! It will start as little particles of white papery substance floating around your pool anytime you agitate the surface from swimming or brushing, and it can evolve into a pool so cloudy you can't see a foot down, with huge sheets of water mold floating around in the pool.

I've seen it firsthand in a biguanide pool: The customer asked that I come biweekly for my cleaning service rather than weekly, and they insisted that they'd take care of the chemicals. Well, two weeks later, I'm brushing sheets of mold off of the pool's surface and dealing with a severe white water mold outbreak.

It happens fast, and when it does you have to act just as fast to get it under control. Otherwise, you may end up being better off draining the pool, sanitizing and wiping it all down, and starting over with fresh water.

Preventing white water mold

Preventing this fungus from growing is all about circulation and sanitation, just like all the other pesky organisms that want to grow in your pool. It's more likely to start when the weather and sun are at their hottest, so make sure you start keeping an eye out for it in the hot summer months. Like pink slime (see the section "Finding the origins of pink slime," earlier in this chapter), start by adding more than your usual hydrogen peroxide maintenance dose and running your filter for longer periods of time. I wouldn't recommend less than 10 hours a day, during the day. After you see the start of white water mold, start the cleanup process right away.

Treating white water mold in a chlorine pool

Here's one of the reasons chlorine is so great: You'll rarely get this water mold in your pool. If your water is sanitized and circulated, getting white water mold in a chlorine pool should be next to impossible. If you do get it, there's likely an outside reason that leads to it becoming a problem. It's not as simple to rectify as pink slime (which I talk about in the section "Treating pink slime in chlorine," earlier in this chapter), only because it'll start in the pool and not in the skimmer, so there's a little more elbow grease involved in getting rid of it.

DEALING WITH A MILD CASE OF WHITE WATER MOLD IN CHLORINE

In a mild case of white water mold — for example, the water is clear with the beginning stages of what looks like tissue paper floating around — you'll want to follow these steps:

1. **Balance your water.**

    In any situation where the water is starting to grow something, always start with balancing. Chapter 9 gives you the how's and why's of balancing your pool water.

2. **Brush down the pool really thoroughly.**

   All surfaces should be rustled up, even the ones you think look okay.

3. **Clean your filter.**

   If you have a cartridge or DE filter, there's a good chance it's caught some of the water mold you had growing.

4. **Shock the pool heavily with a chlorine-based shock.**

   Start with a minimum of a double dose of your maintenance shock.

5. **Add a treatment dose of a copper-based or polyquat algaecide.**

   That amount will be listed on the label of the algaecide bottle.

6. **Let the pool filter for 24 continuous hours.**

7. **After 24 hours, check your water's chlorine level.**

   You want to make sure it's still high.

8. **If your chlorine level has dropped dramatically, repeat Steps 2 through 7 as many times as needed.**

   You're likely still dealing with live water mold if your chlorine level takes a plunge.

   You want to keep your water's chlorine level high and the filter clean during all of this.

TIP

You know you've successfully freed yourself from white water mold when the water is clear, and you hold a steady chlorine level over 5 ppm over a 24-hour period.

DEALING WITH A SEVERE CASE OF WHITE WATER MOLD IN CHLORINE

If you're dealing with a severe case of white water mold, your steps are similar to what you do for a mild case (see the preceding section), but with an extra step.

To start, a severe case of white water mold looks like this: a very cloudy pool with a tissue paper–like substance floating in the pool, stuck to the walls, and in your skimmer baskets and filter. And when I say very cloudy, I mean you can't see the bottom of the pool.

In this case, you'll want to follow these steps:

1. **Balance your water.**

   Flip to Chapter 9 for the lowdown on water balancing.

2. **Brush down everything.**

   You want to remove the water mold from the surfaces of the pool as thoroughly as you can by brushing every square inch of the pool as well as you can, even if you can't see the areas that you're brushing.

3. **Shock the pool heavily by using a triple dose of your preferred chlorine shock.**

   I personally like liquid for this step because it is the most fast-acting shock that tends to be the least expensive, especially for large doses.

4. **Floc the pool 12 to 24 hours later.**

   Allow all of the suspended particles to fall to the bottom of the pool over the next few days. (See the section "Floccing your pool," earlier in this chapter.)

5. **Vacuum your pool to waste as thoroughly as you can.**

   The more you can remove, the closer you will be to a clear clean pool.

6. **Shock the pool again, using a single dose of shock.**

   By now, the pool should look significantly better.

7. **If your pool doesn't look clear, repeat Steps 2 through 5, using a different kind of floc in Step 4.**

TIP

For any remaining cloudiness or water mold that you see around, I recommend continuous filtration and possibly using a filter aid or liquid clarifier for the small pieces. You should be able to clear up this cloudiness in a few days, so if you don't see the results you're looking for in that time, refer to Chapter 4 to be sure your filter is working properly or seek help from your trusted local pool store.

Treating white water mold in a biguanide pool

Getting white water mold in a biguanide pool is a much more likely situation than water mold in chlorine, so I'd be ready for a small amount of either water mold or pink slime in the middle of every summer.

DEALING WITH A MILD CASE OF WHITE WATER MOLD IN BIGUANIDE

If you find that your biguanide pool has white water mold, hopefully you caught it in the beginning stages, where you have minor cloudiness and only a little bit of floating water mold around. If this is the case, you're in luck because the treatment is fairly simple. Follow these steps:

1. **Test your water.**

   You want to make sure that all of your balancing chemicals are in the ranges they're meant to be, along with your biguanide levels.

2. **Clean all cleanable pool-related items that may have touched the water in the past week or two.**

   That includes floats, ladders, bathing suits, cleaning equipment, and the inside of DE or cartridge filters. You'll want to use a water-and-bleach solution to ensure the mold is completely taken care of.

3. **Add a minimum of a double dose of hydrogen peroxide shock to your pool.**

   You'd add 2 gallons of hydrogen peroxide per 10,000 gallons of water if you're using 27.5 percent hydrogen peroxide products.

4. **Brush that pool down very thoroughly.**

   Make sure you get every surface agitated. This can really be done right before or right after the addition of your shock. I like to brush right before shocking to be sure the pool is perfectly prepped for the next step and things haven't settled or started growing again.

5. **Run your filter 24 hours a day until the pool is clear.**

6. **Clean your filter well anytime it needs it until the pool is clear.**

   This may be once a day in some cases, so be sure to keep up with it.

TIP

7. **(Optional) Use either a water-and-bleach solution or an acidic wash on your DE or cartridge filter element after the water mold situation seems to be completely fixed.**

   This step just ensures that you have no residual traces of the water mold in the filter that could lead to another bloom.

I would also keep your peroxide levels nice and high for a few days after the treatment process as well, just to make sure the mold doesn't come back.

DEALING WITH A SEVERE CASE OF WHITE WATER MOLD IN BIGUANIDE

If your water mold case has gotten out of control and has taken over the pool, you are in for a little more work. Follow these steps:

1. **Balance your water.**

2. **Clean everything that has come into contact with the pool's water by using a water-and-bleach solution.**

3. **Add a triple dose of your hydrogen peroxide shock into the pool.**

4. **Brush the pool very well.**

5. **Floc the pool with a floc of your choice.**

   Follow the steps on the bottle exactly to make sure you're not wasting a product's potential and your time.

6. **After the floc has had the proper amount of time to settle, vacuum to waste.**

7. **Repeat Steps 3 and 4.**

   The pool should be in much better shape than when you started.

TIP

8. **If the pool looks the same or only marginally better, repeat Step 5.**

   You might possibly try a different floc this time.

9. **Run your filter for 24 hours a day for a few days.**

   The remaining particles of water mold should be filtered out easily. Use a filter aid or clarifier to get the pool perfect at a faster rate if you want to.

If you have no success after following the preceding steps, or even only partial success, be sure to get in touch with a local pool professional whom you trust and who's knowledgeable about treating a biguanide pool. You may have outside variables preventing a proper cleaning process.

I recommend cleaning your filter at the end of treatment and keeping your peroxide levels on the high end for a few days after treatment to ensure the mold stays away.

Staining and Discoloration from Metals

Staining and discoloration can be a frustrating problem. Nobody wants their pretty pool looking dirty when it's not. The main culprit for stains and discoloration are metals in your water. (Algae also causes discoloration; see the section "Is it algae, or is it metals?" earlier in this chapter, for details on treating algae issues.)

Stains occur when the metals that are in your water become oxidized from your chemicals and deposit themselves on your pool's surfaces. Metals can discolor your pool water a wide range of colors — green, brown, yellow, black, or even purple (that one's my favorite). If you add chlorine or bromine to your pool and the water changes from clear and blue to clear and literally any other color, you're likely dealing with metals in the water. Not all of them are inherently dangerous, but they all like to cause staining if left untreated.

You can find metal stain identification kits online or at local pool stores that come with multiple products that allow you to experiment on a stain and see which treatment works best. These kits can be super helpful, and they're easy to use. But if you don't want to spend money to find out what products you need to spend money on for treatment, you can always consult your local pool store or follow some the tips I offer in the following section.

If you have a pool that has a light-colored surface, it's almost impossible to not have some staining or discoloration. You'll just come to accept some of them because trying to keep your brand new perfectly white plaster pool that perfect white color forever may end up driving you crazy. Figuring out some quick and easy treatments is going to be the first step, and not panicking will be the second one.

So, before you pull your hair out trying to correct every little stain on your pool wall, let me explain the harm they may cause. Short answer? They do nothing. The stain itself won't hurt a bather, affect your chemicals, or damage the pool's surface. Just like a coffee stain on your white t-shirt doesn't ruin the shirt's integrity, a pool stain just makes it less visually appealing. So, if you do not make the stain go away, it won't actually hurt anything.

You may, however, want to treat the high metal concentration that's causing the stain or discoloration. The following section helps you identify which metal is in your water, and the section "Treating your water for metals," later in this chapter, discusses getting rid of it.

Identifying the problem-causing metal

When you have metals in the water, they can discolor the pool water and cause staining. Knowing how to treat them varies slightly on what metal you are dealing with, or if it is a metal at all! Sometimes, algae like black algae or yellow mustard algae can give the appearance of metal staining, and green algae can cause a hue of green to the water that looks like it could be copper and vice versa. What you want to identify first and foremost is whether the discoloration is from metals or if it's organic.

For staining, this is the easy way to figure out what you're dealing with:

>> **Rub a vitamin C tablet on a stain.** If the stain lifts, you're dealing with metals.

>> **Shock the pool and brush any stains.** If the water discoloration gets worse or stays the same, it's likely metals. If the stain easily brushes off, or the water becomes less green or clears up, it's from something organic, such as algae (see the section "Is it algae, or is it metals?" earlier in this chapter).

When dealing with water discoloration, there are three main colors: green, brown, and purple. Sometimes, the brown can look yellow, and the purple can appear almost black. Based on the color of your water, you can identify what metal you're dealing with. Here's a list:

>> **Copper causes green:** Green is always going to be from copper. Think of it like the Statue of Liberty going from copper to green because of oxidation. I've seen copper become an issue in a pool by using too much copper-based algaecide. Or maybe it's being stripped from an old copper heat exchanger in a gas heater that may not even run anymore. Or it might simply come from the source water that was added to the pool.

>> **Iron causes brown (or yellow):** Brown or yellow comes from iron in the water. That's almost always from your source water. So if you're filling the pool from a well, be ready for this because iron is very commonly prevalent in wells.

>> **Manganese causes purple (or black):** The purple (or, in bad cases, it can look black) that you'll get is one of the most beautiful shades of purple you'll ever see in your life — you may never want to fix it! This purple comes from manganese, which is naturally occurring in groundwater, mostly seen in countries like China, Australia, and Africa Manganese. In the U.S., it is a less common occurrence and is a more rare metal to deal with.

One thing all of these staining metals will have in common is that they'll first appear to get worse with the addition of chlorine. The stains they create will vary from a yellowish discoloration on white or light-colored surfaces, and they can expand to look like rust is oozing from the walls. If you've ever seen a toilet or shower tinted yellow or orange from hard water, it is really the same thing. It can sometimes also look like coffee stains.

Treating your water for metals

Luckily, no matter what kind of metals you're dealing with, the treatment is basically the same. In cases where you're dealing with just water discoloration, you really only need one product, and that's a metal-sequestering chemical. But adding that product to your pool isn't the only step; there's always the prep work!

Follow these steps to remove the metal from your water:

1. **Get your water tested and balanced.**

   Some metal-removing chemicals will have specific parameters for your pH, alkalinity, and chlorine levels, so be sure to get your pool as close to those numbers as possible.

2. **Add in the metal-sequestering chemical and let it work its magic.**

   Most metal-sequestering chemicals are liquid and can be poured right into the pool water, but read the label of the chemical you are using for proper instructions.

3. **Leave your pool filter running for at least 24 hours.**

   Don't add any chlorine in that time frame because it can counteract the metal remover you added before it gets a chance to do its job.

TIP

   I also don't recommend shocking the pool for at least four days after introducing the metal-removing chemical so that you can be sure you don't reverse the effects of that chemical.

A sequestering agent works by bonding a bunch of ions together so that they become a large enough clump that a filter can filter them out. Different filters have different recommendations. If you have a

>> **DE filter:** You don't need any additional chemicals added. Just backwash and add new DE as needed. (Flip to Chapter 3 for how to backwash your pool and for dealing with your DE filter.)

>> **Cartridge filter:** You don't necessarily need any additional chemicals, but I've found that using a natural clarifier will cause those already larger clumps of ions to cling to other clumps of ions and become even larger and easier to filter out. Bigger clumps will make your filtration cycles go further in a shorter period of time.

>> **Sand filter:** I recommend using both a powdered filter aid and a natural clarifier if you have a sand filter. The filter aid will cause your filter to be more efficient, and the natural clarifier will make the cleanup process go even faster.

In most cases, the metal-sequestering agent you're using will recommend a thorough filter cleaning after 24 to 48 hours of filtration time. Be sure to follow all of the steps so that you're not adding chemicals for nothing.

If you're dealing with staining on your pool wall, steps, or anything else, follow these steps:

1. **Test and balance your water.**

2. **Add in ascorbic acid at a rate of ½ pound of ascorbic acid per 10,000 gallons of water.**

   The ascorbic acid will remove the stains from the pool's surface immediately and put those metals back into the solution of the water so that the metal-sequestering agent can remove them completely.

3. **Add in the metal-sequestering chemical.**

   Most metal-sequestering chemicals won't actually remove stains that have already been deposited on the surface. Those stains may lighten after you introduce a metal-sequestering chemical to the pool water, but rarely will they go away completely.

4. **Run the filter for 24 hours.**

   Let the filter run on Recirculate, if you have that option, but the stains should be gone within the hour. The extra 23 hours is to be sure the sequestering agent has plenty of time to remove the metals from the solution from the water.

If you didn't add in the metal-sequestering agent after adding the ascorbic acid, your stains will reappear in a matter of weeks, sometimes days. If you don't remove the metal from the water, you won't ever take care of the root of the problem. But if you're looking for quick fixes before an event to take the yellow out of your steps, ascorbic acid works instantly and is very satisfying. Plus, it's safe to swim in only 15 minutes after adding. In severe stain cases, you may need to repeat the process of adding in the ascorbic acid until the stains are completely gone.

When Your Water Stinks

Nobody likes it when they smell bad, and I can't imagine anyone likes it when their pool smells bad. But, unfortunately, it's not an uncommon occurrence. The big thing about stinky water is figuring out why it smells. There are three really common kinds of pool water smells:

» Chlorine (the most common, and probably most controversial)

» A moldy/musty smell

» The smell of fish

All pool water smells are bad smells — I want to start with that. A strong chlorine smell isn't an indicator of a clean pool, and as you can imagine, neither are the other two. Water smells are indicators of something beyond what you may be able to see, and they're a red flag that will alert you about a situation in your water.

Fixing a strong chlorine smell

I'm pretty sure that anyone who has ever stayed at a hotel that has an indoor pool could find where the pool was based on the smell alone. I think we've all been conditioned to believe that the chlorine smell was a way to tell whether the pool was sanitary, the smellier the cleaner. Well, I have some very unfortunate news for you — clean chlorine has little to no smell. I go into this subject in detail in Chapter 10.

Knowing the source of a strong chlorine smell

What smells is actually something called *chloramines,* or combined chlorine. *Combined chlorine* is when your existing chlorine molecules in the water have attached onto organic contamination in the water and haven't burned through it completely. This bonding will result in the chlorine being nearly useless, and chloramines can cause skin and eye irritation, along with putting out a strong chlorine odor.

If you remove the lid of a chlorine shock bottle and smell the inside of the cap, you'd notice that the smell is minimal, if not untraceable. If you stick something dirty against the inside of the lid, such as a fingertip, and then smell the lid again, you'd notice a dramatic change in the strength of the scent. Chlorine will release a gas when it combines with any organic contaminant in the water. In public pools — especially public pools with poor ventilation — the smell is magnified due to the amount of large of organic matter introduced into the pool regularly. So, that smell isn't telling you that the water is clean; it's telling you that it's dirty.

Treating a strong chlorine smell

How do you fix a strong chlorine smell? You need to shock the pool.

The question I usually get now is, "If my combined chlorine is high, why would I want to add more chlorine?" The answer is because you need to add chlorine to help burn off what's causing the combined chlorine.

In residential outdoor pools, a combined chlorine high enough to cause skin and eye irritation, along with that chlorine smell, can build up within a week. In commercial pools, it's more likely daily. In some cases, such as when your free chlorine levels are already in their ideal 2-to-3 parts per million (ppm) range, you can use a non-chlorine shock, such as potassium monopersulfate, to help break up the combined chlorine without raising the chlorine levels.

It is really important that you test your water a minimum of weekly to ensure that you're not getting a combined chlorine level of over 0.5 ppm. By keeping your combined chlorine level low, you can prevent all of the bad side effects and help make sure that any chlorine you do have in the pool is free and ready to kill fresh bacteria.

Dealing with a musty/moldy or fishy smell

Musty and fishy are less common scents that you'll experience in a pool, but if you ever do smell them, they're easy to identify and correct.

If you have a musty/moldy smell

A musty or moldy smell is an indication of the start of organic growth, and that happens when your sanitizer drops too low for too long. Most of the time, you'll recognize this scent in pools that have solar covers or heaters because the water will release steam, which will allow the smell to travel more freely. When you smell this musty/moldy scent, the reason is simple: Your water has no chlorine in it (less than 0.5 ppm).

Treating this smell is fairly simple. Just follow these steps:

1. **Test and balance your water.**

2. **Shock the pool.**

   Your shock treatment can be a normal dose. Or, if you're noticing a little bit of cloudiness to the water, you can double it.

TIP

3. **Add in a treatment dose of your maintenance algaecide.**

4. **Brush down the walls of your pool.**

5. **Let the filter run for a 24-hour cycle.**

   This step ensures that you're getting proper distribution of the chemicals that you've added. This step will also allow your filter to catch any floating particles that you may have from the start of an algae or water mold.

If you have a fishy smell

Now, a fishy smell is definitely a lesser known problem (thankfully!). I've only ever experienced it in a biguanide pool, and the smell comes from having high levels of hydrogen peroxide in the pool. The levels have to be really high to get this smell as a side effect, but it's possible.

The treatment is fairly simple: Just lower the hydrogen peroxide levels. The only problem with that is there isn't really an easy way to do that outside of partially draining and refilling your water. If you're dealing with a fishy smell, the easiest thing to do is just let it dissipate on its own. It may take a few weeks, but it will eventually go away.

Preventing Rashes and Burning Eyes

One of the most common complaints about a pool is going to be these two things: burning eyes and rashes. If you're having bathers complain about skin and eye irritation, the problem is likely not your chlorine (if you even have a chlorine-based pool); it's everything else. I've tried my very hardest to stress the importance of water balance in many areas of this book, and this is going to be another one.

No one wants to have a pool that's basically a hostile environment for humans, but more often than it should be, that happens. A clear pool does not mean a safe pool. If you're basing your pool water quality on how it sparkles in the sunlight and not how it reads on a test strip, you're doing it wrong.

And those same things that cause skin and eye irritation are the same things that will prematurely wrinkle and fade your liner or wear down your rubber gaskets. Keeping your water bather-friendly won't only prevent you from having red, bloodshot eyes, but also keep you from ruining your pool investment.

If it's not allergies, it's a water imbalance

I have customers tell me all the time that either they or their kids are allergic to chlorine because they always break out in a rash after swimming. The reality is that a chlorine allergy is very rare; you or your family member has *irritant dermatitis*, which is a sensitivity reaction to chlorine or the pool's lack of proper water balance. The water balance reason is a way more likely scenario, although a chlorine allergy or chlorine-caused irritant dermatitis is still possible.

I don't want to dismiss the possibility of a real chlorine reaction or allergy, but before jumping to conclusions, test your water. The two main culprits are a high combined chlorine level or a too-high or too-low pH level:

>> **Combined chlorine:** Chlorine at it's ideal range of 2 parts per million (ppm) isn't going to cause any skin irritation in the vast majority of people. But, a combined chlorine of 2 ppm absolutely will. The average chlorine parts per million in city water is between 1 and 4 ppm or milligrams per liter (mg/L). So, if your shower doesn't bother you, a properly balanced pool shouldn't, either.

>> **Water pH:** The number one cause of skin and eye irritation outside of combined chlorine is your water's pH. The acidity level in your pool is the most important variable in the entirety of your pool. It's what will fade and wrinkle liners, break down rubber gaskets, rust stainless steel, and cause burning eyes and rashes.

The pH of the human eye is 7.4 and introducing anything outside of the 7.2-to-7.8 range to your eye will likely cause irritation. For some perspective, the average pH of shampoo is between 3.6 to 5.5, and we all know how much that burns getting in your eyes. Unfortunately, improper water care is not short of abundance and I've seen a pool pH of below 5.0 almost as often as I've seen one at 7.4. (Eye irritation is also caused by a high pH, so it goes both ways.)

Not only does the pH being out of range cause the bathers physical discomfort, but it's also making it so your sanitation, which you use to prevent people from getting sick, is a fraction as effective as it should be. So, all around, having your water unbalanced — especially your chlorine and pH levels — will cause all sorts of problems, including the ones blamed on chlorine alone.

How to correct the imbalance problem

To establish a solution to your water imbalance and create a regiment of preventative actions, in very simple terms, you need to get your water tested! Stop assuming your pool is fine because it's clear. Stop comparing your pool to the lake that you swim in every summer. Stop assuming that your pool is maintenance free and that chemicals are a scam. None of that is true, and all of those assumptions will lead your pool down a path to quick destruction.

I go over taking care of your pool water quite a bit in Chapter 9, but testing your water at home weekly is so important. And if you don't want to do that, at least get it tested biweekly or monthly at your local pool store. The tests at pool stores are designed to get your pool water into the perfect balance, and if you follow the steps given to you by the pool store testing system, your pool will be perfectly balanced. It's a few minutes of work every week or a few hours of work once a month, but either way, it's a small amount of effort to keep you, your bathers, and your pool safe.

My Pool Uses Up Chlorine Quickly

Chlorine, although it's incredibly effective, can also be somewhat of a chore, depending on the time of the year. In the middle of summer, it's not out of the ordinary to have your chlorine levels drop and algae grow. In the middle of the summer, there's a lot of sun and a lot of use. Both of those things will lead to a pool that's likely to let algae grow because of a sanitation drop. It becomes especially bad at times where the weather alternates from sunny and 90 degrees, to a massive rainfall, and then back to sunny. An environment like that is a perfect storm for a chlorine pool to *yo-yo* (meaning it is constantly jumping from low to high and rarely perfect).

There are also outside variables that can cause chlorine to dissipate quickly, and sometimes you may not even understand why. We call that a chlorine demand, which you can read about in the section "The elusive chlorine demand," later in this chapter. If you have a chlorine pool, at least once in your lifetime, you'll run into a situation where you shock the pool on a Tuesday morning, and the chlorine is gone by Wednesday night. It's a pain, but it's usually very fixable.

The common causes of disappearing chlorine

Here are the main reasons your chlorine may not be holding:

>> **Poor water balance:** This may come as a shock to you if you've read any other parts of this book (where I've mentioned it only about 20,000 times), but your water balance plays a huge part in the functionality of your sanitation. Two factors in your water balance may be at fault:

- *Low CYA levels:* Your cyanuric acid (CYA) is what prevents the chlorine from dissipating in UV rays. So, if your pool sits in direct sunlight for 10 hours a day in the middle of July when it's over 90 degrees Fahrenheit for five days in a row, your CYA will come in really handy. If it's low, say good-bye to your free chlorine!

- *Low pH levels:* Your pH also plays a huge part in water balance because it directly affects the reaction time chlorine has. A slightly high pH of 7.8 causes your chlorine effectiveness to drop 17 percent. At 8.0, your chlorine is half as efficient. And at 8.5, it's like you don't have chlorine at all. With low pH, your chlorine is in hyperdrive and will burn off quickly. Your pool's water balance is so important in every aspect of the pool-owning process, so keeping it where it needs to be is necessary.

TIP

>> **Phosphates:** These are another big reason to not hold chlorine levels. The phosphates themselves don't actually lower your chlorine levels, but the acceleration of the growth of algae in your pool will cause your chlorine to have to work extra hard to keep the algae at bay.

If your phosphates are over 500 ppm and you're having trouble keeping chlorine in the pool, consider taking the steps to use phosphate removers and get your pool back into a more sustainable condition (see the section "Check those phosphates," earlier in this chapter).

>> **High water temperature:** Keep in mind how water temperature affects your chlorine usage. There's a reason bromine is more popular in hot tubs than chlorine — chlorine doesn't hold up against the heat well. If you keep your water temperature very high, you're more likely to go through a lot more chlorine than the average person.

The elusive chlorine demand

A *chlorine demand* is when your pool has a certain amount of organic matter in the water and it's requiring a certain amount of chlorine to get rid of that organic matter. The problem with a chlorine demand is that you can't truly identify its source. You can guess and say maybe it's fertilizers, tree pollen, or black mold in your pipes or under the liner, but that's all it will ever be, a guess. When you have a chlorine demand, you will find that the water will be perfectly clear and balanced, but you can't hold chlorine no matter what you do. You could shock the pool with a double dose of chlorine shock and then have a chlorine reading at basically zero 12 hours later (that's not normal!).

Before jumping to a chlorine demand as your problem, verify that chlorine demand is, in fact, your problem:

REMEMBER

>> If your water isn't crystal clear, don't assume chlorine demand; identify and fix whatever is causing the cloudiness first.

A true chlorine demand usually takes place when the water is perfectly clear and has no visible and obvious reasons to cause your chlorine to not hold.

>> Check your water balance. Make sure your pH and CYA are exactly perfect.

>> Do a shock test.

To do a shock test, follow these steps:

1. **At 8 p.m., add a double dose of 12.5-percent liquid chlorine into your pool.**

   A double dose is at a rate of 2 gallons of liquid chlorine for every 15,000 gallons of pool water.

2. **Allow your filter to run overnight.**

3. **At 8 a.m., test your pool's chlorine levels.**

   If your chlorine is still high come morning, you don't have a chlorine demand. If it has dropped to normal ranges or lower, you likely have a demand.

TIP

If you believe you have a chlorine demand, have your water tested at a pool store. Most pool stores can perform a chlorine demand test to determine the amount of chlorine needed in one dose to cure the problem. In some cases, I've seen a chlorine demand that required over 70 gallons of liquid shock at one time to break through it. As you can imagine, that created a whole other set of problems.

You may wonder why a chlorine demand has to be treated all in one dose, and I'm going to try to explain it to you in the way that it was explained to me by one of my favorite teachers. Picture your chlorine demand like an overdrawn bank account. If you have a deficit of $100 and you deposit $25, do you have any money? No, because you're still $75 in the hole. Did you make the problem better? Yes, but you didn't fix your problem just yet. But, if you deposit $101, you fixed your deficit and still have $1 to spare.

So, when the pool professionals perform a chlorine demand and inform you that you need 25 gallons of liquid chlorine, but you add only 5 gallons, you won't worsen your problem, but you'll still be in a chlorine demand. And if you decided to add 5 gallons a day for five days, rather than 25 gallons all at the same time, but it rained on Day 3 or people used the pool on Day 4, that contamination adds to your deficit, so you'll never fully meet that chlorine demand.

If you're ever in a situation where you have a chlorine demand, follow the instructions that you get from the pool pros and add what's needed; otherwise, you'll chase your tail and become very frustrated with a situation that has a simple solution.

4

The Part of Tens

Chapter **13**

(Almost) Ten Tools You Didn't Know You Needed

W hen it comes to taking care of a pool, my philosophy is, easier is better. If you're working on your pool and say to yourself, "I wish they invented something that did this for me," I can pretty much guarantee it exists out there somewhere. This chapter talks about some of my favorite tools that make life with your pool easier.

Skimmer Socks

Skimmer socks are fine mesh bags that fit inside the basket in your skimmer. Each of these socks has an elastic band on the top, which allows it to hold in place. These socks catch bugs, pine needles, and even oils. It may be one of the most lifesaving tools to ever exist during pollen season!

In New Hampshire, our spring pollen season has gotten so bad that you could write a message on your car in the pollen that falls on it. As pollen season gets worse, pools take the brunt of it all. The pollen isn't only a pain because the majority of filters can't filter it out (because it's so fine of a particle), but it also makes an excellent source of food for algae. That means the more pollen you get, the more likely you are to get algae, and therefore the more chlorine and algaecide you go through, and the more you need to clean your filter.

If you have a diatomaceous earth (DE) or cartridge filter and get a big explosion of pollen in your area, your pressure will rise more quickly than you're used to because your filter gets clogged with all of that sticky yellow pollen. So, wouldn't it be nice if you could catch the pollen before it got to your filter?

That's where skimmer socks come in. Most of the time, you can buy them in a pack of five, and you can just keep swapping them out, rinsing and reusing. They do begin to deteriorate over time, as you can imagine, so after they start to get holes bigger than a dime, it's time to toss them and get new ones. You can use them to help corral anything on the surface of your pool; it doesn't have to be just for pollen.

WARNING

Although skimmer socks work incredibly well, you have to make sure you keep an eye on them and clean them regularly. They can clog quickly and cause a lot of resistance for the pump, which could lead to your motor burning out. Use them when you need to, but never leave them unattended for more than a day. I recommend dumping out the large debris and rinsing it with a hose any time you see it is getting full.

Cover Funnel

Here's a product that I'm sure you've never heard of: the Cover Funnel. It's made by Klever Klever Innovations and has a lot of benefits. If you're in a climate where you winterize your pool by using a safety cover, then a cover funnel may be perfect for you.

How often do you open your pool in the springtime to find it's a lovely shade of emerald green? Or worse, maybe it got really bad and turned black! Well, the best way to prevent gross things growing in your pool over the winter is to add chemicals to your water until it freezes, and then add chemicals after the water starts to thaw.

If you have a cover on the pool, there's no real way to add in chemicals unless you pop off a couple of springs from the pegs in the ground and poor chlorine or algaecide in there. Not only is that procedure a lot of work, but it also doesn't really give you a great way to spread the chemicals around for maximum efficiency.

Well, with the Cover Funnel, you can easily add chemicals right underneath the cover without undoing anything! Figure 13-1 shows how the Funnel slides easily under a pool cover.

Follow these steps to use the Cover Funnel:

1. **Slide the 3-foot-long pipe underneath the cover.**

   Position it so that the opening for the funnel is face up and as much of the pipe is under the cover as you can fit while still having room for the support leg to go down.

2. **After you have the run where you want it, pull down the locking leg stand.**

   This stand ensures that the Funnel will stay in place on its own.

3. **Pour the shock into the top of the Funnel.**

   No splashing, and the shock doesn't back up into the top.

4. **Move the funnel around to multiple locations around the perimeter of the pool to distribute your chlorine throughout the pool.**

   The Funnel is lightweight, so you can do this distribution with ease.

FIGURE 13-1:
The easy 3-step process to use the Cover Funnel.

Klever Klever Innovations

TIP

The best time to use the Cover Funnel, even if you don't do it in the fall when you first cover your pool, is once a month after there's consistently warm weather (meaning about 50 to 60 degrees Fahrenheit or above), and then again a few days to a week before you plan to fully open the pool. The chlorine will kill any algae that may have already formed, along with preventing anything else from starting. You already have to shock the pool when you open it, so why not start earlier and have a cleaner start?

The Cover Funnel doesn't have to be used only when the pool is closed; it can be used at any time if you want to prevent the chlorine from splashing on you when you add it. I have a few customers who use their Cover Funnels all year, and they swear by them.

REMEMBER

Don't use more than one chemical at a time through the Funnel. If you want to add a second kind of chemical to the pool by using the Cover Funnel, be sure to thoroughly rinse the tool by using flowing water for at least two minutes. Rinsing out the Funnel will ensure there's not accidental mixing of incompatible chemicals.

Specialty Removal Tools

Certain pieces of pool equipment have tools specifically made for opening, or closing, or loosening, or tightening each particular piece. Here are a few types that are nice to have on hand:

>> **A wrench for threaded pump lids:** Some pumps have a special wrench to remove the lid available. A common pump that has a wrench is the Hayward Super II Pump. The wrenches are different for the different models they go to. To know if your pump has a wrench available, present the make and model of your pump to a local pool professional or check it out on the internet.

>> **A wrench for the lid of sand filters:** This tool is for removing the lid of sand filters that have a dome on the top and their multiport valve on the side. The Hayward S200 and S240 sand filter and the Pentair Tagelus and Triton each have an available dome wrench for purchase.

>> **A wrench for a tablet chlorinator:** Having a wrench makes removing the lid easier. Hayward makes one for their in-line and off-line chlorinators, and so does Pentair and King Technology.

>> **A return removal tool:** Those pesky eyeball returns get stuck more often than any other pool part that I've ever dealt with, and it's almost always because someone overtightened them. This tool inserts into the center of the eyeball piece so you have better leverage and grip to remove the stuck piece.

>> **A safety cover removal and installation tool:** This long metal tube with a notch cut out on the end allows you to install and remove the springs for your safety cover.

Battery-Operated Vacuums

Cordless pool vacuums can be used for quick and easy self-contained cleaning, so you don't have to take out all of your vacuuming equipment for spot touch-ups before a party. This type of product has so many options and variations, from a little cylinder that uses D batteries and turns on with a switch to a robotic cleaner that moves on its own. These styles are worth looking into:

» **Manual battery-operated vacuum:** This type of vacuum is simple to use and is fairly inexpensive (between $90 and $300, depending on the model). They come in a variety of sizes, from small ones intended for hot tubs to larger ones that can hold a half gallon of debris. And the rechargeable battery works for up to 60 minutes at a time. They're lightweight and attach to any standard telescopic vacuum pole, and most of these vacuums that you buy new come with a one-year warranty.

They are best used for spot cleaning your pool or doing a full vacuum on a small fairly clean pool. The internal vacuum bag is not very large so you would not be able to vacuum a pool with more than a hand full of large debris.

» **Battery-operated robotic vacuum:** These vacuums are good for small messes and pools that are on the smaller side. They hold their charge for 80 to 90 minutes, with only a four- to six-hour charge time. They're completely cordless, which gives them great mobility and poses zero risk for bathers. They clean only larger debris on the floor of the pool, but overall, these little guys are pretty great for being so simple.

» **Motorized leaf bagger vacuums:** This type of vacuum has no attachment other than your telescopic pole, and it has a motor that includes an impeller. The impeller sucks the leaves up into a large bag that can hold a lot of debris. This vacuum holds its battery charge for two to three hours, and it's light-weight and easy to use.

TIP

I love this type of pool vacuum for spring and fall cleanups if you have a lot of leaves at the bottom that you don't feel like scooping. You may need to empty the bag a few times, but it's a lot less labor-intensive than scooping.

Organizers

For me, there's nothing worse than a cluttered pool area. I think your pool is supposed to be an oasis, a staycation that allows you to relax and unwind. It's definitely not a relaxing situation when your pool toys and cleaning tools are all over the deck. Well, lucky for you, there are great little organizers for all of that stuff! Here are a few types to keep your pool stuff from getting cluttered:

» **Float holders:** For your pool floats, there are a variety of organization tools that can help you out. Some are simple, such as a hook, and hold just circular ring floats. Some are more complex, such as a free-standing unit with drawers, shelves, and slots. I personally like the ones that are on the simpler side but can hold multiple kinds of floats. They're usually made with a plastic or PVC frame, so they're completely resistant to elements and salt. They don't take up a lot of space, and they're inexpensive and lightweight to move. The more elaborate ones are really pretty and made a great option, too.

>> **Equipment holders:** For your cleaning equipment, such as vacuums, brushes, and poles, you can find a few holder choices, too. Some of the simpler ones are small hooks that can either hang on a chain link fence or screw into a wooden fence. They can hold hoses and multiple poles, which you can leave with your heads attached. You can also find some more elaborate equipment holders that also usually screw into a wooden surface. These options can hold all of your brush, skimmer, and vacuum heads, along with one pole.

>> **Outdoor patio storage bins:** These bins are very helpful for storing smaller pool items, such as goggles and fins, or small toys. But they're also a great place to store your chemicals. A lot of the bins that I've come across are plastic and both water- and weatherproof. A bin like this will save you from having to store harsh chemicals such as chlorine in your garage or shed. Chemicals should be stored in a temperature-regulated area when possible.

A Good Pole

I know this one seems sort of silly, but I have been in the pool business for too long not to express my opinions on the need for a good pole. This section is for you if you've ever

>> Had a telescopic pole that constantly collapses, no matter how tight you make the cam

>> Been brushing or scooping leaves and had your pole snap or bend in half

I personally have experienced both of the preceding mishaps when I was using subpar pool poles.

For a long time, my dad (who's my mentor) and a few of my coworkers really liked using the fiberglass poles. Those poles tended to last the longest and had some of the best durability to them. The major problem with them was that if they saw the daylight for too long, they would start to leave fiberglass splinters. I don't know if you've ever experienced a fiberglass splinter, but trust me, it's not enjoyable! Fiberglass poles also would inevitably break, or the cam would stop tightening enough, and I would be left buying another new pole.

Well, a few years ago, I discovered push-button vacuum poles. Instead of a tightening plastic cam, they have a button that you push in. And then you can adjust the telescoping half of the pole to one of multiple holes for whatever height you want. When I tell you that this changed my opinion on vacuum poles forever, I am not kidding. They are so much easier to use than telescopic poles with cams, they don't collapse mid-brush, and they're incredibly durable.

Critter Savers

I don't know about you, but I am really not a big fan of finding deceased critters in a pool. They're icky, smelly, and unsanitary (not to mention a little sad). Especially if you live in a wooded or marshy area, you deal with it the worst. I'm here to inform you that manufacturers make a special little tool that gives those little animals a way to escape. I have seen them called frog logs, critter savers, and escape ramps, but regardless of what you call it, the concept is the same.

This wildlife rescue device includes a small weighted bag that sits on the pool deck and a netted ramp that leads down to a small floating pad that stays in the pool against the wall. Any time a small animal ends up in the pool, it can swim to the floating platform and easily escape up the netted ramp. This kind of device is a really big help for woodland creatures because they're less likely to survive falling into a pool than a newt or frog.

Critter savers come in a variety of styles and are usually less than $20. I recommend them to all of my customers because I'm a big animal lover, and I really don't enjoy finding animals at the bottom of the pool or in the skimmer basket.

Smart Water Monitors

Summertime can be a very busy time, and getting out to test your water may seem like just one more annoying thing on your to-do list. How would you like it if you could just open a phone app and see your pool water's up-to-the-minute condition? Yep, there's a device for that!

Water monitors are devices that float in your pool and send you digital readings of your pool's condition. It's all taken care of through a simple app, and these monitors' accuracy is pretty incredible. They can test your pool water's chemical readings and take its temperature, and some can even read the salt content of your pool water. They tend to be a slightly expensive investment, but it takes the headache out of owning a pool.

When you can see the chemical readings of the pool on your phone, it helps you keep the pool chemicals balanced all of the time — and that will save you huge amounts of money and time in the future. I know that getting to the pool store for a water test isn't always a top priority on a beautiful 90-degree day, especially in an area where pool stores are few and far between. So easily having a way to check your chemistry and have accurate readings to make small adjustments on the fly is priceless, in my opinion.

Quality Test Kits

I can't stress enough the importance of proper chemical balancing, so being able to accurately read those numbers is essential. There are a lot of brands of test kits — and a lot of styles, as well. So figuring out which test kit is a good one can seem intimidating. But I'm here to make it easier:

>> **Test strips:** Many people like to use the test strips that come in the small bottle that includes a simple chart. Although those strips are perfectly fine for quick checks once a week, they're not perfectly accurate, so they can't get you exact numbers. They have a lot of variables that can cause inaccuracy. And on top of that, the colors are completely open to interpretation. You can use these strips for checkups, but I wouldn't say that they're your best testing method.

>> **Liquid drop test kits:** The most accurate at-home testing method is liquid drop test kits. There are a lot of brands of these test kits, but the most well-known is Taylor. Pentair test kits are also great. And all brands offer a few options that can test either everything or only a few things.

But the best part of liquid drop test kits is that you can buy only replacement reagents when you need them. The reagents over time will either run out or expire, and not having to buy a whole new test kit every time is pretty helpful.

TIP

>> **Pro tests:** If you have the ability to test your pool water at a pool store that has high-tech testing equipment, that should be done at least three times a year. Testing your pool regularly by using a pro's system gives you a proper history of your levels.

Chapter **14**

Ten Pool Products to Stock Up on in Spring

I f you're anything like me and you love saving money (keep an eye out for those early spring-pre-season sales!), then knowing how to supply your pool for an entire season is preferable so that you can get it all while it's on sale. What exactly you'll need will vary from pool to pool, or area to area; but, in general, this chapter should give you a place to start. These estimates are for a season that's primarily from Memorial Day to Labor Day (14 weeks), so if your season is longer, consider sizing up.

Getting Set with Plenty of Sanitizer

Sanitation is one of the most important methods of keeping your pool clean. Whether you're using chlorine, bromine, biguanide, or salt, you'll always need a sanitizer throughout your season. Here are some numbers to keep in mind for stocking up on sanitizer, depending on which type of system you use:

» **For chlorine or bromine systems:** When using tablets, the amount for both of these products is about the same. The best rule is to buy it at 1 pound of tablets for every 1,000 gallons of water your pool has. So, a 10,000-gallon pool will go through about 10 pounds of chlorine or bromine tablets in a season.

If you overbuy, no harm! Tablets won't go bad if they're stored in a temperature- and humidity-controlled dark location.

>> **For a salt-to-chlorine generator system:** Estimating how much salt you'll need can be tricky. If you have a pool that uses a salt-to-chlorine generator and you drain your pool 18 inches below the top to winterize, then you end up diluting your salt content when you fill it back up in the spring. Your best bet is to test the salt level after the pool is clean and has been circulating for more than two days after you open it for the season. I recommend purchasing at least three 40-pound bags of salt for every 10,000 gallons of pool water.

>> **For a biguanide system:** You add 1 pint of biguanide sanitizer for every 10,000 gallons of water once a week. So, if you're getting chemicals for 14 weeks (the amount of time between Memorial Day and Labor Day), you estimate 3.5 bottles (typically sold in ½-gallon size) for every 10,000 gallons of water for a season. I recommend getting an extra bottle or two in case your starting levels are low (below 30 ppm).

Having Enough Oxidizer

Oxidizers are used to shock your pool for weekly maintenance or for anytime you run into issues like algae or cloudy water (you can read all about oxidizers in Chapter 11). Figuring how much oxidizer (also known as a *shock product*) you need for a season is relatively standard. And, to make it easier, most oxidizers will have an average dose of either 1 pound of oxidizer per 10,000 gallons of water or 1 gallon of oxidizer for every 15,000 gallons of water.

Obviously, the amount you'll need varies, depending on the quality and percentage of chemical you're buying, so I'll break it down based on your sanitation system:

>> **Chlorine-based oxidizers for pools that are chlorine, bromine, or salt based:** I recommend adding an additional 6 pounds or 3 gallons of oxidizer for every 10,000 gallons of water per seasonal amount; to be safe, store enough for emergencies and for initial startup and winterization.

Based on which product you decide to use, take the numbers given in Table 14-1 and multiply them by how many weeks you have in a season to get the correct amount of product that you need:

TABLE 14-1

Weekly Doses of Chlorine-Based Oxidizers

Oxidizer	Percentage	Amount	Gallons of Water
Cal hypo	65%	1 lb.	10,000
Cal hypo	75%	1 lb.	15,000
Dichlor	99%	1 lb.	10,000
Sodium hypo	12.5%	1 gal.	15,000
Potassium monopersulfate	42%	1 lb.	10,000

>> **A biguanide-based system:** You really have only one option for a shock product if you use biguanide, and that would be hydrogen peroxide. This product typically comes in gallon form, with 1 gallon treating 10,000 gallons once a month. I recommend getting an additional 6 gallons of hydrogen peroxide per 10,000 gallons of pool water for the season, for initial startup and winterization, as well as in case you need to shock it really hard in the middle of the season.

Loading Up on Algaecide

You definitely want to have enough algaecide on hand to prevent and combat any algae growth during the pool season. Now, this is a little tricky because there are so many kinds of algaecides out there to choose from. In Chapter 11, I go pretty in depth on the different kinds of algaecides and why you may choose one over another. But to make things extra complicated, those types of algaecides can also come in different percentages. I list the types with their ideal percentages in Table 14-2, along with their maintenance weekly dosing:

TABLE 14-2

Weekly Algaecide Doses

Algaecide	Percentage	Amount	Gallons of Water
Quaternary	50%	1.5 fl. oz.	10,000
Polyquat	60%	2–3 fl. oz.	10,000
Copper-based	3%	1.5 fl. oz.	10,000

The initial dose and winterization dose for these algaecides range around 6 to 8 fluid ounces per 10,000 gallons of water. And if you need an algae treatment for an algae bloom, you'll need around 15 fluid ounces per 10,000 gallons of water. So be sure to apply those numbers to your season supply. Algaecides usually come in quart-size bottles, which contain 32 fluid ounces, so some quick math should help you out figure out how many bottles you will need for your pool size. Follow any instructions printed on the bottle.

Staying Efficient with Enough Alkalinity Increaser

Alkalinity increasers are available to help increase your total alkalinity levels in order to do their job of protecting the pH from rapid fluctuation. The alkalinity increaser is made with sodium bicarbonate (sometimes also called sodium hydrogen carbonate). How much alkalinity increaser you need to add to your pool can vary, based on the weather and use of the pool, but on average, I've found that you can start with a certain amount and work your way up if you need to.

REMEMBER

Your initial dose for an alkalinity increaser typically ends up being around 1 pound for every 1,000 gallons of water. So a 10,000-gallon pool will usually start off needing 10 pounds of alkalinity increaser right from the start.

From there, you'll likely need more alkalinity increaser when the pool is used, when rain falls, or even when other chemicals are added to the pool water. In Chapter 9, I go over the importance of keeping your pool water's alkalinity up and how it's affected by various factors. I estimate that, with regular use of the pool in average weather conditions (not excessive heat or rain), you'll use an additional 5 pounds of alkalinity increaser every four to six weeks.

TIP

If it was my pool, I'd get about 20 pounds of alkalinity increaser for every 10,000 gallons of water to make sure it lasts a 14-week season.

Prepping yourself with enough Calcium Hardness Increaser

Calcium hardness is added in to keep the pool from becoming corrosive, and you add calcium hardness increaser (calcium chloride) to raise those levels. Similar to alkalinity (see the preceding section), calcium hardness is something you have to start off balancing initially by using a large amount of calcium carbonate.

Your season supply of calcium hardness increaser can vary depending on whether you have a plaster- or vinyl-surface pool because calcium ranges are different for those two styles. Here are some estimates to follow:

>> **For plaster pools, pebble tech pool, or any other surface susceptible to etching:** Get 15 pounds of calcium hardness increaser for every 10,000 gallons of water to start and have an additional 10 pounds of calcium hardness increaser for every 10,000 gallons of water to maintain it throughout the season.

>> **For vinyl and other surface types:** You're okay getting 10 pounds of calcium hardness increaser for every 10,000 gallons of water for initial balancing, and then 5 pounds of calcium hardness increaser for every 10,000 gallons of water to maintain it.

TIP

The only real way calcium levels decrease is if they're diluted by water that contains low levels of calcium, such as rainwater or most source water. If you're in an area that has very soft water or where there's a lot of rainfall, it may be worth getting a little extra calcium hardness increaser!

Getting the Right Amount of pH Adjusters

Having to adjust your pool water's pH throughout the season is inevitable, so making sure you have the proper chemicals is a must. Proper pH balance is the most important level to watch because acidic or basic water affects everything (swimmers, equipment, chemicals, and surfaces). I really think that pH increasers and decreasers are something that you should have on hand at all times.

To estimate the amount of pH decreaser you may need, follow these guidelines:

>> **If you have a plaster pool or a salt-to-chlorine generator (or both):** You're much more likely to need pH decreaser throughout the season because of the high pH created from the base levels of the pool's surfaces. This is the same for pools that use salt-to-chlorine generators because the salt cell produces a pH of about 13 every minute that it's producing chlorine. That will keep your pool water's pH high pretty consistently, so have plenty of pH decreaser on hand. My recommendation for these types of pools is 4 to 6 pounds of pH decreaser for every 10,000 gallons of water. Go for the high end of that estimate if you have both a plaster pool and a salt-to-chlorine generator.

>> **If you have a vinyl liner or fiberglass pool:** These surfaces don't cause any kind of fluctuation in your pH, so you can have closer to 2 to 4 pounds of pH decreaser for every 10,000 gallons of water to last you a season. But if you keep your pool very warm, you're likely to have a higher pH.

For pH increasers, it's basically the opposite of what I said for decreasers. Follow these guidelines:

» **For plaster pools or salt pools (or both):** You'll likely never use a pH increaser, and if you do, you should also be checking your alkalinity levels. Alkalinity increasers have a high pH (about 8.3), so remember that any time you add it, it will be increasing your pH at the same time. (You can read more about alkalinity in the section "Staying Efficient with Enough Alkalinity Increaser," earlier in this chapter.) You'd probably be safe if you have only 1 pound of pH increaser for every 10,000 gallons of water to last a whole season — or may even multiple seasons.

» **For vinyl or fiberglass pools, or pools that use chlorine tablets as their main sanitizer:** Keep 1.5 to 2 pounds of pH increaser for every 10,000 gallons of water.

Having Cyanuric Acid on Hand

Cyanuric acid (CYA) is the chemical used to protect your chlorine from the sun. This is a product that not all pools will need, and some pools may need higher CYA levels than others. This level really doesn't change outside of being diluted, so after it's in range, it's good for a while. Bromine and biguanide pools don't need CYA. Neither of these chemical systems use stabilizer as a part of balancing. But you need CYA if you have a chlorine or saltwater pool.

The ideal range for your CYA is between 30 and 50 parts per million (ppm). If you're using regular chlorine tablets or powder, you can have your CYA levels on the lower end. Salt-to-chlorine-generated pools will be on the higher end. I'd estimate you'd need around 3 pounds of CYA for every 10,000 gallons of water if you're using chlorine tabs or powder, and 5 pounds of CYA for every 10,000 gallons of water for salt pools. These amounts should be more than enough for startup and maintenance.

Keeping Up Your Supply of Diatomaceous Earth

Filter media is something that most people forget about in the spring because it isn't a chemical. From experience, getting fresh filter media in the beginning of the year is crucial. When I say filter media in this context, I mostly mean the diatomaceous earth (DE) filter medium because that's really the only one that's changed out regularly throughout the season. Plus, you are starting off with a filter that has no media in it at all because it would've been cleaned off last fall!

Here's how to determine how much diatomaceous earth you need for your DE filter (which can vary depending on the size of your filter):

>> **Pools smaller than 10,000 gallons:** Pools this size use a filter that takes 4 pounds of DE or less in the beginning of the season, so a 10-pound bag ends up being enough for a season.

>> **For pools larger than 10,000 gallons:** I recommend getting the larger 25-pound bag of DE to ensure that you have plenty of this media if you need to backwash your pool water a few times.

>> **For algae-prone pools:** If your pool is notorious for getting algae, I would get a 25-pound bag no matter what because you will end up going through more media every time you backwash.

Getting All the Clarifiers You Need

I feel that clarifiers should be on your shelf for "just in case" moments. If you're in a pinch because it's the middle of summer and you have a party in two days, you will be glad you have these items at your disposal.

If you have a diatomaceous earth (DE) filter, you won't need any of these clarifiers, but all other filters could benefit from them.

A natural liquid clarifier is safe, easy to use, and fast acting, so having a quart of that around never hurts. When it comes to filter aids or flocculants, I think it's helpful to have either a 2-pound bottle of flocculant or a cellulose filter aid, as well, in case you need extra help. These clarifiers may not be a necessity, so if you're looking to save some money, you can wait to purchase these when you actually need them.

Having Other Products in Reserve

A few products I recommend that you have on hand are phosphate removers, borates and enzymes, and metal removers. All of these products might prove useful for pool owners, and more often than not, they're needed at one time or another. Here are some reasons to keep these products in your pool storage area:

>> **Phosphate removers:** A necessary product these days because salt-to-chlorine generators are becoming more popular. It's also more common that phosphates are being added to drinking water to protect underground pipes. Phosphates can be kind of pesky, and if they're left untreated, they can lead to a complicated pool season. Using phosphate removers can help prevent algae and improve your chemical efficiency. If you have a salt pool, get 2 quarts of a standard phosphate remover for the season. For other pools, you can get just 1 quart — or even hold off until you actually need it.

>> **Borates and enzymes:** A few of my favorite add-ons for your pool water. They're excellent for softening the pool water, preventing algae growth, and keeping your chlorine from having to work so hard to keep your pool sparkling and beautiful. Here's what you'll want to have on hand:

- *Borates:* If used as directed, you'll use about 15 pounds of borates for every 10,000 gallons of water per season.

- *Enzymes:* Around 5 ounces of the product for every 10,000 gallons or water once a week. Enzymes are typically sold in quart-sized bottles for maintenacne, so 32 fluid ounces will last around six weeks for a 10,000-gallon pool. If you are in an area where the pollen season is brutally bad, I would get a treatment enzyme as well, one that is designed for cleanup purposes.

>> **Metal removers or stain- and scale-controlling products:** Really helpful if you have hard source water. They help tremendously to keep staining at bay and to eliminate trace metals that you may have in the water. The initial dose is usually 1 full quart or metal remover for every 10,000 gallons of water. So if you have hard water, I'd keep an initial-dose-worth in your pool shed at all times. It's a safe product to use in the middle of summer because you can swim right after adding and works efficiently.

TIP

It also wouldn't hurt to have some ascorbic or citric acid on hand if stains do appear because of metals. They're fast-acting stain removers that will lift the metal from the affected area and put those metals back into solution. Then you can use your metal remover to take the metals out of the water completely.

IN THIS CHAPTER

» **Dealing with unwanted (and unsanitary) additions to the pool**

» **Making accommodations for a pool dog**

» **Getting broken glass safely out of your pool**

» **Correcting when the wrong chemicals end up in the pool**

» **Handling nature's wrath**

Chapter **15**

Ten Nightmare Mishaps and How to Handle Them

Y ou never think it will happen to you, but sometimes it does. I've heard some wacky stories in my career; some are more common than others. In this chapter, I cover some of the most common mishaps that I see in the wonderful world of pool ownership and how to gracefully handle them with as little panic as possible.

Someone Peed in My Pool

If you have kids, or know someone who has kids, or just see movies of kids in pools, then you know that pool pee is 100 percent a possibility. In fact, I think it's more of an inevitable situation — not so much if, but when. Now, this isn't something I consider okay to do in a pool, but if I had to choose between someone peeing in a pool and any of the other things I cover in this chapter, I'd choose the pee.

Although urine isn't something I think very many persons would enjoy swimming in, it's really not terribly dangerous. The chlorine levels in your pool at the regular 2 to 4 parts per million (ppm) will be enough to sanitize the compounds in urine and make it safe. When urine gets in the water, combined chlorine is created (I cover combined chlorine in Chapter 10). A good indicator that urine is present in your pool is a strong chlorine smell. (Hence public pools being very stinky — it's from all of that dirty chlorine in the water.)

TIP

To handle pee in your pool, shock your pool by using a regular dose of oxidizer. (Use more oxidizer if the pool is cloudy.) If you're using biguanide chemicals, such as Baquacil or SoftSwim, use a full gallon of your shock for every 10,000 gallons of pool water. Then, let the pool filter run continuously for a 24-hour period, and all can be forgotten.

Someone Pooped in My Pool

If someone goes Number 2 in your pool, treat it immediately. The reason fecal matter in your pool is such an issue is because of the bacteria that may be involved in why it even ended up in your pool in the first place. If it's regular poop, your chlorinated water should kill the bacteria. But, if it's diarrhea caused by viruses, those viruses can be spread through the water after the accident and infect others. Treat the water, no matter which type of accident occurs.

If the feces are solid, the protocol involves following these steps:

1. **Have all swimmers exit the pool immediately.**

2. **Remove any fecal pieces from the water and dispose of them in a sanitary manner.**

   Anything you use to remove the feces from the pool should be thoroughly sanitized afterward (or disposed of), too.

3. **Add in a small dose of your sanitizer or oxidizer to raise your chlorine levels to over 2 parts per million (ppm).**

4. **Wait one hour.**

   After one hour, the pool is perfectly safe to swim in, and you can all pretend it didn't happen.

Remember diarrhea is usually from an issue inside the body such as a virus. You want to take stricter precautions to prevent anyone from becoming ill after this type of incident. If the accident is in the form of diarrhea, follow these steps:

1. **Have all swimmers exit the pool immediately.**

2. **Remove as much of the fecal matter as possible and dispose of it in a sanitary manner.**

   Thoroughly sanitize anything you used to remove the fecal matter or dispose of those items, as well.

REMEMBER

3. **Add a double dose of your shock oxidizer.**

4. **Run the pool filter for a 24-hour period before re-entering and test every 8 hours to be sure the chlorine level stays high on your test kit for the full 24-hour period.**

During any treatments, always be sure your pH is in proper range to ensure that oxidizer is as effective as possible. Test with your home test kit before and after treatment.

I Found a Dead Animal in the Pool

This can be a common occurrence when you're a pool owner. Some people definitely have it worse than others, but it's never fun finding a critter belly-up in the pool. Honestly, most of the time, a dead animal in the pool isn't a big health threat to humans, other than being very unpleasant. Based on what type of animal you find, you want to treat it accordingly:

» **Small animals:** When you're dealing with a small animal, such as a squirrel or chipmunk, within the first 30 minutes, your regular chlorine levels should kill any and all bacteria that could have been introduced. Remove the animal and allow an hour before entering the pool to give your chlorine time to sanitize any bacteria.

» **Larger animals:** If you're dealing with something about the size of a cat, you'll have more bacteria to kill. Remove the animal and make sure you raise your sanitation levels to over 3 parts per million (ppm) by adding in a partial dose of your oxidizer. Allow the pool water a few hours of filtration before swimming, just to be safe.

» **Raccoons:** The reason I specify raccoons in this list is because they're more likely to be infected with a worm called Baylisascaris, which can easily spread to humans. The eggs of this worm are resistant to chlorine, thus making the treatment of your pool a little bit different after finding a raccoon in it.

   If you find a dead racoon in your pool, start by removing the deceased animal, and then shock the pool with your regular oxidizer. (Be sure the pH is in range to ensure the chemicals are 100% effective.) Then filter the pool continuously for 24 hours. Filtering for this length of time should turn over the pool enough times to filter out any eggs that may be in there. You'll want to be sure to sanitize your filter, as well:

- *For a DE filter:* Remove the internal assembly with gloves. Clean off all of the media and double bag as much as possible by hand and then spray off the residual. You can spray the internal assembly and the inside of the filter tank down with a mild bleach for extra sanitization if desired. Then you can reassemble the filter, and all pesky eggs should be eliminated.

- *For a sand filter:* Remove the sand and start fresh, you can spray the inside of the tank with a mild bleach solution after the tank is empty of sand for extra sanitation.

- *For a cartridge filter:* Rinse thoroughly and use an acidic cleaner on the cartridges before returning them to the filter.

My Dog Took a Dip

Most dog and pool owners will run into this scenario pretty often. My dogs personally don't love the pool, but I certainly know of plenty of dogs who can't get enough of the water. The tricky part with dogs swimming in your pool is that your filter can get clogged with fur and they can make keeping up with maintenance more difficult.

TIP

Normal chlorine levels will help any bacteria that may have been on the dog from becoming a problem. But, a dog swimming in the pool will introduce more contaminants than a human will. Treat your pool as if a dozen kids had just gone swimming. Hit it with a small dose of oxidizer after each swim that your dog takes to help keep your pool clean.

REMEMBER

The real problem you'll face with your faithful friend in the pool is dog hair causing issues. Dog hair will clog your filter very quickly, so always pay attention to your filter pressure if you have a dog that swims regularly. As the filter gets dirty the pressure will rise on the pressure gauge. Once it reaches 7 to 10 psi higher than it started at when it was clean, it is time for the filter to be backwashed or cleaned out.

Also check your skimmer and pump baskets every few days if a dog is swimming daily; the fur can clog up the baskets and cause strain on the pump motor. A dog swimming definitely will introduce a lot more contaminates into the pool water than a human will, so treat your pool like ten kids just went swimming after your dog is done. If you hit it with a small dose of oxidizer after every swim, you will be safe!

The Wind Blew My Glass Table In

First things first, don't panic. Getting broken glass out of the pool takes a cautious process. If you end up with broken glass in your pool and try to fix it quickly and without taking your time, you can cause more harm than good. Breathe. After you're calm and have a clear visual of the situation, follow these steps:

1. **Shut off your filter.**

2. **Remove the frame of the table from the pool.**

    Be very careful with this step, especially if you need to get into the pool to do it. Have someone assist you and wear protective footwear. Getting the frame out will allow you to be able to assess the amount of glass you're looking for and to see whether there's any damage to the pool surface.

3. **(Optional) Drain the pool.**

    Technically, the best way to properly deal with this situation is to drain your pool. For obvious reasons, this may be too much to ask to fix the situation, but it really is the safest way. If the table fell into one corner on the shallow end, you may be able to get away with not draining the pool completely, just enough to expose the shallow end.

TIP

If you have a liner pool, I recommend having some pool liner patches on hand, readily available, just in case.

4. **Vacuum the pool.**

    Depending on whether you drained your pool, you need to approach vacuuming in different ways.

If you were able to drain the pool, follow these steps:

1. *Gently sweep the floor of the pool with a household broom.*

2. *Shop-vac the bottom of the pool to collect all the glass pieces.*

   Be sure to wear protective footwear so that you don't cut your feet.

WARNING

If you didn't empty the pool, follow these steps:

1. *Invest in an in-line vacuuming canister.*

2. *Connect one end of the canister to your suction port in the skimmer and the other end to your vacuum hose.*

3. *Carefully and tediously vacuum the pool by hand.*

   I've found it's safest to hold the end of your vacuum hose in your hand and swim around vacuuming up the pieces of glass. The vacuum canister will prevent the glass from possibly causing damage to your pipes or filter system.

I Accidentally Added Chlorine to My Biguanide Pool

This doesn't happen too often, but when it does, it can be pretty catastrophic to the pool. Unfortunately, if you're using Baquacil, SoftSwim, or any other biguanide-based chemical systems, you can't introduce chlorine into that pool without a very intense chemical reaction. I used to demonstrate this reaction in a jar with my new employees to show them on a small scale how quickly it happens. It usually occurs when you're a new pool owner and buy some shock; the clerk doesn't know you mean for a biguanide pool, and you don't ask. Or maybe you hire a pool service company that's unfamiliar with biguanide pools or unaware that biguanide and chlorine aren't compatible, and the pool service employees just throw chlorine in. The possibilities are endless, and the reaction is always the same — ugly.

To start, the pool will get really cloudy and turn a yellow-brown color. It may also foam on the top and typically has a strong chlorine odor because of the combined chlorine that's being created in the reaction. Because of all that combined chlorine, it will also be incredibly irritating to the skin and eyes of anyone who dares to take a dip in it while it's in this condition. It takes a few days to correct itself completely.

Follow these steps if you're faced with a biguanide-chlorine reaction:

1. **Don't swim in the pool.**

   If you want to be in the smelliest, most aggressive type of water, then feel free to jump in — but I promise it won't be fun!

2. **Allow your filter to run continuously.**

   The reaction will dwindle while the chlorine levels lower, but you still need to filter out the physical side effects, and that takes time.

3. **Add in sodium thiosulphate, also known as chlorine neutralizer.**

   This will lessen the reaction of the chlorine with the biguanide and speed up the wait time before swimming again.

4. **After the water is back in decent shape, get the pool tested somewhere that does professional testing.**

   You want to make sure your numbers are all where they need to be and that you don't need to make some adjustments.

TIP

As a bonus, you can test your water for chlorine, too, and see if there are any residual chloramines in the pool that need another day to dissipate so that you can swim comfortably.

After the pool looks good and tests well, you're good to proceed as normal.

I Dumped Motor Oil in My Pool

Before you call me crazy, I just want to say that motor oil ends up in pools enough that I felt it necessary to discuss it. If you do your own oil changes, it's not uncommon to put the old oil in gallon jugs that you have lying around, and sometimes those gallon jugs are former liquid chlorine or hydrogen peroxide bottles. When a mix-up happens and oil ends up in a pool, the hapless pool owner typically doesn't add the whole gallon. But it's still a pain to clear any amount of oil out of the pool.

To treat motor oil in your pool, follow these steps:

1. **Shut off the filter.**

2. **Remove as much oil as possible, acting quickly.**

   You can use a pool skimmer net, ideally with some sort of fabric on it to help catch and absorb as much oil on the surface as possible. The skimmer net on its own won't be fine enough, so add in something fabric, such as a sock or a rag. It won't get all of the oil, but it's a start.

3. **Add in a treatment enzyme product.** Enzymes are amazing at breaking down the oil in the pool and will begin destroying the oil the second it's added to the water.

   Be sure you are adding an enzyme designed for treatment and not maintenance, because the maintenance ones will work, but not as quickly and effectively.

4. **Use a scum remover.**

   For all residual oil, you can use something called a Scum Bug or any other kind of scum remover. These products will attract the oil to them and remove the leftover oil on the surface. The best place to put one of these tools is in the skimmer because that is where a lot of the surface oil will be pulled into.

5. **Turn the filter on and allow it to run for a few days.**

   Keep the filter running until all the oil is gone.

6. **Clean your filter by using a degreasing filter cleaner.**

   After the oil seems completely removed from the water, clean your filters thoroughly with a degreasing filter cleaner to make sure there's no oil left in or on your filter that may hinder proper circulation or filtration.

After all the oil is gone, you're good to continue pool life as normal.

A Tree Fell in My Pool

When something like a tree falling into your pool happens, there's not much you can do but sigh. I always feel so terrible for a customer going through a problem like this because it's almost never a quick, easy fix. Here are a few things to keep in mind when a tree falls on your pool:

» **Assess the damage.** How you make this assessment depends on the type of pool you have:

- *Above ground pool:* Look for structural damage to the wall or railings. If you're really lucky and things look more dented than crushed, it's like getting a dent in your car. Most of the time, it's just cosmetic — and although it may not look the prettiest, it's still functional.

- *Inground pool:* See whether the pool is still holding water and look for large breaks or cracks in the surrounding surface. To be honest, if a tree falls on an inground pool, the majority of the damage is usually done to the liner or cover.

>> **Contact your insurance company.** Most of the time, your insurance will want a professional to quote the repair costs, so get in touch with pool companies near you to get a proper evaluation and estimate.

Unfortunately, acts of nature that cause damage to the pool aren't covered under any warranty, even if the pool is a week old. If you're hoping to have things covered and not pay out of pocket, insurance is the only way to do it.

>> **Let a professional handle removal and repairs.** Depending on what you need done, there may be leaf cleanup duty on your end, but most of this work should be done by people who are trained and insured. More damage can easily be caused during the tree removal process, so you don't want to be responsible for that if you can avoid it. Hopefully the cleanup and repair processes go smoothly.

There Are Thousands of Tiny Black Bugs in My Pool

If you know what I'm talking about when I mention these little pests, you're probably rolling your eyes right now. These tiny bugs, called springtails, live in large swarms and tend to enjoy your pool as much as you do. We pool pros see them mostly in the middle of summer, but you can get them any time of the year. They can't fly, and they can't swim (but they're light enough to not break the water's surface tension by standing on it). And if you try to touch them, they jump into the air the same way that fleas do. They're annoying little pests that drive many pool owners crazy, so let me give you some pointers:

>> **Break the water's surface tension so that the bugs sink.** After they sink to the bottom of the pool, vacuum out their bodies and go about your business. You can reduce the surface tension in a couple of ways:

- *Buy a product at your local pool store called Bug Off.* This product will do exactly what you need.

- *Make a mixture of water and dish soap.* Spray the mixture around the border of the pool's surface, and then spritz the surface of the pool evenly.

    The biggest downside to using dish soap is the obvious side effect of suds and an oil slick effect on the pool's surface. That will filter out over time, but that's why I prefer the chemicals made for pools that are designed to perform specific tasks.

>> **Get skimmer socks and place them over your skimmer baskets.** This fine mesh is enough to filter out the tiny bugs and allow you to remove them from the pool after they die.

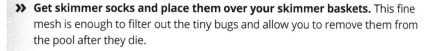

>> **Prevent moisture and limit light use.** These bugs love lights and moisture, so to prevent them swarming your pool as much as possible, limit your pool light use and keep your pool area as dry as you can and clear of leaves, which may trap water and attract the bugs. If you offer a less attractive environment for the springtails, you may be able to avoid getting them at all.

REMEMBER

Because of their tiny size, you can try to skim springtails off of the pool's surface, but it may not work very well. They're tiny enough that they can fit through your pool net, and you end up spreading them around.

My Pool Is Popping Out of the Ground

It's completely possible for your pool to pop out of the ground, and the repair isn't easy. When I say "popping out of the ground," I do mean that literally. In certain scenarios, where the ground's water level is too high, *hydrostatic pressure* (this is when ground water pushes on below ground surfaces like pools) can form that presses against the pool wall, causing an inground pool to be forced from its place in the ground.

When this happens, there really isn't much you can do as the pool owner to fix it. The process requires disconnecting your electrical, plumbing, and decking, removing the pool, re-digging the hole, and reinstalling the pool. It's absolutely something that must be done by professionals.

But how does this happen? How can you prevent it? First, let me explain what's actually happening. When you put a pool into the earth and fill that pool with water, that water puts its hydrostatic pressure against the inside of the pool. On the opposite side, the groundwater is also applying hydrostatic pressure to the outside of the pool. And those two pressures equal each other out. So, the only way for this battle to be lost is for the underground pressure to be stronger than the pressure inside the pool. That happens if you drain a pool when the water table of your groundwater is high, such as right after rain, especially severe rain.

WARNING

Your job as the pool owner is to not drain your pool during a time when the groundwater water table is high. I know this seems like what you're supposed to do if the water is overflowing, but it's far from the correct move.

TIP

Wait until the water table seems to have returned back to normal. That really just means to wait until the ground around the pool isn't saturated. Sometimes, you can begin to drain the pool slowly, but I honestly believe your best step is to call a local pool professional and get their opinion. Or have them drain the pool for you to ensure that you're doing it correctly and safely.

Index

filters. *See also* cartridge filters; diatomaceous earth
filters; sand filters
  backpressure from dirty, 86–87
  connecting
    for above ground pools, 120–123
    for inground pools, 134–135
  floor cleaning jets, strain on, 36
  multiport valve on
    Backwash setting, 55
    Closed setting, 58
    common settings, 55–57
    Filter setting, 55
    overview, 54–55
    Recirculate setting, 57
    Rinse setting, 57
    Waste setting, 57–58
    Winter setting, 58
  overview, 9, 40
  recommended, 54
  running after adding winter chemicals, 166
  for temporary pools, 30
  winterizing, 173–177
first aid kit, 109
fishy smell, fixing, 319–320
flash-freeze preparations, 198–200
float holders, 331–332
floating chlorinators, 250
floats, removing for winter, 169
floccing pool
  calcium hardness, adjusting, 231
  cloudy water, treating, 290–291
  overview, 286
  vacuuming to waste, 148–149
  white water mold, treating, 311
flocculants, 57, 290
floor drain, 34–35
floor jets, 36
flow rate, 59–60
folding pool cover, 118–119, 127–130
following directions on chemicals, 244
food grade DE, 53
frames for above ground pools, 21–22
free form pools, 25, 206
freezes, preventing damage in open pools from, 198–200
frequency of testing, 207

G

gallon jugs as weights for cover, 187
gallons of water in pool, calculating, 204–207
gaskets, replacing, 92, 98–99
gates, safety, 107–108
glass, removing from pool, 347–348
glass media, 42
granular chlorine, 251–252
green algae
  algaecides, adding, 294
  cloudy water after treating, 284
  overview, 292–293
  running filter, 295
  shocking pool, 294
  testing for, 293
  troubleshooting for, 295
  vacuuming, 294
grid DE filters, 50–51, 79–80
grommets, on cover, 182
ground, pool popping out of, 27, 352
gunite-plaster pools
  brushing, 150–151
  calcium hardness, effect on, 229
  general discussion, 27–28
  overview, 26
  pH levels in, 219

H

hair and lint trap housing, 173
hand railings, replacing upon opening, 132–133
handle of multiport valve, loosening, 99–100
hard water, 227
Hayward T-Cell 15 salt generator, 40
Hayward Vari-Flo sand filter, 55
heads, vacuum, 140–142, 145
heaters, 10, 177
height of pool wall, 22
high calcium, 229–231
high CYA levels, dealing with, 238–239
high pH, symptoms of, 218–219
hiring professionals versus DIY, 15–16
home tests, 208–211
homeowners' insurance, 107

purchasing chemicals, 242

purge plug, 191

push-button vacuum poles, 333

Q

quality test kits, 334

quartz, 42

quat algistats, 277–278, 337

R

racoons, 345–346

railings, replacing, 132

reagent test kits, 209–210

Recirculate setting, multiport valve, 57, 69, 86, 135–136

rectangular pools, 25, 204–205

red algae

in biguanide pools, 305–308

in chlorine pools, treating, 304–305

overview, 303–304

signs of, 304

regenerative DE filters, 51

regular bead liner, 22–23

regular skimmer heads, 151

Remember icon, 3

removing sand, 71

replacing sand, 72–73

rescue devices, 108–109

resin frames, 22

responsible ownership, 11–12

return plug, removing, 123

Return port, 121

returns

blowing out, 194–196

floor, 36

identifying lines, 189

installing plugs, 170–171

overview, 35

removal tool, 330

removing eyeball, 168–169

wall, 35

winter hardware, removing, 131

rings, life, 108

rings inside of filters, 48–49

Rinse setting, multiport valve, 43–45, 57

robots

cleaners, 39, 154–158

solar skimming, 158–159

round pools, 20–21, 206

rubber expansion plugs, 131, 170–171, 190

rules of use, establishing, 109–110

running, rules against, 110

S

sacrificial anode, 255

safety, chemical. *See* chemical safety

safety, pool. *See* pool safety

safety covers

general discussion, 105–106, 183

peg anchors, 133–134, 172

putting on, 185

removal and installation tool, 330

removing, 126–129

water level for, 167

safety fencing, 105

safety hook, 109

safety lines, 109

safety vacuum release system (SVRS), 108

salt cells, 177, 258

salt-to-chlorine generators

blowing out returns, 194

calcium hardness, 228

general discussion, 38–40

hooking up, 123

overview, 14, 245, 253–254

stocking up on salt, 336

saltwater, corrosion from, 18

saltwater pools

boosting salt system, 257

chlorine in, 14, 253

costs of salt system, 256–258

effects of saltwater on pool and equipment, 254–255

feel of saltwater, 255

frames for, 22

overview, 254

pool types for, 258–259

use of chemicals in, 256

Y

Z

About the Author

Kristine Blanchard started working on pools with her dad when she was only 5 years old. For years and years, she would tag along with her father while he took care of his weekly pool maintenance customers, cleaning out the baskets in hopes of finding a frog or skimming the leaves with a pole that was much too big for her. She always loved the atmosphere of being out in the sun by the water, hearing her dad sing the wrong words to a song he had listened to 10,000 times. There was also a love for the challenge of learning how pool chemicals' active ingredients worked, under threat of being pushed into the water! Her love for this industry started young and grew as she did.

At 17, she got her first job working at a local pool store — the one her father had worked at for 30 years. It was here that she began to learn by reading the pool tips written by the owner, taking the pool school classes alongside customers to absorb as much information as possible, and being sent to numerous training seminars all over the East Coast. During all that time, learning everything she could through books and classes, she was also working alongside her dad out in the field, becoming familiar with pools and filter systems of all styles. She did hundreds of pool openings, winterizations, and filter installs and repairs, and she began doing the weekly maintenance for the established customers that her father had. After six years of working hard out in the field and in the store in the summertime — sometimes working 90-plus days consecutively between the two — she was offered the Assistant Manager position at her store.

From there, she began focusing on teaching — not only the new employees who started at the company, but also the customers who came through the store all day. She started designing and teaching her own pool schools and attending more classes to better educate herself on subjects in which she wanted more expertise. All of this while still maintaining her weekly service customers, year after year. In 2019, she strayed away from pools to try her hand at something else she had a passion for: dogs. After years of fostering dogs in her home, she wanted to try working with them more closely at a dog daycare and grooming facility. But, as any other lifer in the pool industry would understand, once you're in, it's hard to leave.

Kristine started a new career at Paquette Pools and Spas in Hooksett, New Hampshire, where she has taken on the role of Assistant Manager once again and has continued to educate customers and employees in the store. She still works on pools out in the field from time to time to keep her mind sharp and to help the service crew whenever they need it. Since coming back to the pool industry, she has been selected to write this book, along with winning the prestigious Future Leadership award from Pleatco during its annual competition. Her drive, experience, and knowledge will keep expanding with every year that she works in the swimming pool industry.

Dedication

I dedicate this book to two people: my dad Tod, who my first and best teacher, and Dennis DiPaolo, the original owner of the first pool store I worked at. If it wasn't for my dad introducing me to this industry so early, and Dennis making sure that I had every opportunity and tool I needed to advance, none of this would have been possible.

Author's Acknowledgments

There is so much that lead me to this point, and a lot of that was through the knowledge and experience other people have taught me. Someone who got me to this point was one of my previous coworkers and a former boss, Stephanie McCormack. She was always an excellent teacher who never slowed down and taught me some of the tricks I still use today.

The technical reviewer Patrick McEwen is the former General Manager at the first pool store I worked at and is now a coworker at my current company. He is one of the most well-rounded and knowledgeable pool guys you will ever meet, and if there is something he doesn't know, he will find the answer quickly and never forget it. He is the only other person outside of my father who is educated in not only the chemistry and in-store hands-on experience like I am, but also has decades of in-field experience under his belt, too. He is one heck of a pool guy!

Last, I want to thank the entire Wiley team for giving me the opportunity to write this book and being a part of a huge highlight in my career and life. This was an experience I never thought I would get, and I am so thankful to have had it. Special thanks to Linda Brandon — she constantly assured me I was doing great when I was feeling overwhelmed and under-delivering. Her patience and kind words are what kept me focused and calm while writing this book for you all.

Publisher's Acknowledgments

Acquisitions Editor: Steve Hayes

Development Editor: Linda Brandon

Copy Editor: Laura K. Miller

Technical Editor: Patrick McEwen

Proofreader: Debbye Butler

Production Editor: Tamilmani Varadharaj

Cover Image: © nazarovsergey/Shutterstock